Word-of-mouth Learning

New Chinese Phonetic Common Course

(The Multi-media Teaching Version in Chinese / English)

口耳之学

——新编汉语发音通用教程

（中英文多媒体教学版）

主　编　刘　伶

副主编　张　黎

编委会　刘　伶　张　黎　武建义　胡金燕
肖　刚　刘　昕　曹　茜　唐月华
李莉芳　刘晓霭　莫　超　刘小虎
贺　群　王金娥　侯一农　刘晓燕
何茂活　王　荣　孙雪英　孙丽静

兰州大学出版社

图书在版编目(CIP)数据

口耳之学:新编汉语发音通用教程/刘伶主编. —兰州:兰州大学出版社,2011.12

ISBN 978-7-311-03763-5

Ⅰ.①口… Ⅱ.①刘… Ⅲ.①汉语拼音—对外汉语教学—教材 Ⅳ.①H195.4

中国版本图书馆 CIP 数据核字(2011)第 245983 号

策划编辑 李 晖
责任编辑 锁晓梅
装帧设计 管军伟

书 名 口耳之学
——新编汉语发音通用教程(中英文多媒体教学版)
主 编 刘 伶
副 主 编 张 黎
出版发行 兰州大学出版社 (地址:兰州市天水南路 222 号 730000)
电 话 0931-8912613(总编办公室) 0931-8617156(营销中心)
0931-8914298(读者服务部)
网 址 http://www.onbook.com.cn
电子信箱 press@lzu.edu.cn
印 刷 甘肃澳翔印业有限公司
开 本 787mm×1092mm 1/16
印 张 19.25(插页 10)
字 数 405 千
版 次 2011 年 12 月第 1 版
印 次 2011 年 12 月第 1 次印刷
书 号 ISBN 978-7-311-03763-5
定 价 48.00 元(含光盘)

目 录
Contents

老当益壮 大业盛德 …… 甘晖 I
前言 …… III
说明 …… V
第一章 现代汉语语音概说 …… 001
第一节 语音的形成 …… 002
第二节 现代汉语语音简介 …… 004
第三节 记音符号 …… 005
第二章 普通话声母及发音 …… 012
第一节 唇音 …… 016
b …… 016
p …… 020
m …… 023
f …… 026
第二节 舌尖前音 …… 030
z …… 030
c …… 034
s …… 036
第三节 舌尖中音 …… 040
d …… 040
t …… 042
n …… 045
l …… 048
复习一 分辨 n 和 l 声母 …… 051
第四节 舌尖后音 …… 053
zh …… 053
ch …… 056
sh …… 059
r …… 062

复习二 分辨 zh ch sh 和 z c s 声母 …… 065
第五节 舌面音 …… 068
j …… 068
q …… 070
x …… 072
第六节 舌根音 …… 075
g …… 075
k …… 077
h …… 080
复习三 分辨 f 和 h 声母 …… 083
第七节 零声母 …… 085
第三章 普通话韵母及发音 …… 088
第一节 舌面单韵母 …… 091
ɑ …… 093
o …… 096
e …… 099
复习一 分辨 o 和 e 韵母 …… 101
ê …… 102
i …… 104
u …… 108
ü …… 112
第二节 特殊单元音韵母 …… 116
-i[ʅ] …… 116
-i[ʅ] …… 120
er …… 124
第三节 复韵母 …… 129
ɑi …… 130
ei …… 132
ɑo …… 135
ou …… 137
iɑ …… 140
ie …… 142
uɑ …… 145
uo …… 148
üe …… 151
iɑo …… 154

iou …… 157
uai …… 160
uei …… 163
第四节 鼻韵母 …… 166
an …… 166
ian …… 171
uan …… 173
üan …… 177
en …… 179
in …… 182
uen …… 187
ün …… 189
ang …… 192
iang …… 195
uang …… 198
eng …… 200
ing …… 203
ueng …… 207
ong …… 210
iong …… 213
复习二 分辨前鼻韵母和后鼻韵母 …… 215
第四章 普通话声调及变调 …… 218
第一节 普通话声调的分类 …… 219
第二节 调号 …… 221
第三节 变调 …… 223
第五章 音节 …… 226
第一节 音节的结构 …… 227
第二节 音节的拼合 …… 227
第三节 普通话声、韵拼合方法 …… 228
第四节 普通话声、韵拼合规律 …… 228
第六章 语音阅读和汉字的书写 …… 230
第一节 古典诗文阅读 …… 231
孔子语录（八则节选）…… 231
孟子语录（五则节选）…… 237
礼记·礼运大同篇 …… 240
诫子书 …… 242

读太宗十思疏 …… 243
陋室铭 …… 247
格言 …… 248
江城子 …… 249
石灰吟 …… 250
第二节 现代诗文阅读 …… 251
一 现代诗歌 …… 251
二 历史小故事 …… 257
三 散文 …… 259
四 童话故事 …… 261
五 笑话 …… 265
六 人文常识 …… 266
第三节 汉字的书写 …… 270
一 汉字的特点 …… 270
二 汉字的形体 …… 273
三 现行汉字合体字的结构 …… 276
四 现行汉字的笔画 …… 277
五 现行汉字的笔顺 …… 280
六 现行汉字常用偏旁（部首） …… 281
练习一 汉字书写 …… 286
练习二 汉字游戏 …… 288
后记 …… 291
诗画欣赏 …… 293

老当益壮 大业盛德

《口耳之学——新编汉语发音通用教程》序

今年盛夏的一日傍晚，我接到刘伶老师的电话，他说自己主编的一本现代汉语语音教材将要出版，因我在兰大时曾经关注、关心过此事，便嘱我写个序。我诚惶诚恐，老师写书，学生何德何才，岂敢作序！然而，长者命，不得辞。权且再当一回学生，叙叙我和刘老师三十多年的缘分，聊聊对书稿的印象。

我是恢复高考后兰州大学录取的第一届学生，当时的中文系四十几位老师各有绝活，刘老师给我们讲授“现代汉语”课程。上过中文系的都知道“现代汉语”课程比文学课难得多，而刘老师却把课讲得活泼而有趣。毕业后，我又留在兰州大学工作，于是和刘老师更多了一层同事的缘分，有了更为密切的接触。

刘老师一直致力于语音教学与研究，治学勤奋，功底深厚，对语音及方言的研究造诣颇深，成就显著。从上世纪七八十年代起，刘老师就对甘肃方言中的语音问题进行了调查与研究，曾在日本国立东京外国语大学亚非言语与文化研究所《亚非言语与文化》发表了《广韵音系与敦煌音系》《甘肃张掖方言声母“tʂ，tʂ‘，ʂ”与“k，k‘，f，v”的分合》，还出版了《敦煌方言志》等著作。在教学方面，早在1986年，他就编制了《现代汉语语音》动画教学片，当时就受到国家教委、国家语委的高度重视，徐世荣、李行健等专家还给予了高度评价，并建议修改后及早出版，惜因故未能付梓，堪属憾事，然其价难泯。

时光流转，直至今日，刘老师已届耄耋之年，仍心萦斯事，不顾年高，孜孜不倦地对该教学片进行了大幅修订，使之在内容和形式上更加完善，并名为《口耳之学——新编汉语发音通用教程（中英文多媒体教学版）》。书中有不少亮点，让人耳目焕然一新。

首先，让语音发音能“看得见”。语音教学，首重发音。但语音一发即逝，既不能传之远方，也不能流于后世。教者不好教，学者无兴趣，以至于语音教学庶显无味。而本教材通过动态的视频图形表现了发音时的生理机能，达到视听直观的效果，为学习者了解某个声母、某个韵母发音的唇、齿、舌、腭以及声带、鼻腔的动态和作用提供了直观而形象的途径，让学习者由听得到转变为既听得到又看得见，对语音不仅“知其然”，而且“知其所以然”，对于模仿发标准音是大有帮助的。这样的改革和创新，对语音教学意义甚大。

其次，中国传统文化精神贯穿全书。汉语作为文化的载体，深深地印上了中华民族悠久而多姿多彩的历史文化印记。这本教材虽然主要讲汉语发音，但是却紧紧围绕着中国传统文化而展开，全书选编了古典诗词六十余首并配有精美的国画，附在每个汉语拼音字母之后，并有释义和相关提示。每首诗词均有标准朗诵发音的光盘，不仅为学习者提供了汉语标准发音示范，而且可以激发学习者对汉语诗歌的兴趣；全书还有不少丰富有趣的汉语俗语、成语、绕口令以及大量的中华经典选文，如孔孟语录、诸子名言、贤臣良将言谈笔录、《礼记》《三字经》《弟子规》等；另外，本书将汉字也纳入了学习范围，让学习者在学发音时还能了解汉语的书写规范。全书有看、有读、有听、有写，还有唱，让人读后印象深刻、倍感有趣。同时相信，该作之行世，既属学界之幸事，亦必将使汉语语音和中华文化的学习者获益！

总之，《口耳之学——新编汉语发音通用教程（中英文多媒体教学版）》这一教材的内容、材料相当丰富，涉及面广，弥补了我学生时代没有全面系统了解语音知识的遗憾，读后印象深刻、获益良多。突然忆起《易·系辞上》曰：“富有之谓大业，日新之谓盛德。”刘老师八十有余，犹自笔耕不辍。“老骥伏枥，志在千里”，这种精神，是我读此书得到的更大收获。

遵嘱说了以上的话，不当之处，敬请指正。

甘晖

2011年8月20日于陕西师范大学

前 言

汉语是汉民族早期的民族共同语。现代汉语是现代汉民族的共同语，它是**“以北京语音为标准音，以北方方言为基础方言，以典范的现代白话文著作为语法规范的普通话”**。

汉语源远流长，是世界上使用人口最多的语言。

汉语是联合国大会和安理会法定的六种工作语言之一。

汉语是我国各兄弟民族自觉选择的共同交际的语言。

要学习汉语，必须得认识汉字：要认识汉字，就得知道汉字的读音，由于汉字不是拼音文字，要学会汉字的读音，还需要学会一套记音符号。《汉语拼音方案》正是给汉字注音的有效工具，也是我国各兄弟民族和外国朋友了解汉语、学习汉语必需的一个步骤。

一般认为，学习语言重在听、说、读、写，但光靠这些还不够完善，若能在学习中清楚地看见每个语音的真实发音过程，就会学得更快、更好、更准确，能更科学地了解和矫正汉语发音中的错误。本教程是以《汉语拼音方案》为标准，用动态形式显示普通话语音声母、韵母、声调等成音时口、舌、喉、鼻、气流等在口腔中活动变化的全过程。其目的在于更有效地提高普通话教学水平，让汉语语音学习能够看得见、听得清、读得准、说得好，把汉语语音学习的直观性、真实性、形象性和科学性统一起来，力图为国内外各级各类学校普通话语音教学提供一部理想的视听教材。

Preface

Chinese is the early language of the Han nationality, and modern Chinese is the language of the modern Han nationality. Modern Chinese is a mandarin which takes Beijng dialect pronunciation as its standard pronunciation, northern dialect as its basic dialect and the canonical modern vernacular literary works as its grammatical norm.

Chinese has a long history and is used by almost 27% of the world's population.

Chinese is one of the six legal working languages at the UN General Assembly and the Security Council.

Chinese is the common lingua franca which is voluntarily chosen by our brotherly minority nationalities.

To learn Chinese, you have to learn Chinese characters. To learn Chinese characters, you must, firstly, know its pronunciation. Since Chinese is not written with the alphabetic characters, in order to master its pronunciation, you should learn a set of phonetic symbols. At present, *The Scheme for the Chinese Phonetic Alphabet* is an effective tool for the phonetic notation of Chinese characters as well as a necessary step for both our brotherly minority nationalities and foreign friends who want to know and learn Chinese.

It is well known that the best way in learning a language is to practice listening, speaking, reading and writing. However, only these are not enough. If you can see clearly, from the mouth, the real pronouncing process of every phonetic alphabet, you will surely learn it faster, better and more precisely. Moreover, you will definitely know and correct the errors during your pronunciation more scientifically. The media course which is based on *The Scheme for the Chinese Phonetic Alphabet*, presents the whole changing processes of the mouth, tongue, larynx, nose, air, *ect*. in the dynamic way, when we pronounce an initial, a final as well as the tone. Herein, the purpose of the book is to improve the level of *Putonghua* teaching skill and to make the Chinese *Pinyin* learning more direct, real, visual and scientific. Finally, we try hard to provide all kinds of schools home and abroad, where *Putonghua* phonetics is taught, with an ideal audio-visual textbook.

说 明

一、编写指导思想

语言是口耳之学，它是通过语言的物质外壳——语音表现出来的。没有语音就没有语言。因此，学习语言必须首先学习语音，而语音又是通过人的发音器官表现出来的，所以了解语音的成音过程是学好一种语言的关键。学习汉语也不例外。

《口耳之学——新编汉语发音通用教程（中英文多媒体教学版）》依据《汉语拼音方案》体例，编撰、制作了本教程及光盘，目的在于展示汉语语音的声母、韵母、声调发音时，人的唇、齿、牙、腭、喉、声带、气管、鼻腔、气流等发音器官在口腔中变化活动的全过程。让每个声母、韵母、声调的发音不仅能听得到，而且能看得见，使语音学习由“听、说、读、写”变为“看、听、读、写、说”，从而显示语音学习的形象性、实用性、趣味性、真实性和科学性。

二、教程体例和教材特点

1. 教程体例

本教程发音动画的光盘与教程的书面内容相辅相成，图文并茂，动静结合，使看、听、读、写、说的学习更加具体、直观、逼真、生动、形象。教程所附动画时长约 100 分钟；歌曲 15 首，约 60 分钟；诗朗诵 67 首，约 25 分钟；共计 32 个课时。书中未规定各章节课时进度，教师可根据不同教学对象的具体情况灵活掌握，自学者也可根据自身情况安排学习进度。

2. 教材特点

（1）动态因素教学

动态音素教学，重视单音教学和发音的准确性。本教程重在“动态”，即以观看视频的方式，看、听和读本单元的语音。一个单元展示一个发音，视频同步展示出侧面口腔内舌头的变化及其语音器官的部位、声带动态、气流走向及正面口形、声音和字母。

（2）鲜明的中国文化特色

本教程以承载鲜明中国文化的俗语、成语、绕口令、孔孟语录、诸子名言、古今诗词、中国歌曲及中国国画为趣味汉语素材，进行语流教学。语流教学强调从会话入手，一开始就教短语或句子，音素在会话练习中逐步得到纠正。我们在直观、真实的动态音素教学的基础上，为学生提供准确清晰的汉语发音，强调在语流中学习并纠正语音。学生通过阅读、吟诵、聆听注有汉语拼音的具有浓厚的中国文化底蕴的语料，不仅可以纠正他们的偏误发音，培养其语感，促进音义的结合，收到事半功倍的效果，而且可以让学生领略到汉语及中国文化的博大与精深。另外，每章节的语料中都配以相关意境的中国水墨画，给读者带来愉悦的阅读感受和想象空间，引领读者从不同的角度去品味中国文化的情境和意蕴。这部分的教学目的在于通过传统的背诵、讲述等方式理解汉语语音，并能通过背诵材料增加汉语语音语感，还能从文句的上下文语境中理解意义和汉语语法。

（3）语音选读

为了给汉语学习者提供更多的汉语语音阅读资料，在本教程主体内容之后，编者还选录了“古典诗文”和“现代诗文”，并填注了拼音和相关注释和译文，以供学习者方便使用。

（4）汉字与书写

除了听辨音之外，汉字的学习和掌握对学习者也很重要。本教程简略选编了“汉字与书写”部分作为语音教学的补充。对汉语的特点、字形、笔画、笔顺和常用的部首作了简单的介绍与说明，其中对汉字字形、笔顺等内容以视频的方式进行了展示。这样，在学习汉语语音之外，对汉字文化感兴趣的学习者可以在此基础上继续深造，而不愿再学习汉字的学习者有了这些基本的汉字书写认读能力后，也可以为以后的汉语学习打下基础。

（5）双语讲解

本教程包括语音视听、字词听读和诗文听读，并配有相应的中英文讲解和相关视频、音频。

三、适用对象

本教程在国内可作为开设“现代汉语”课程的大专院校、职业院校（大学语文）推广普通话语音教学的参考教材，也可作为中小语文课、幼儿园识字学话的参考教材；在国外也可作为孔子学院和一些大学、中学教授汉语的语音教材。

本教程所选用的听读练习素材，在内容上和语言上都经过了不同程度的修改，拼音中该发生变调的声调一律未标原调，标变调，以便于对外汉语教学和外国留学生练习语音。谨此向所选材料的原作者致谢，并敬请原作者理解。教程中如有任何不当之处，敬请读者予以指正，以便进一步修订。

编者：刘伶 张黎

Instruction

I. The Main Idea of the Book

In learning a language, we should use our mouths and ears because a language is presented by its sounds. Therefore, we can say that there is no language without sounds. To learn a language, you should, at first, learn its pronunciations, which are presented through the vocal organs. Thus, the key point to learning a language well is to know how to pronounce every sound, and this is no exception to learning Chinese.

Therefore, according to *The Scheme for the Chinese Phonetic Alphabet*, we compiled and produced a new course book on Chinese Pinyin pronunciation, which is accompanied by a Video CD. The content of the VCD is to make clear the whole changing processes of the vocal organs in the oral cavity such as the lips, teeth, tongue, palates, larynx, vocal cords, trachea, nasal cavity, flow of air and so on .By using this new book, you can not only hear, but also watch clearly the articulation of each initial, final as well as tone. Herein, we study pronunciation is not only a matter of listening, speaking, reading and writing, but also watching, listening, speaking, reading and writing. Hence the study tends to be more visual, practical, real and scientific.

II. The Structure and Characteristics of the Book

1. The Structure of the Book

The course book consists of two parts: the one is paper book, the other is the attached VCD. In the CD attached the book, besides the animation of the pronunciations, there are many moving and static scenes and pictures, which are used to make watching, listening, reading, writing and speaking more specific, visual, life-like and vivid. The CD animation attached to the book, about 1,950 minutes long, is divided into four parts: initials, finals, tones and syllables, about 32 school hours. However, we did not fix the schedule, so, teachers can arrange the lessons based on the different situations of the students. In particular, the VCD, being complementary to the book, can be used not only at class, but also in extracurricular study. That is to say, you can pick it up without a teacher.

2. The Characteristics of the Book

(1) Dynamic Phoneme Teaching

Dynamic phoneme teaching makes the teaching of the tone and the pronunciation accurate. The animated content on the VCD makes the students to see the exact pronunciation of the vocal organs. Each unit demonstrates different pronunciation. The audio and video are broadcasted simultaneously. Displayed on the screen are the parts of the mouth offered in both front view and profile view, the movements of the tongue, air flow, the sounds as well as the letters.

(2) Vivid Chinese Culture

We offered many Chinese proverbs, tongue twisters, Confucius and Mencius collected sayings, and the pre-Qin thinkers' famous sayings, ancient and modern poetry, Chinese songs and Chinese traditional paintings, which bear Chinese culture vividly, will be used to the pronunciation variations teaching as the interest-teaching materials. During the pronunciation variations teaching, the phrases or the sentences from the conversation will be taught at the beginning, and the pronunciations of the phonemes are gradually corrected during the conversation. We provide the accurate and clear Chinese pronunciation for students based on dynamic phoneme teaching; it can help students to correct the wrong pronunciation at language class. Students may not only learn their pronunciation by correcting mistakes, but also develop their language sense through watching clearly, reading loudly and listening carefully Chinese culture language materials, which are marked with *Pinyin* in the Chapter Seven. They can help the students to master Chinese language, to understand greatness and profoundness of Chinese culture. Moreover, each unit's language materials are matched with some traditional Chinese paintings, which can bring the readers joyful reading and active imagination. They guide the readers to taste Chinese culture in different view. The teaching aim of this part in the book is to make the readers learn Chinese pronunciation by ways of recitation and speaking. Using these methods, the readers can not only improve their sense of Chinese language, but also understand the meanings of words and Chinese grammar in the proper context.

(3) Selected Reading on Chinese Pronunciation

In order to provide more reading materials on Chinese pronunciation, we select some classical poems, fables and stories in the book. They are divided into two groups: the first are ancient Chinese classics and the second are materials selected from modern works. For convenience of the readers' reading and learning, we mark the notes and the reading materials with *Pinyin*, and attach the classical text with translation in modern Chinese.

(4) Chinese Characters and Their Writing

Besides hearing how to distinguish between similar pronunciations of Chinese character, it is also important to learn how to write these as well. We carefully compiled the Chinese Characters and their writing part of the book as a supplement. The strokes, the order of the strokes, components, radicals and rules of writing Chinese characters are showed. Their shapes and the stroke order will be displayed on the screen. The readers, who are interested in learning the traditional culture contained by Chinese characters, can study Chinese language further on the foundation offered by this book; As for the readers who don't want to continue with Chinese language learning will at least have a firm foundation, which is helpful to their future Chinese learning.

(5) Bialingual Explanations

The book is compiled of three components namely seeing, listening and reading of Chinese pronunciation of Chinese words, poems and stories. The exercises and explanations in the book are both in Chinese and in English. The CD and MP3s on Chinese pronunciation accompany to our book.

III. The Target Reader of the Course Book

At home, the book applies to modern Chinese course in colleges and vocational schools. It can also be used as a reference book in primary, secondary schools and kindergartens to popularize mandarin. Overseas, it applies to the Confucius institute and a number of universities and secondary school where Chinese is taught.

The listening and reading materials in this course were adapted to a certain degree in its contents and languages, and the tones which should be changed are marked changed tones instead of original tones. In order to be convenient to Chinese teaching and foreigers practising Chinese. We are thankful to the original author of the selected materials and his understanding. We welcome corrections from readers for further adaptation.

The Compilers: Liu Ling & Zhang Li

第一章 现代汉语语音概说

Chapter I Summary of Modern Chinese Pronunciation

★ 语音的形成

★ 汉语普通话以北京音为标准音。它是以一个汉字为一个音节的。每个音节包含声母、韵母和声调。现代汉语普通话有21个辅音声母和零声母、39个韵母、4个声调。

★ 《汉语拼音方案》和国际音标

第一节 语音的形成

Section I Taking Form of Pronunciation

语言是人类最重要的交际工具。语言是通过语音形式表现出来的。那么，语音又是如何形成的呢？

Human language is the most important tool of communication. Language is presented through the manner of articulation. So, how dose the articulation take form?

语音是我们说话时肺部呼出的气流，通过支气管、喉头、声带、咽头、小舌、软腭、舌根、硬腭、舌面、舌尖、齿龈、上下齿、双唇等不同的阻碍变化以及口腔、鼻腔的共鸣调节而形成的。口腔的开合、元音舌位高低的变化是通过下颌（下巴颏儿）的升降来完成的。

Speech sound is the air exhaled from the lungs when we speak. It takes form through different changes of the windpipe, larynx, vocal cords, soft palate, lingual root, hard palate, blade of the tongue, tip of the tongue, alveolar, upper and lower teeth, lips, *etc.*, and the resonance of the oral and nasal cavities. The opening and closing of the oral cavity and the changes of the tongue places are completed through raising and lowering the lower jaw.

鼻腔	nasal cavity	喉	larynx
鼻孔	nostril	舌根	lingual root
齿龈	gum	小舌	uvula
上齿	upper teeth	腭	palate
下齿	lower teeth	软腭	soft palate
上唇	upper lip	硬腭	hard palate
下唇	lower lip	舌	tongue
肺	lung	舌尖	tip of the tongue
气管	windpipe	舌面	blade of the tongue
食道	oesophagus	口腔	oral cavity
声带	vocal cords		
咽	pharynx		

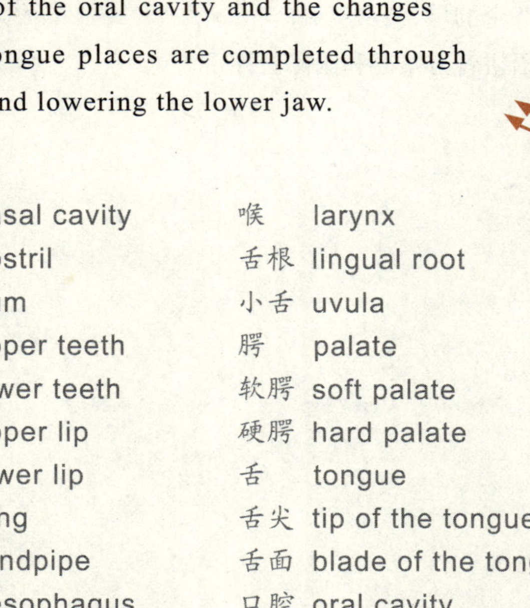

图 1-1 人体发音器官部位示意图
Figure 1-1 Places of the Vocal Organs

普通话的声母、韵母、声调的发音就是这样形成的。图 1-2 中和教学光盘中的成音状况，分别用侧面口腔中发音器官活动变化图、元音舌位移动图、正面口形图、字母、声调走向图表示。图中带箭头的实线表示气流强的音，带箭头的虚线表示气流弱的音。

So are formed the initials, finals and the tones of these pronunciations. The formation of all the speech sounds are presented by the places of the mouth from right, in front and in profile, the variation of the vocal organs, the places of the tongue and the trends of the tones. In Figure 1-2, the sounds with strong air are shown in the arrow of solid line and the sounds with weak air are shown in the arrow of dotted lines.

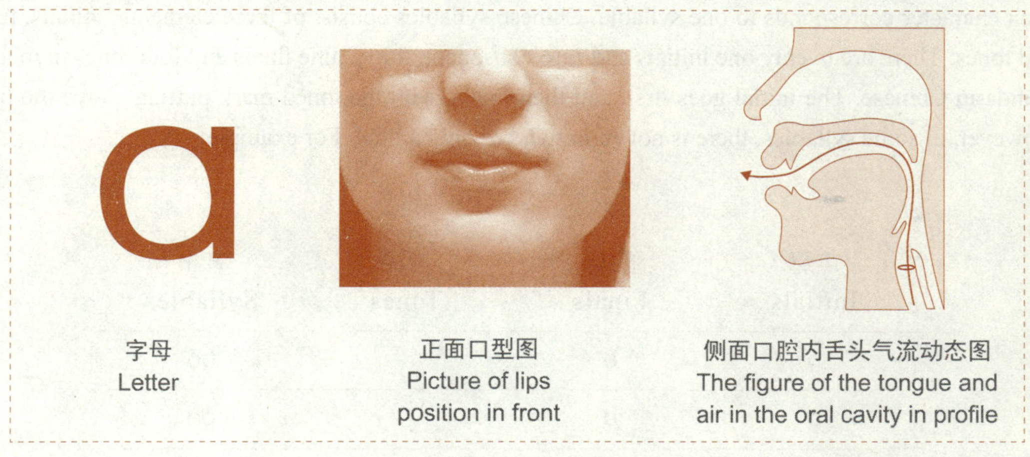

图 1-2
Figure 1-2

说话是人们运用有声语言在声波中通过口耳进行交际的语言形式。图1-3表示口耳之间的关系；图1-4表示口耳之间的声波传送。

Speaking is a language form,which people use phonic language to communicate with each other by word-of-mouth. Figure 1-3 shows relationship between the mouth and the ears. Figure 1-4 illustrate transmission of sound-wave between the mouth and the ears.

图 1-3 口耳关系示意图
Figure 1-3 Schematic illustration of relationship between the mouth and the ears

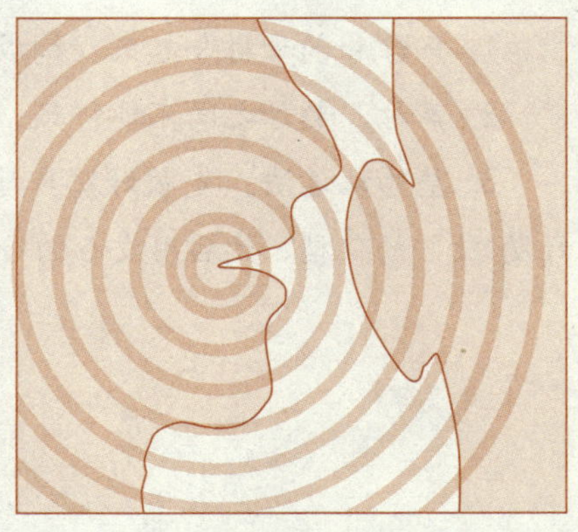

图 1-4 口耳之间声波传送示意图
Figure 1-4 Schematic illustration of sound-wave between the mouth and the ears

第二节 现代汉语语音简介

Section II Introduction of Modern Chinese Pronunciation

汉语普通话以北京音为标准音。它是以一个汉字为一个音节的。每个音节包含声母、韵母和声调。现代汉语普通话有21个辅音声母和零声母、39个韵母、4个声调。声母在前，韵母在后，声调在韵母上，但有的音节只有韵母没有声母。例如：

The phonology of *Putonghua* is based on the Beijing dialect of mandarin Chinese. In Chinese, each character corresponds to one syllable. Chinese syllables consist of three elements: initials, finals and tones. There are twenty one initials and zero consonant, thirty-nine finals and four tones in modern mandarin Chinese. The initial goes first, and then finals, with the toned mark putting above the final. However, in some syllables, there is not an initial, but only a final. For example:

声母 Initials	韵母 Finals	声调 Tones	音节 Syllables
b	o	ˉ	bō
p	ɑ	ˊ	pá
m	u	ˇ	mǔ
/	ɑi	ˋ	ài
/	in	ˊ	yín
/	o	ˇ	wǒ

【提示】

1. 声母和韵母拼合起来，构成一个音节，就是拼音。

2. 声母、韵母之间不能停顿。

3. 整体认读法。先做好发声母的准备，然后读带声调的韵母。例如“波”，先摆好发“b”的口型，然后用发ō的气流冲开紧闭的双唇并连成音节，就发出了“bō”音。

第三节 记音符号

Section III Symbols to Mark Pronunciation

1.《汉语拼音方案》 *The Scheme for the Chinese Phonetic Alphabet*

《汉语拼音方案》是记录现代汉语语音系统的一套符号和拼音规则。主要用途是给汉字注音。它由字母表、声母表、韵母表、声调符号、隔音符号五部分组成。

The Scheme for the Chinese Phonetic Alphabet is formulated by the state for the Chinese phonetic alphabet and its spelling rules. The main purpose of it is to mark Chinese Characters with phonetic alphabets and spell correctly *Putonghua*. It includes Alphabet, The Table of Initials, The Table of Finals, Tone Marks and Syllable-Dividing Marks.

字母表

The Table of Alphabet

字母：	Aɑ	Bb	Cc	Dd	Ee	Ff	Gg
名称：	ㄚ	ㄅㄝ	ㄘㄝ	ㄉㄝ	ㄜ	ㄝㄈ	ㄍㄝ
	Hh	Ii	Jj	Kk	Ll	Mm	Nn
	ㄏㄚ	ㄧ	ㄐㄧㄝ	ㄎㄝ	ㄝㄌ	ㄝㄇ	ㄋㄝ
	Oo	Pp	Qq	Rr	Ss	Tt	
	ㄛ	ㄆㄝ	ㄑㄧㄡ	ㄚㄦ	ㄝㄙ	ㄊㄝ	
	Uu	Vv	Ww	Xx	Yy	Zz	
	ㄨ	ㄪㄝ	ㄨㄚ	ㄒㄧ	ㄧㄚ	ㄗㄝ	

1. V 只用来拼写外来语、少数民族语言和方言。

V is used to spell the loan words, language of the minorities and some dialects.

2. 字母的手写体依照拉丁字母的一般书写规则。

The script of the letters is based on the Latin letters.

声母表
The Table of Initials

字母：	b	p	m	f	d	t	n	l
名称：	ㄅ玻	ㄆ坡	ㄇ摸	ㄈ佛	ㄉ得	ㄊ特	ㄋ讷	ㄌ勒
	g	k	h		j	q	x	
	ㄍ哥	ㄎ科	ㄏ喝		ㄐ基	ㄑ欺	ㄒ希	
	zh	ch	sh	r	z	c	s	
	ㄓ知	ㄔ蚩	ㄕ诗	ㄖ日	ㄗ资	ㄘ雌	ㄙ思	

在给汉字注音的时候，为了使拼式简短，zh ch sh 可以省作 ẑ ĉ ŝ。

When annotate the *Pinyin* for each character, we use ẑ ĉ ŝ instead of zh ch sh to make them much easier.

韵母表
The Table of Finals

	i ㄧ 衣	u ㄨ 乌	ü ㄩ 迂
a ㄚ 啊	ia ㄧㄚ 呀	ua ㄨㄚ 蛙	
o ㄛ 喔		uo ㄨㄛ 窝	
e ㄜ 鹅	ie ㄧㄝ 耶		üe ㄩㄝ 约
ai ㄞ 哀		uai ㄨㄞ 歪	
ei ㄟ 欸		uei ㄨㄟ 威	
ao ㄠ 熬	iao ㄧㄠ 腰		
ou ㄡ 欧	iou ㄧㄡ 忧		
an ㄢ 安	ian ㄧㄢ 烟	uan ㄨㄢ 弯	üan ㄩㄢ 冤
en ㄣ 恩	in ㄧㄣ 因	uen ㄨㄣ 温	ün ㄩㄣ 晕
ang ㄤ 昂	iang ㄧㄤ 央	uang ㄨㄤ 汪	
eng ㄥ 亨的韵母	ing ㄧㄥ 英	ueng ㄨㄥ 翁	
ong （ㄨㄥ）轰的韵母	iong ㄩㄥ 雍		

1.“知、蚩、诗、日、资、雌、思”等七个音节的韵母用 i，即：知、蚩、诗、日、资、雌、思等字拼作 zhi, chi, shi, ri, zi, ci, si。

The finals of “知、蚩、诗、日、资、雌、思” is i. Herein,the *Pinyin* of each character is zhi, chi , shi , ri , zi , ci and si respectively.

2. 韵母儿写成 er，用作韵尾的时候写成 r。例如：“儿童”拼作 ertong，“花儿”拼作 huar。

The final 儿 can be written as er. If it is used in the end of the final, it can be changed into r.Therefore, we write ertong for “儿童” and huar for “花儿”.

3. 韵母せ单用的时候写成 ê。

When we use the single せ, it can be written as ê.

4. i 行的韵母，前面没有声母的时候，写成 yi（衣），ya（呀），ye（耶），yao（腰），you（忧），yan（烟），yin（因），yang（央），ying（英），yong（雍）。

When there is no initials in front of the final i,the *Pinyin* of 衣，呀，耶，腰，忧，烟，央，英，雍 can be written yi, ya, ye, yao, you, yan, yin, yang, ying, yong respectively.

u 行的韵母，前面没有声母的时候，写成 wu（乌），wa（蛙），wo（窝），wai（歪），wei（威），wan（弯），wen（温），wang（汪），weng（翁）。

When there is no initials in front of the final u, the *Pinyin* of 乌，蛙，窝，歪，威，弯，温，汪，翁 can be written wu , wa , wo , wai , wei , wan , wen , wang and weng respectively.

ü 行的韵母，前面没有声母的时候，写成 yu（迂），yue（约），yuan（冤），yun（晕），ü 上两点省略。

When there is no initials in front of the final ü, the *Pinyin* of 迂，约，冤，晕 can be yu, yue, yuan and yun. And the two dots on ü are omitted.

ü 行的韵母跟声母 j，q，x 拼的时候，写成 ju（居），qu（区），xu（虚），ü 上两点也省略；但是跟声母 n，l 拼的时候，仍然写成 nü（女），lü（吕）。

If the final ü is used after the initials j, q and x, the two dots on it are omitted. So, ju（居），qu（区），xu（虚） can be pronounced as ju, qu and xu. However, there exist the two dots when it is after n and l.

5. iou，uei，uen 前面加声母的时候，写成 iu，ui，un。例如 niu（牛），gui（归），lun（论）。

When there is an initial before iou, uei and uen, they are changed into iu, ui and un respectively such as niu（牛），gui（归）and lun（论）.

6. 在给汉字注音的时候，为了使拼写简短，ng 可以省作 ŋ。

When we write the *Pinyin* for the characters, we often use ŋ instead of ng in order to make it shorter and easier.

声调符号
Tone Marks

阴平	阳平	上声	去声
ˉ	ˊ	ˇ	ˋ
High-level tone	Rising tone	Falling-rising tone	Falling tone

声调符号标在音节的主要元音上。轻声不标。例如：

A tone mark is usually on the main finals of a syllable. There is no mark when it is a neutral tone. For example:

妈 mā	麻 má	马 mǎ	骂 mà	吗 ma
（阴平）	（阳平）	（上声）	（去声）	（轻声）

隔音符号
Syllable-Dividing Marks

ɑ，o，e 开头的音节连接在其他音节后面的时候，如果音节的界限发生混淆，用隔音符号（'）隔开。例如：pi'ɑo（皮袄）。

If a syllable, beginning with ɑ, o or e, follows some other syllables, we usually use (') to separate them to avoid mixing them up. For example: pi'ɑo.

2. 国际音标 International Phonetic Alphabet (IPA)

国际音标是国际语音学会1888年制订的一套记音符号，是现在国际通用的语音符号。后附汉语拼音字母、注音符号和国际音标对照表。

The International Phonetic Alphabet (IPA) is an alphabetic system of phonetic notation. It was devised by the International Phonetic Association in 1888. It was devised to regulate the sounds of spoken languages. The Table of the Chinese Phonetic Alphabet, Phonetic Symbols and International Phonetic Alphabet is attached.

汉语拼音字母、注音符号和国际音标对照表

The Table of Chinese Phonetic Alphabet, Phonetic Symbols and International Phonetic Alphabet

拼音字母 Phonetic Alphabet	注音符号 Phonetic Symbols	国际音标 IPA	拼音字母 PA	注音符号 PS	国际音标 IPA	拼音字母 PA	注音符号 PS	国际音标 IPA
b	ㄅ	[p]	z	ㄗ	[ts]	iɑ	ㄧㄚ	[iʌ]
p	ㄆ	[p‘]	c	ㄘ	[ts‘]	ie	ㄧㄝ	[iɛ]
m	ㄇ	[m]	s	ㄙ	[s]	iɑo	ㄧㄠ	[iɑu]
f	ㄈ	[f]	ɑ	ㄚ	[A]	iou	ㄧㄡ	[iou]
Á	ㄪ	[v]	o	ㄛ	[o]	iɑn	ㄧㄢ	[iɛn]
d	ㄉ	[t]	e	ㄜ	[ɣ]	in	ㄧㄣ	[in]
t	ㄊ	[t‘]	ê	ㄝ	[ɛ]	iɑng	ㄧㄤ	[iɑŋ]
n	ㄋ	[n]	i	ㄧ	[i]	ing	ㄧㄥ	[iŋ]
l	ㄌ	[l]	-i（前）	ㄭ	[ɿ]	uɑ	ㄨㄚ	[uA]
g	ㄍ	[k]	-i（后）	ㄭ	[ʅ]	uo	ㄨㄛ	[uo]
k	ㄎ	[k‘]	u	ㄨ	[u]	uɑi	ㄨㄞ	[uai]
(ng)	ㄫ	[ŋ]	ü	ㄩ	[y]	uei	ㄨㄟ	[uei]
h	ㄏ	[x]	er	ㄦ	[ɚ]	uɑn	ㄨㄢ	[uan]
j	ㄐ	[tɕ]	ɑi	ㄞ	[ai]	uen	ㄨㄣ	[uən]
q	ㄑ	[tɕ‘]	ei	ㄟ	[ei]	uɑng	ㄨㄤ	[uɑŋ]
/	ㄬ	[ȵ]	ɑo	ㄠ	[ɑu]	ueng	ㄨㄥ	[uəŋ]
x	ㄒ	[ɕ]	ou	ㄡ	[ou]	ong	ㄨㄥ	[uŋ]
zh	ㄓ	[tʂ]	ɑn	ㄢ	[an]	üe	ㄩㄝ	[yɛ]
ch	ㄔ	[tʂ‘]	en	ㄣ	[ən]	üɑn	ㄩㄢ	[yan]
sh	ㄕ	[ʂ]	ɑng	ㄤ	[ɑŋ]	ün	ㄩㄣ	[yn]
r	ㄖ	[ʐ]	eng	ㄥ	[əŋ]	iong	ㄩㄥ	[yŋ]

汉语拼音字母歌

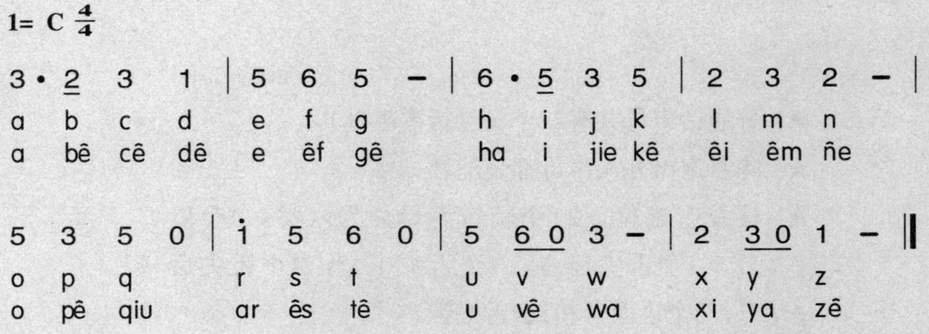

1= C $\frac{4}{4}$

3 • 2 3 1 | 5 6 5 – | 6 • 5 3 5 | 2 3 2 – |
a b c d e f g h i j k l m n
a bê cê dê e êf gê ha i jie kê êi êm ñe

5 3 5 0 | i 5 6 0 | 5 6 0 3 – | 2 3 0 1 – ‖
o p q r s t u v w x y z
o pê qiu ar ês tê u vê wa xi ya zê

第二章　普通话声母及发音

Chapter II　Initials and Their Pronunciation in *Putonghua*

★ 普通话声母共有22个（包括零声母）。

★ 除零声母外，声母都是辅音。

★ 按发音部位，21个辅音声母分为六类：4个唇音，3个舌尖前音，4个舌尖中音，4个舌尖后音，3个舌面音和3个舌根音。

★ 零声母中“y，w”，是起隔音作用的字母。

普通话的辅音声母共有 21 个：b, p, m, f, z, c, s, d, t, n, l, zh, ch, sh, r, j, q, x, g, k, h。它们的发音不同是由于发音器官接触、阻碍变化和方法的不同而形成的。可分为七类五种。

There are a total of twenty-one initials in *Putonghua*. They are b, p, m, f, z, c, s, d, t, n, l, zh, ch, sh, r, j, q, x, g, k, h. Their different pronunciations are caused by the various contacts as well as the changes and manners of impediments of the vocal organs. They can be divided into 7 categories and 5 kinds.

从发音部位上分为：双唇音、唇齿音、舌尖前音、舌尖中音、舌尖后音、舌面音、舌根音七类；从发音方法上分为：塞音、塞擦音、擦音、鼻音、边音五种。其中 b, p, d, t, g, k 发音时先堵后开，是塞音；z, c, zh, ch, j, q 先堵塞后摩擦，是塞擦音；f, s, sh, r, x, h 发音时不堵塞全摩擦，是擦音；m, n 从鼻孔出气，是鼻音；l 发音时从舌头两边出气，是边音；m, n, l, r 发音时声带振动，是浊音；其他声母均为清音。另外，b, d, g, z, zh, j 发音时气流较轻较弱，是不送气音；p, t, k, c, ch, q 发音时气流较强，是送气音。

From the point of various places of articulation, they can be divided into 7 categories:bilabial, labio-dental, supra-dental, alveolar, retroflex, dorsal and velar. From the manners of articulation, they can be divided into five categories:occlusive, affricate, fricative, nasal and lateral. Among the articulations, b, p, d, t, g and k belong to the occlusive; z, c, zh, ch, j and q belong to the affricate; f, s, sh, r, x and h to the fricative; m and n to the nasal; and l to the lateral. And among all the initials, m, n, l and r are voiced because they are produced with a vibration of the vocal cords. Except from these, all the other initials are unvoiced. Moreover, b, d, g, z, zh and j are un-aspirated because they are produced with very weak air. p, t, k, c, ch and q are aspirated.

普通话声母总表
The Table of Initials in *Putonghua*

声母 \ 发音方法 / 发音部位			塞音 Occlusive 清音 Unvoiced 气流弱音 Unaspirated	塞音 Occlusive 清音 Unvoiced 气流强音 Aspirated	塞擦音 Affricate 清音 Unvoiced 气流弱音 Unaspirated	塞擦音 Affricate 清音 Unvoiced 气流强音 Aspirated	擦音 Fricative 清音 Unvoiced	擦音 Fricative 浊音 Voiced	鼻音 Nasal 浊音 Voiced	边音 Lateral 浊音 Voiced
唇音 Labial	双唇音 Bilabial	上唇下齿 Upper Lip and Lower Teeth	b [p]	p [p‘]					m [m]	
唇音 Labial	唇齿音 Labio-dental	上齿下唇 Upper Teeth and Lower Lip					f [f]			
舌尖前音 Dental Sibilant		舌尖上齿背 Tip of the Tongue and Upper Back of Teeth			z [ts]	c [ts‘]	s [s]			
舌尖中音 Alveolar		舌尖上齿龈 Tip of the Tongue and the Upper Gum Teeth Ridge	d [t]	t [t‘]					n [n]	l [l]
舌尖后音 Retroflex		舌尖硬腭前 Tip of the Tongue and the Front of the Hard Palate			zh [tʂ]	ch [tʂ‘]	sh [ʂ]	r [ʐ]		
舌面音 Palatal		舌面硬腭 Front of the Tongue and Middle Hard Palate			j [tɕ]	q [tɕ‘]	x [ɕ]			
舌根音 Velar		舌根软腭 Back of the Tongue and Soft Palate	g [k]	k [k‘]			h [x]			

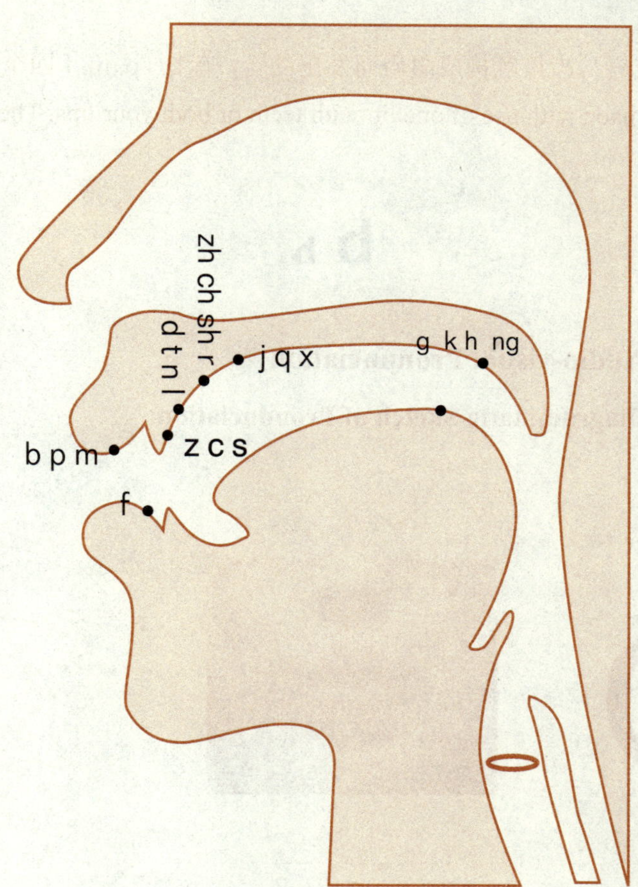

图 2-1 口腔内声母发音部位图
Figure 2-1 The picture of initial pronouncing position in oral cavity

现根据“总表”顺序，学习声母。

Now, we will learn the initials according to the order in the above table.

第一节 唇音
Section I Labials

唇音，是双唇或唇与齿接触构成阻碍而发出的音，有b，p，m，f四个。（详见“总表”）

Labial, a sound made with use of one lip with teeth or both your lips. There are four kinds of labial, b，p，m and f.

b b

一 语音视听 Audio-visual Pronunciation

1. 发音示意图 Diagrammatic Sketch of Pronunciation

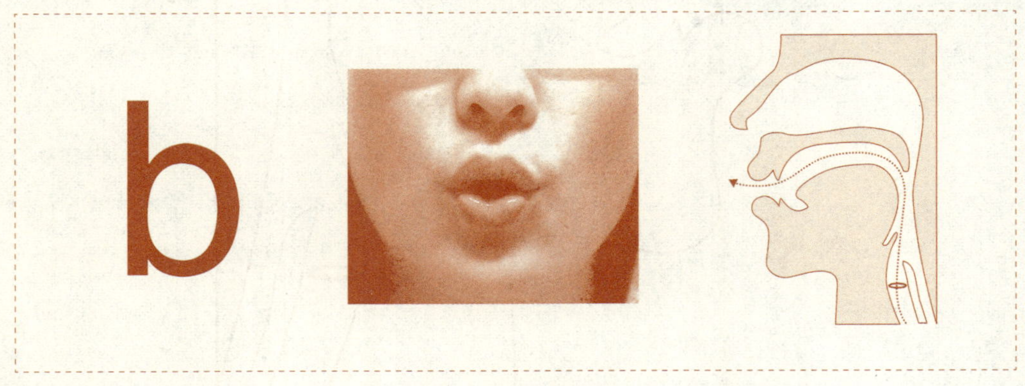

2. 发音特点 Characteristics of Pronunciation

b [p] 双唇、清、弱气流、塞音。发音时，双唇紧闭，弱气流冲开双唇阻碍成音。

b [p] A bilabial, unvoiced, weak airstream, occlusive sound. It is produced by keeping the lips tightly closed and the weak airstream bursts the lips open to form the sound.

二 听读词语 Listen and Read the Following Words

巴	bā	bar
拔	bá	pull
把	bǎ	handle

爸	bà	father
包	bāo	bag
宝	bǎo	treasure
报	bào	newspaper
标本	biāoběn	sample
背包	bēibāo	backpack
白布	bái bù	white cloth

【提示】

汉语是声调语言，声调有区别意义的作用。

如：巴（bā）、拔（bá）、把（bǎ）、爸（bà），体现了汉语普通话在发音时声调高低、升降的变化。

三　速读短语，注意加点字的声母 Read Phrases Quickly, Pay Attention to the Initials of the Characters Marked with Dots

八九不离十	bā jiǔ bù lí shí	about right, very near
白日做梦	bái rì zuò mèng	spin daydreams
不得了	bù déliǎo	terrible; horrible
宝刀不老	bǎo dāo bù lǎo	the man is old , but not his sword; elderly person still at the height of their skills

四　跟读绕口令，注意句中加点字的声母 Read the Tongue Twister Following the Teacher, Pay Attention to the Initials of the Characters Marked with Dots

Bābān biāobīng bēi bēibāo, bēibāo biāobīng bēi bàobiǎo.
Biāobīng bēibāo bēi biāoběn, bēibāo biāobīng bái bùbāo.

八班标兵背背包，背包标兵背报表。
标兵背包背标本，背包标兵白布包。

五　听诵古诗，给诗中加点的字注上声母 Listen and Recite the Ancient Poem, Write the Initials for the Characters Marked with Dots

游园不值

宋 · 叶绍翁

应怜屐齿印苍苔，小扣柴扉久不开。

春色满园关不住，一枝红杏出墙来。

【提示】

全诗写诗人春日游园观花的所见所闻，写得十分形象而又富有理趣。这首诗情景交融，千古传诵。诗人去朋友家游园看花，长满苍苔的路上遍印着诗人木屐钉齿的繁荣痕迹，敲了半天柴门，没有人来开。诗人从露在墙头的一枝杏花想象出满园的春色，说：“园门虽然关得紧，春色却是关不住的啊！”

叶绍翁：南宋中期诗人，字嗣宗，号靖逸，祖籍建安（今福建建瓯），本姓李，后嗣于龙泉（今属浙江）叶氏。生卒年不详，是江湖派诗人。他的诗以七言绝句最佳，有诗集《靖逸小集》，著有《四朝闻见录》。

六　听歌学声母，给歌词中加点的字注上声母 Learn Initials by Listening to a Song, Write the Initials for the Characters Marked with Dots in the Lyrics

读书郎

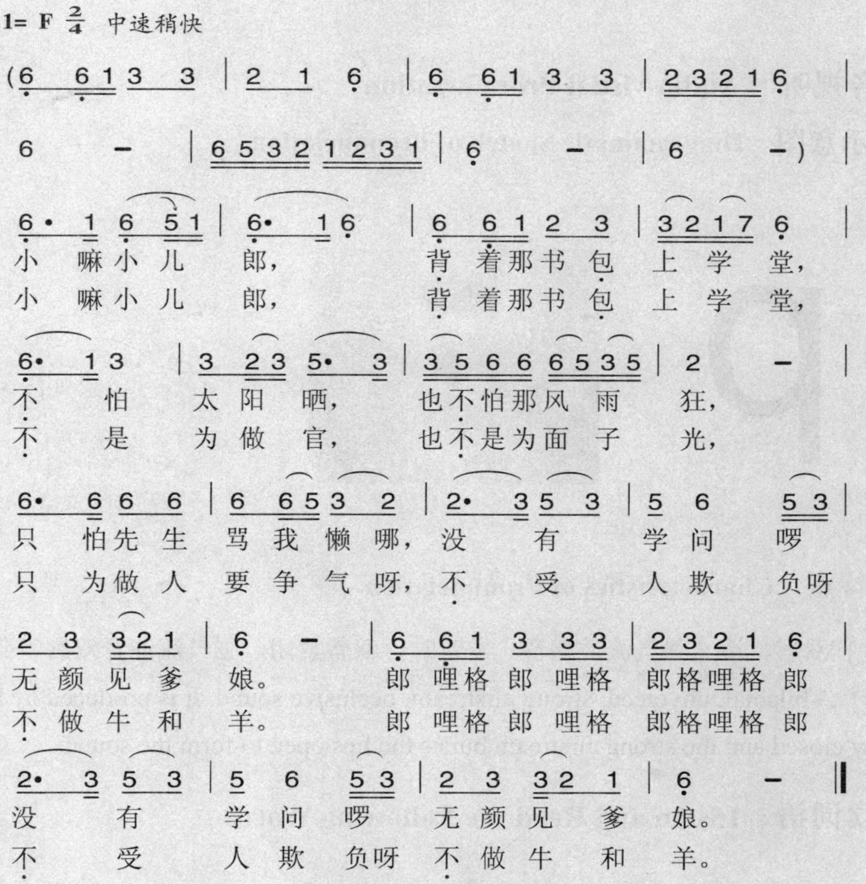

1= F $\frac{2}{4}$ 中速稍快

(6 613 3 | 2 1 6 | 6 61 3 3 | 23216 |

6 – | 65321231 | 6 – | 6 –) |

6· 1 6 51 | 6· 16 | 6 61 2 3 | 32176 |
小 嘛 小 儿 郎， 背 着 那 书 包 上 学 堂，
小 嘛 小 儿 郎， 背 着 那 书 包 上 学 堂，

6· 1 3 | 3 23 5· 3 | 3566 6535 | 2 – |
不 怕 太 阳 晒， 也 不 怕 那 风 雨 狂，
不 是 为 做 官， 也 不 是 为 面 子 光，

6· 6 6 6 | 6 653 2 | 2· 3 5 3 | 5 6 53 |
只 怕 先 生 骂 我 懒 哪， 没 有 学 问 啰
只 为 做 人 要 争 气 呀， 不 受 人 欺 负 呀

2 3 321 | 6 – | 6 61 3 33 | 23216 |
无 颜 见 爹 娘。 郎 哩 格 郎 哩 格 郎 格 哩 格 郎
不 做 牛 和 羊。 郎 哩 格 郎 哩 格 郎 格 哩 格 郎

2· 3 5 3 | 5 6 53 | 2 3 32 1 | 6 – ‖
没 有 学 问 啰 无 颜 见 爹 娘。
不 受 人 欺 负 呀 不 做 牛 和 羊。

【提示】

“不”的变调

“不”单念或者用在词尾末尾，声调不变，读原调。例如：不（bù）、偏不（piānbù）。

“不”在非去声（一、二、三声）前，不变调。例如：不吃（bùchī）、不同（bùtóng）、不想（bùxiǎng）。

在以下情况，“不”会发生变调：

1. 在去声（第四声）前，读第二声。例如：不怕（búpà）、不是（búshì）、不受（búshòu）、不做（búzuò）。

2. “不”在相同的动词中间，读轻声。例如：来不来（lái bu lái）、找不找（zhǎo bu zhǎo）、开不开（kāi bu kāi）。

3. “不”在可能补语中读轻声。例如：做不好（zuò buhǎo）、来不了（lái buliǎo）。

“不”的变调现象只出现在口语中，书面上调号不变，但本书为方便学习者，将变调后的调号标记出来。

p p

一 语音视听 Audio-visual Pronunciation

1. 发音示意图 Diagrammatic Sketch of Pronunciation

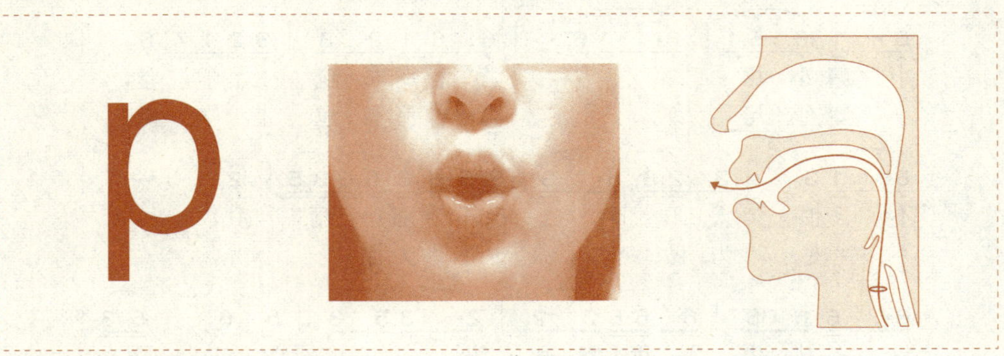

2. 发音特点 Characteristics of Pronunciation

p [p‘] 双唇、清、强气流、塞音。发音时，双唇紧闭，强气流冲开双唇阻碍成音。

p [p‘] A bilabial, unvoiced, strong airstream, occlusive sound. It is produced by keeping the lips tightly closed and the strong airstream bursts the lips open to form the sound.

二 听读词语 Listen and Read the Following Words

1.

批	pī	criticize
皮	pí	fur
匹	pǐ	match
拼	pīn	spell
品	pǐn	taste
乒乓	pīngpāng	table tennis
拼盘	pīnpán	cold platter
婆婆	pópo	mother-in-law
批评	pīpíng	criticize
品牌	pǐnpái	brand
皮袍	pípáo	furred robe

【提示】

b 的气流弱，p 的气流强。

2.

奔跑	bēnpǎo	run
跑步	pǎobù	run, jog
别跑	biépǎo	don’t run
拼搏	pīnbó	fight with all one’s might for the victory in a battle or competition
鞭炮	biānpào	firecrackers
背叛	bèipàn	betray
配备	pèibèi	allocate,provide
普遍	pǔbiàn	universal
布匹	bùpǐ	cloth
旁边	pángbiān	beside
爆破	bàopò	blow up
瀑布	pùbù	waterfall
绑票	bǎngpiào	kidnap (for ransom)
赔本	péiběn	loose money

三 速读短语，注意加点字的声母 Read Phrases Quickly, Pay Attention to the Initials of the Characters Marked with Dots

碰钉子	pèng dīngzi	be rebuffed; hit a snag
跑买卖	pǎo mǎimai	be a travelling businessman
破旧立新	pò jiù lì xīn	destroy the old and establish the new
平平安安	píngping-ānān	safe and sound; without an accident or danger

四 跟读绕口令，注意句中加点字的声母 Read the Tongue Twister Following the Teacher, Pay Attention to the Initials of the Characters Marked with Dots

Yuàn li yǒu gè pén, pén li fàngzhe jǐgè bōli píng, měngrán láile yízhènfēng, fēng chuī pén yáo píng pèng pén lái píng pèng píng, pīngpīng-pāngpāng pīngpīng-pāngpāng,pén guài píng lái píng guài fēng, fēng chuī pén fān píng pò fēng bù píng.

院里有个盆，盆里放着几个玻璃瓶，猛然来了一阵风，风吹盆摇瓶碰盆来瓶碰瓶，乒乒乓乓乒乒乓乓，盆怪瓶来瓶怪风，风吹盆翻瓶破风不平。

【提示】

一阵（yīzhèn），读“yízhèn”，是“一”的变调现象。

“一”的变调

“一”在单念或出现在词句末尾以及在序数中声调不变，“一”读阴平（一声）。如：一（yī），十一（shíyī），第一（dìyī），统一（tǒngyī）。

在以下情况中，“一”会发生变调现象：

1.“一”在去声（四声）字前，读阳平（二声）。如：一样（yíyàng），一向（yíxàng），一架（yíjià），一阵（yízhèn）。

2.“一”在非去声（一、二、三声）字前，读去声（四声）。如：一般（yìbān），一天（yìtiān），一年（yìnián），一条（yìtiáo），一早（yìzǎo），一晚（yìwǎn）。

3.“一”出现在两个相同的动词中间时，读轻声。如：想一想（xiǎng yi xiǎng），看一看（kàn yi kàn），走一走（zǒu yi zǒu），试一试（shì yi shì）。

“一”的变调现象只出现在口语中，书面上调号不变。为了方便学习者，本书将“一”变调后的调号标记出来。

五 听诵古诗，给诗中加点的字注上声母 Listen and Recite the Ancient Poem, Write the Initials for the Characters Marked with Dots

凉州词

唐·王翰

葡萄美酒夜光杯，
欲饮琵琶马上催。
醉卧沙场君莫笑，
古来征战几人回？

【提示】

《凉州词》：词牌名。此诗写了西北边陲的军旅生活，将士们视死如归、乐观的精神，是边塞诗的名篇。

王翰，字子羽，晋阳人。其作以《凉州词二首》最负盛名。有文集十卷，今存诗一卷。

m m

一 语音视听 Audio-visual Pronunciation

1. 发音示意图 Diagrammatic Sketch of Pronunciation

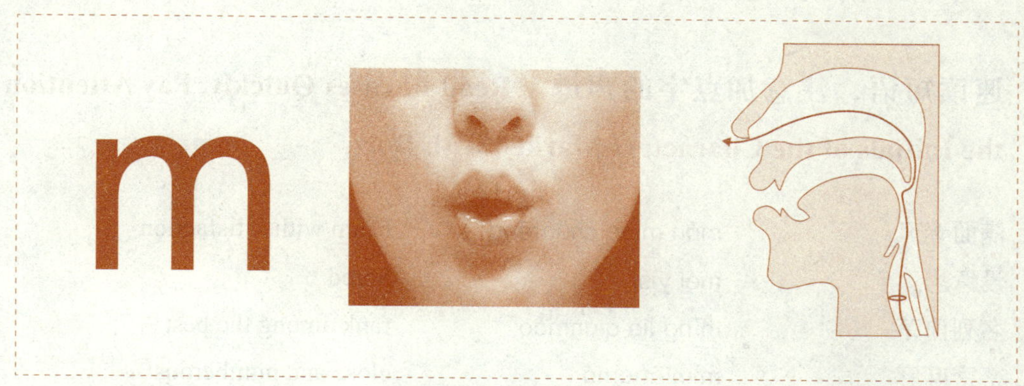

2. 发音特点 Characteristics of Pronunciation

m [m] 双唇、浊、鼻音。发音时，双唇紧闭，气流通过鼻腔冲出鼻孔成音。

m [m] A bilabial, voiced, nasal sound. It is produced by keeping the lips tightly closed and the airstream flow out of the nose through the nasal cavity.

二 听读词语 Listen and Read the Following Words

嘛	má	modal particle
马	mǎ	horse
骂	mà	curse
磨	mó	grind
墨	mò	ink
忙	máng	busy
妈妈	māma	mama
眉毛	méimao	eyebrow
麻木	mámù	numb
妹妹	mèimei	sister
买卖	mǎimai	business

【提示】

妈妈（māma），眉毛（méimao），妹妹（mèimei），买卖（mǎimai）中第二个汉字读得又轻又短，是汉语普通话中的轻声现象。在拼写中，轻声音节无调号。例如:

啊 a 用在句末，表示感叹。

吧 ba 用在句末，表示征求某人的意见、建议、要求或是温和的命令。

吗 ma 用于疑问句句末。

三 速读短语，注意加点字的声母 Read Phrases Quickly, Pay Attention to the Initials of the Characters Marked with Dots

满面春风	mǎn miàn chūnfēng	beam with satisfaction
没意思	méi yìsi	bored
名列前茅	míng liè qiánmáo	rank among the best
密密麻麻	mìmi-mámá	close and numberous

四 跟读绕口令，注意句中加点字的声母 Read the Tongue Twister Following the Teacher, Pay Attention to the Initials of the Characters Marked with Dots

Máotóng yán mò mò mǒ Máotóng yímò mò,
Méixiāng tiān méi méi mǐn méixiāng liǎngméi méi.

毛童研墨墨抹毛童一脉墨，
梅香添煤煤抿梅香两眉煤。

【提示】

研墨：磨墨。在书写前，手捏墨锭在砚台里的水中绕磨成墨汁的过程。

墨锭：干墨块的名称。松木、煤、炭等燃烧时熏下的黑烟（烟子）加入石墨等搅拌成黑团，再放入模具中烘压成大小不等的扁平条形干墨块。

砚台：用精选石料雕琢成磨制墨汁的器皿，又叫砚。砚台在中国源远流长，台型精美，著名的有歙（xī）砚、洮砚、端砚、澄泥砚等。被誉为文房四宝（纸、墨、笔、砚）之一。

砚台

五 听诵古诗，给诗中加点的字注上声母 Listen and Recite the Ancient Poem, Write the Initials for the Characters Marked with Dots

咏怀古迹二首（其二）

唐·杜甫

画图省识春风面，环佩空归月夜魂。
千载琵琶作胡语，分明怨恨曲中论。

【提示】

此诗是作者在昭君出生地昭君村看到昭君墓而写。

画图：古代皇帝选妃凭画像美不美而定。昭君本美，因她没给画师行贿而画丑不选。后被选派出塞和番，客死番邦。她作的“琵琶曲”千古流传。

杜甫（公元712—公元770），河南巩县（今巩义市）人。字子美，自号少陵野老，杜少陵，杜工部等，盛唐大诗人，世称“诗圣”，现实主义诗人，世称杜工部、杜拾遗，代表作“三吏”（《新安吏》《石壕吏》《潼关吏》）“三别”（《新婚别》《垂老别》《无家别》）。他忧国忧民，人格高尚，一生写诗一千五百多首，诗艺精湛，被后世尊称为“诗圣”。

六 学唱下面这首歌，并给带点的字注上声母 Learn the Following Song and Write the Initials for the Characters Marked with Dots

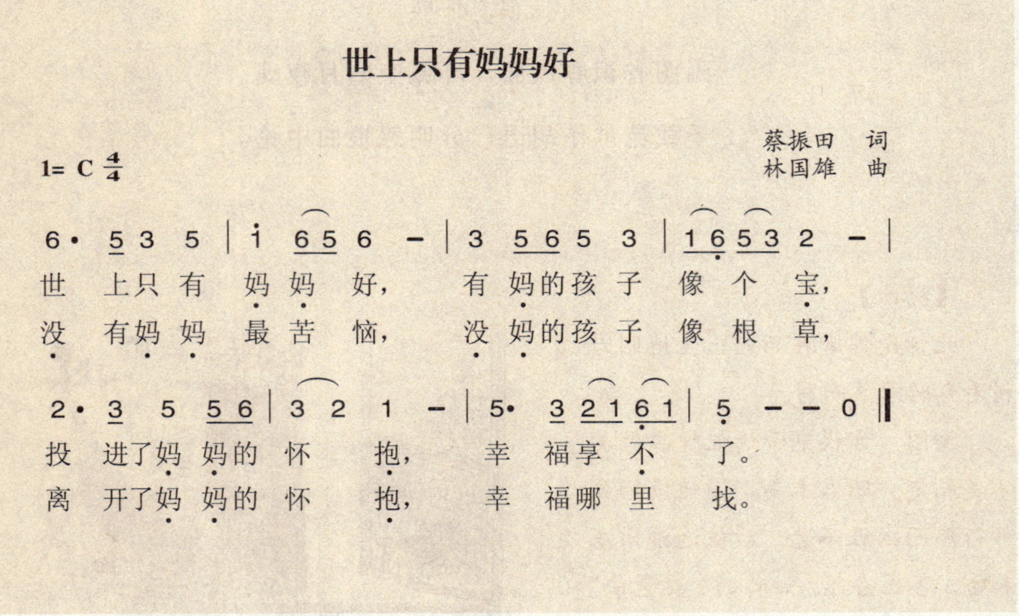

f f

一 语音视听 Audio-visual Pronunciation

1. 发音示意图 Diagrammatic Sketch of Pronunciation

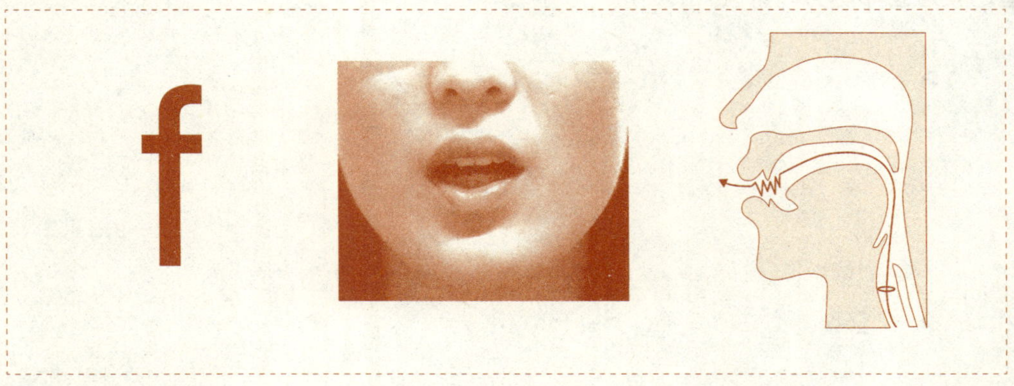

2. 发音特点 Characteristics of Pronunciation

f [f] 唇齿、清、擦音。发音时，上齿切下唇，气流通过齿唇缝隙摩擦成音。

f [f] A labio-dental, unvoiced, fricative sound. It is produced by raising the lower lip against the upper teeth and the airstream comes out of the interstice between the lower lip and the upper teeth.

二 听读词语 Listen and Read the Following Words

方	fāng	square
房	fáng	house
放	fàng	release
夫	fū	man
府	fǔ	mansion
父	fù	father
方法	fāngfǎ	method
犯法	fàn fǎ	break the law
非凡	fēifán	extraordinary
夫妇	fūfù	couple
吩咐	fēnfù	instruct

【提示】

“犯法”是两个词，所以拼写时要分写为：fàn fǎ。

三 速读短语，注意加点字的声母 Read Phrases Quickly, Pay Attention to the Initials of the Characters Marked with Dots

发烧友	fā shāo yǒu	devotee; buff; fanatic
翻来覆去	fān lái fù qù	toss and turn; repeatedly
妇孺皆知	fùrú jié zhī	Even women and children know
风言风语	fēng yán fēng yǔ	canard;groundless talk;privately talk about or spread a rumour

四 跟读绕口令和经典选文，注意加点字的声母 Read the Tongue Twister and the Adapted Classic Following the Teacher, Pay Attention to the Initials Marked with Dots

1. Fēngshù lín zhōng yìwō fēng, fēngshù wàibian huā fēnfāng.
Chūnfēng fú xiāng fú sìfāng, fēi lái fēi qù fēngfēng máng.

枫树林中一窝蜂，枫树外边花芬芳。
春风拂香浮四方，飞来飞去蜂蜂忙。

2. Yànyǔ yún："Níng jiào rén fù wǒ, qiè mò wǒ fù rén."

谚语云："宁教人负我，切莫我负人。"

五　听诵古诗，给诗中加点的字注上声母　Listen and Recite the Ancient Poem, Write the Initials for the Characters Marked with Dots

大风歌

汉 · 刘邦

大风起兮云飞扬。
威加海内兮归故乡。
安得猛士兮守四方。

【提示】

兮（xī）：古文言助词，同今“啊”或“呀”。

筑：古乐器之一。

安得：怎能得到。

此歌节选自《史记 · 高祖本纪》。

刘邦（公元前 247—前 195 年），字季，沛县丰邑（今江苏丰县）人。秦末农民起义领袖之一，汉王朝的建立者。他在平定黥布的叛乱之后回归途中路过沛县，便在沛宫设宴召见父老子弟作乐，酒酣时，自己击筑伴奏唱了此歌。这首歌气势宏大，感情深沉，表现出一个创业者夺得政权之后，对于进一步巩固政权的深思远虑。

第二节 舌尖前音
Section II Dental Sibilants

舌尖前音，由舌尖接触或接近上门齿背构成阻碍而发出的音，有 z, c, s 三个。

Dental sibilant, formed with the tip of tongue close to or touching the back of the upper front teeth. There are three dental sibilants, z, c and s.

Z z

一 语音视听 Audio-visual Pronunciation

1. 发音示意图 Diagrammatic Sketch of Pronunciation

2. 发音特点 Characteristics of Pronunciation

z [ts] 舌尖前、清、弱气流、塞擦音。发音时，舌尖抵上齿背，弱气流冲开舌尖，先堵塞，后摩擦成音。

z [ts] A dental sibilant, unvoiced, weak airstream, affricate sound. It is produced by raising the tip of the tongue against the back of the upper teeth and the weak airstream bursts the tip of the tongue with friction through the narrow passage.

二 听读词语 Listen and Read the Following Words

资	zī	capital
子	zǐ	child
字	zì	character

走	zǒu	walk
在	zài	exist
早	zǎo	early
自在	zìzai	free
总则	zǒngzé	profile
祖宗	zǔzōng	ancestor
自责	zìzé	self-reproach

三 速读短语，注意加点字的声母 Read Phrases Quickly, Pay Attention to the Initials of the Characters Marked with Dots

再接再厉	zài jiē zài lì	make persistent efforts
自卖自夸	zì mài zì kuā	praise the goods one sells; praise one' s own wares
综合大学	zōnghé dàxué	university
走神儿	zǒu shénr	wander; be absent-minded

四 跟读经典选文，注意句中加点字的声母 Read the Adapted Classics, Pay Attention to the Initials Marked with Dots

1.

Jiāo yǔ Xué

Suī yǒu zhì dào, fú xué bù zhī qí shàn yě. Gù xué rán hòu zhī bù zú, jiāo rán hòu zhī kùn. Zhī bù zú,rán hòu néng zì fǎn yě; zhī kùn, rán hòu néng zìqiáng yě. Gù yuē: Jiāo xué xiāng zhǎng yě.

教与学

虽有至道，弗学不知其善也。故学然后知不足，教然后知困。知不足，然后能自反也；知困，然后能自强也。故曰：教学相长也。

——《礼记·礼器》

2.

Fùmǔ zài, bù yuǎn yóu, yóu bì yǒu fāng.

父母在，不远游，游必有方。

——《论语·里仁篇》

【提示】

方：方向，地方。

五 听诵古诗，给诗中加点的字注上声母 Listen and Recite the Ancient Poem, Write the Initials for the Characters Marked with Dots

行宫

唐·元稹

寥落古行宫，宫花寂寞红。

白头宫女在，闲坐说玄宗。

【提示】

全诗以皇宫内人、事的变化，深刻、形象地揭示了唐玄宗淫乱朝政、祸国殃民的历史原由。

元稹（779年—831年），唐洛阳人（今河南洛阳）。早年和白居易共同提倡“新乐府”。世人常把他和白居易并称“元白”。

六 听歌学汉语，注意加点字的声母 Learn Chinese by Listening to the Song, PayAttention to the Initials Marked with Dots

渔 光 曲

电影《渔光曲》插曲

安 蛾 词
任 光 曲

1= G 4/4

(1 – – 5̣ | 2 – – 5̣ | 5 – – 3 | 1 – – 0) |

1 – – 5̣ | 2 – – 5̣ | 5 – – 3 | 2 – – – |
云 儿 飘 在 海 空，
东 方 现 出 微 明，

3 – – 2 | 6̣ – – 2 | 1 – – 6̣ | 5̣ – – – |
鱼 儿 藏 在 水 中；
星 儿 藏 入 天 空；

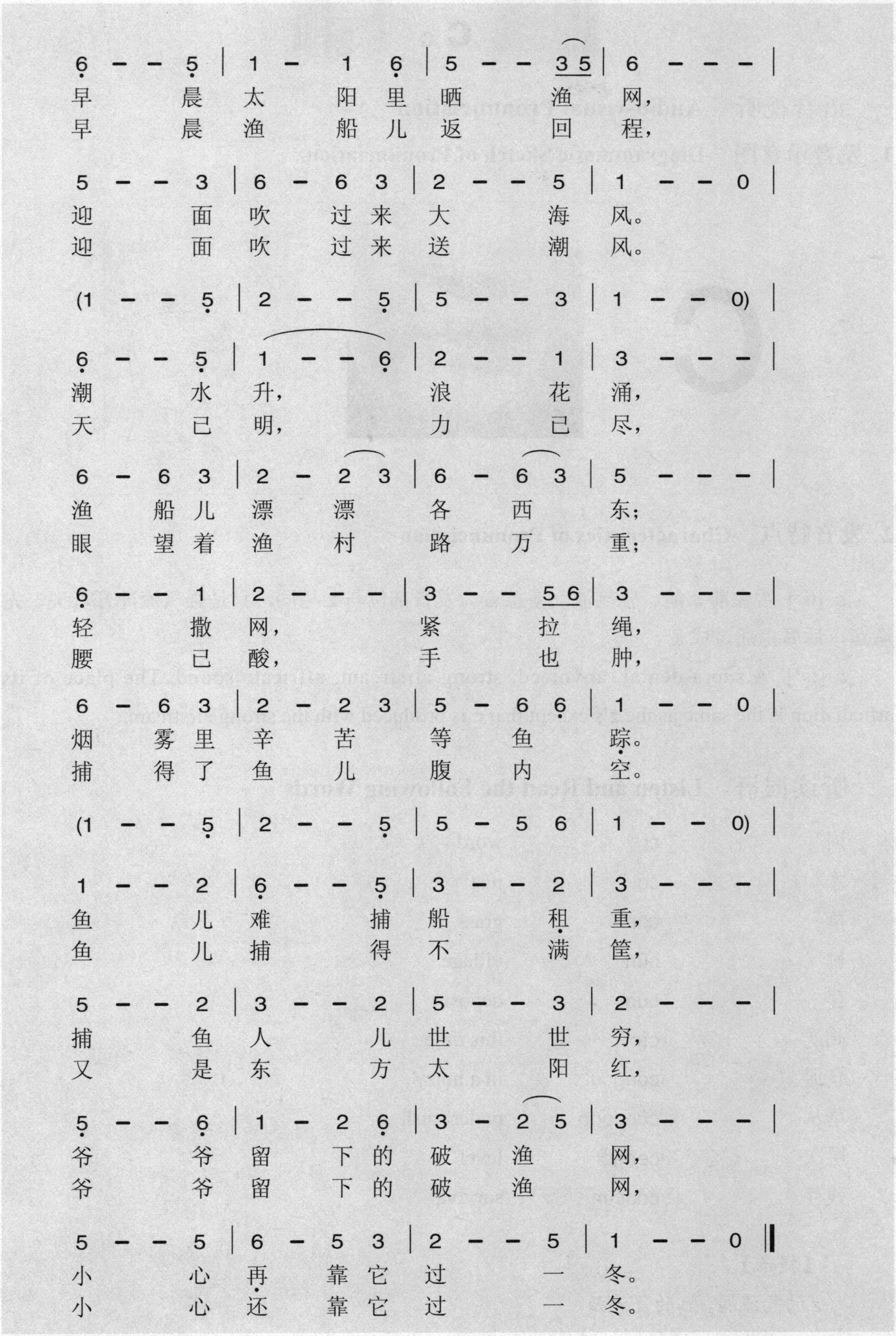

6 – – 5 | 1 – 1 6 | 5 – – 35 | 6 – – – |
早晨太阳里晒渔网，
早晨渔船儿返回程，

5 – – 3 | 6 – 6 3 | 2 – – 5 | 1 – – 0 |
迎面吹过来大海风。
迎面吹过来送潮风。

(1 – – 5 | 2 – – 5 | 5 – – 3 | 1 – – 0) |

6 – – 5 | 1 – – 6 | 2 – – 1 | 3 – – – |
潮水升，浪花涌，
天已明，力已尽，

6 – 6 3 | 2 – 2 3 | 6 – 6 3 | 5 – – – |
渔船儿漂漂各西东；
眼望着渔村路万重；

6 – – 1 | 2 – – – | 3 – – 56 | 3 – – – |
轻撒网，紧拉绳，
腰已酸，手也肿，

6 – 6 3 | 2 – 2 3 | 5 – 6 6 | 1 – – 0 |
烟雾里辛苦等鱼踪。
捕得了鱼儿腹内空。

(1 – – 5 | 2 – – 5 | 5 – 5 6 | 1 – – 0) |

1 – – 2 | 6 – – 5 | 3 – – 2 | 3 – – – |
鱼儿难捕船租重，
鱼儿捕得不满筐，

5 – – 2 | 3 – – 2 | 5 – – 3 | 2 – – – |
捕鱼人儿世世穷，
又是东方太阳红，

5 – – 6 | 1 – 2 6 | 3 – 2 5 | 3 – – – |
爷爷留下的破渔网，
爷爷留下的破渔网，

5 – – 5 | 6 – 5 3 | 2 – – 5 | 1 – – 0 ‖
小心再靠它过一冬。
小心还靠它过一冬。

C c

一 语音视听 Audio-visual Pronunciation

1. 发音示意图 Diagrammatic Sketch of Pronunciation

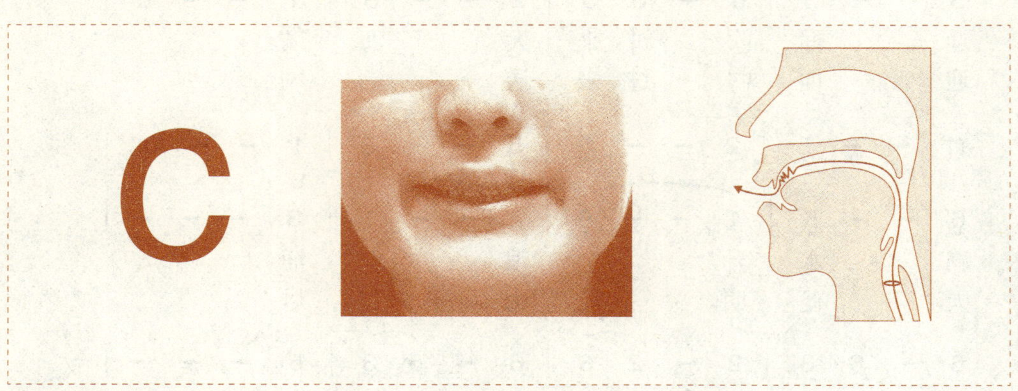

2. 发音特点 Characteristics of Pronunciation

c [ts‘] 舌尖前、清、强气流、塞擦音。发音部位与 z 相同，只是强气流冲开舌尖，先堵塞，后摩擦通过成音。

c [ts‘] A supra-dental, unvoiced, strong airstream, affricate sound. The place of its articulation is the same as the z’s except that c is produced with the strong airstream.

二 听读词语 Listen and Read the Following Words

词	cí	word
才	cái	just
草	cǎo	grass
村	cūn	village
存	cún	deposit
此次	cǐcì	this time
仓促	cāngcù	in a hurry
草丛	cǎocóng	underbrush
层次	céngcì	level
残存	cáncún	survival

【提示】

z 的气流弱，c 的气流强。

三 速读短语，注意加点字的声母 Read Phrases Quickly, Pay Attention to the Initials of the Characters Marked with Dots

财大气粗	cái dà qì cū	money talks; he who has wealth speaks louder than others
层出不穷	céng chū bù qióng	emergy in an endless stream
寸步难行	cùn bù nán xíng	be unable to do anything
粗茶淡饭	cū chá dàn fàn	plain tea and simple food

四 听诵古诗，给诗中加点的字注上声母 Listen and Recite the Ancient Poem, Write the Initials for the Characters Marked with Dots

【提示】

见，音 xiàn，通“现”。

本篇选自《乐府诗集》。敕（chì）勒是我国古代的一个种族，又名铁勒，居住在朔州（今山西北部）。此歌唱出了辽阔、壮丽、生机勃勃的草原风貌，倾注了对祖国无限深厚的热爱之情。

S s

一 语音视听 Audio-visual Pronunciation

1. 发音示意图 Diagrammatic Sketch of Pronunciation

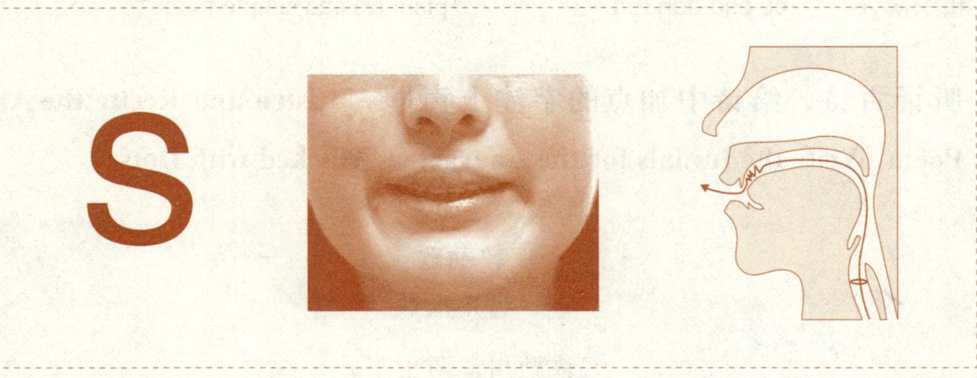

2. 发音特点 Characteristics of Pronunciation

s [s] 舌尖前、清、擦音。发音时，舌尖接近上齿龈，留出窄缝，气流从中摩擦通过成音。

s [s] A supra-dental, unvoiced, fricative sound. It is produced by putting forward the tip of the tongue close to the upper teeth ridge to make a narrow passage and the airstream run out through with friction.

二 听读词语 Listen and Read the Following Words

1.

私	sī	private
俗	sú	conventional
色	sè	colour
松	sōng	pine
扫	sǎo	sweep
色素	sèsù	pigment
洒扫	sásǎo	clean up
三岁	sānsuì	three years old
诉讼	sùsòng	litigate

【提示】

洒扫(sǎsǎo),读“sásǎo”。这是汉语普通话中的三声变调现象。

三声变调

三声音节单念时是原调,如“洒(sǎ)”。但是在与其他三声字连读时,受其影响声调会发生变化。如“洒(sǎ)”和“扫(sǎo)”连读为sásǎo。这种现象只出现在口语中,书面上调号不变。(为方便学习者,本书将“三声字”变调后的调号标记出来。)

常见的有以下几种:

一、两个三声字的变调

两个三声字紧相连,前一个声调从三声(214)变成二声(35)。

	书面	口语	
把柄	bǎ bǐng	bábǐng	handle
板斧	bǎnfǔ	bánfǔ	broad axe
马表	mǎbiǎo	mábiǎo	stopwatch
采买	cǎi mǎi	cáimǎi	select and purchase

二、两个或两个以上三声字的变调

两个或两个以上三声字音节的连读,主要根据词语内部的语义停顿而定。

	书面	口语	
五百/匹	wǔbǎi pǐ	wúbái pǐ	five hundred (horses)
好/补品	hǎo bǔpǐn	hǎo búpǐn	tonic
买把/雨伞	mǎibǎ yǔsǎn	máibǎ yúsǎn	to buy an umbrella

2.

(1) 子孙 zǐsūn descendants
作祟 zuòsuì haunt
自私 zìsī selfish
走私 zǒusī smuggle

(2) 随从 suícóng accompany or followtone's surperior
酸菜 suāncài pickled Chinese cabbage
饲草 sìcǎo forage fodder
私财 sīcái private property

(3) 自从 zìcóng from,since
做操 zuò cāo do exercise
错综 cuòzōng intricate
存在 cúnzài exist

【提示】

“做操”是两个词,所以拼写时应分写为“zuò cāo”。

三 速读短语，注意加点字的声母 Read Phrases Quickly, Pay Attention to the Initials of the Characters Marked with Dots

丧家之犬	sàng jiā zhī quǎn	homeless dog; stray
死对头	sǐduìtou	deadly enemy
酸溜溜	suānliūliū	sour; ache; fell a little envious
缩头缩脑	suō tóu suō nǎo	be timid and shrink from responsiblity

四 跟读绕口令，注意句中加点字的声母 Read the Tongue Twister Following the Teacher, Pay Attention to the Initials of the Characters Marked with Dots

Qīngzǎo pǎo cāo guò dàqiáo，qiáo zuǒ guǒyuán zǎoshù gāo，shùshù jiēmǎn dàxiǎo zǎo，zǐxì kàn， zǐxì zhǎo， qīngzǎor duō，hóngzǎor shǎo，xiǎng chī hóngzǎo bié lái zǎo，sān-sì tiān hòu zài lái kàn， zìzi-zàizai chī hóngzǎo。

清早跑操过大桥，桥左果园枣树高，树树结满大小枣，仔细看，仔细找，青枣儿多，红枣儿少，想吃红枣别来早，三四天后再来看，自自在在吃红枣。

【提示】

枣儿，音 zǎor，汉语普通话中的儿化现象，儿化了的音节读起来是一个音节，写做两个汉字，以“儿”为标志。汉语拼音拼写时，在原来的音节之后加上“r”字母。

五 听诵古诗，给诗中加点的字注上声母 Listen and Recite the Ancient Poem, Write the Initials for the Characters Marked with Dots

相思

唐・王维

红豆生南国，春来发几枝？
愿君多采撷，此物最相思。

【提示】

这是借咏物而寄相思的诗，表达诗人对友人的思念之情。

红豆：又名相思子，一种生在岭南地区的植物，结出的籽像豌豆而稍扁，呈鲜红色。古人常用来象征爱情或相思。

南国：南方。

撷：音 xié，采摘。

王维（701 年—761 年），字摩诘，祖籍山西祁县，唐朝诗人，外号“诗佛”。今存诗四百余首。王维的诗书画都很有名，非常多才多艺。他对音乐也很精通。受禅宗影响很大。

第三节　舌尖中音
Section III Alveolars

舌尖中音，由舌尖接触上齿龈构成阻碍而发出的音，有 d, t, n, l 四个。

Alveolar, which is formed with the tip of the tongue against the bony ridge behind the upper front teeth. There are four kinds of Alveolar: d, t, n and l.

d d

一　语音视听　Audio-visual Pronunciation

1. 发音示意图　Diagrammatic Sketch of Pronunciation

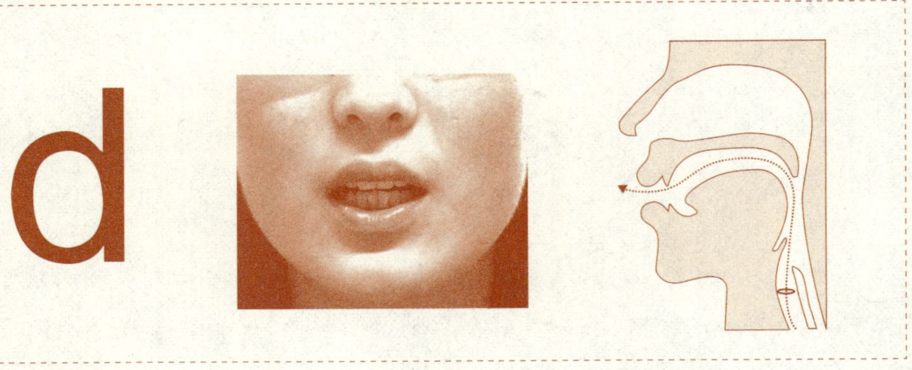

2. 发音特点　Characteristics of Pronunciation

d [t] 舌尖中、清、弱气流、塞音。发音时，舌尖抵上齿龈，弱气流冲开舌尖成音。

d [t] An alveolar, unvoiced, weak airstream, occlusive sound. It is produced by raising the tip of the tongue against the upper teeth ridge and the weak airstream bursts the tip of the teeth to form the sound.

二　听读词语　Listen and Read the Following Words

代	dài	generation
丹	dān	red
斗	dòu	fight

地	dì	field
多	duō	many
打斗	dǎdòu	tussle
到达	dàodá	arrive
当代	dāngdài	contemporary
地点	dìdiǎn	place
电灯	diàndēng	electric light

三 速读短语，注意加点字的声母 Read Phrases Quickly, Pay Attention to the Initials of the Characters Marked with Dots

打抱不平	dǎ bàobùpíng	defend sb. against an injustice
独一无二	dú yī wú èr	unique; unparalleled
吊胃口	diào wèikǒu	stimulate sb.' s appetite with delicious food
到头来	dàotóulái	in the end; finally

四 跟读绕口令，注意句中加点字的声母 Read the Tongue Twister Following the Teacher, Pay Attention to the Initials of the Characters Marked with Dots

Dàdāo duì dāndāo, dāndāo duì dàdāo, dàdāo dòu dāndāo, dāndāo duó dàdāo.

大刀对单刀，单刀对大刀，大刀斗单刀，单刀夺大刀。

五 听诵古诗，给诗中加点的字注上声母 Listen and Recite the Ancient Poem, Write the Initials for the Characters Marked with Dots

静夜思

唐 · 李白

床前明月光，疑是地上霜。

举头望明月，低头思故乡。

【提示】

全诗写的是在寂静的月夜思念家乡的感受。

李白（701—762），字太白，号青莲居士。中国唐朝诗人，有“诗仙”之称，是伟大的浪漫主义诗人。存世诗文千余篇，代表作有《蜀道难》《行路难》《梦游天姥吟留别》《将进酒》《梁甫吟》《静夜思》等诗篇，有《李太白集》传世。

t t

一 语音视听 Audio-visual Pronunciation

1. 发音示意图 Diagrammatic Sketch of Pronunciation

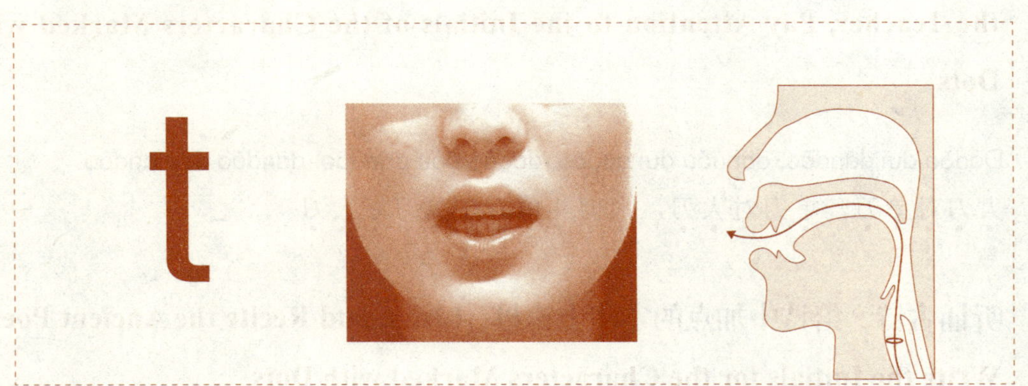

2. 发音特点 Characteristics of Pronunciation

t [t‘] 舌尖中、清、强气流、塞音。发音时，发音部位与d相同，只是强气流冲开舌尖成音。

t [t‘] An alveolar, unvoiced, strong airstream, occlusive sound. The place of its articulation is the same as the d’s except that t is produced with the strong airstream.

二 听读词语 Listen and Read the Following Words

他	tā	he
体	tǐ	body
天	tiān	sky
听	tīng	listen
桃	táo	peach
谈天	tántiān	chat
厅堂	tīngtáng	hall
团体	tuántǐ	group
体贴	tǐtiē	considerate
天堂	tiāntáng	heaven

【提示】
d 的气流弱，t 的气流强。

三 速读短语，注意加点字的声母 Read Phrases Quickly, Pay Attention to the Initials of the Characters Marked with Dots

谈天说地	tán tiān shuō dì	talk about everything under the sun; random talk
讨价还价	tǎo jià huán jià	bargain
天长日久	tiān cháng rì jiǔ	long lasting
土包子	tǔbāozi	clodhopper; (country) bumpkin

四 跟读绕口令和对联，注意句中加点字的声母 Read the Tongue Twister Following the Teacher and the Antithetical Couplet, Pay Attention to the Initials of the Characters Marked with Dots

1.

Dà tùzi,dà dùzi. Dà dùzi de dà tùzi, yào yǎo dà tùzi de dà dùzi.

大兔子，大肚子。大肚子的大兔子，要咬大兔子的大肚子。

2.

Tóngzi dǎ tóngzǐ, tóngzǐ luò, tóngzi lè;
Yātou kěn yātóu , yātóu xián,yātou xián.

童子打桐子，桐子落，童子乐；
丫头啃鸭头，鸭头咸，丫头嫌。

【提示】

桐子：梧桐树的种子。

丫头：口语中对女孩子的俗称。

这是一副对联。

对联：雅称“楹联”，俗称对子。它言简意赅，对仗工整，是一字一音的汉语语言独特的艺术形式。对联艺术是中华民族的文化瑰宝。对联的种类繁多约分为春联、喜联、寿联、挽联、行业联等。

春联：也叫“门对”“春贴”。春节的时候贴在门上的对联。通过贴春联表达自己的美好感受和对未来的美好期盼。每逢春节，家家户户都要精选一副大红春联贴于门上，为节日增加喜庆气氛。

喜联：结婚的时候贴的对联。借此表达夫妻恩爱、家庭和睦的美好意愿。

寿联：做寿的时候贴的对联。多用来祝愿老人健康长寿，幸福安康。

谐音：利用汉字语音的特点，用同音或近音字来代替本字，进而产生辞趣，表达一定的意思。

五　听诵古诗，给诗中加点的字注上声母　Listen and Recite the Ancient Poem, Write the Initials for the Characters Marked with Dots

观书有感

宋·朱熹

半亩方塘一鉴开，
天光云影共徘徊。
问渠哪得清如许？
为有源头活水来。

【提示】

鉴：镜子。

天光：日光。

这是一首借景喻理的名诗。全诗以方塘作比喻，形象地表达了一种微妙难言的读书感受。特别是“问渠哪得清如许，为有源头活水来”两句，借水之清澈，暗喻人要心灵澄明，就得认真读书，时时补充新知识。因此人们常常用来比喻不断学习新知识，才能达到新境界。人们也用这两句诗来赞美一个人的学问或艺术的成就，自有其深厚的渊源。

朱熹（1130—1200），南宋著名思想家、哲学家和教育家，世称朱子。字元晦，号晦庵。他继承和发扬中国传统文化，融汇儒、释、道诸家而建构博大精深的思想体系，对中国文化和人类文明产生了深远的影响。

n n

一 语音视听 Audio-visual Pronunciation

1. 发音示意图 Diagrammatic Sketch of Pronunciation

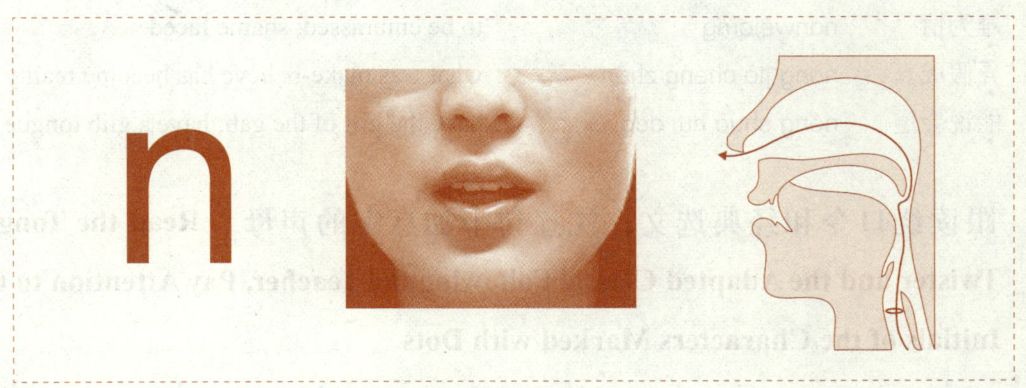

2. 发音特点 Characteristics of Pronunciation

n [n] 舌尖中、浊、鼻音。发音时，舌尖抵上齿龈，气流振动声带从鼻腔通过成音。

n [n] An alveolar, voiced, nasal sound. It is produced by raising the tip of the tongue against the upper teeth ridge and the airstream comes out through the nasal cavity with a vibration of the vocal cords.

二 听读词语 Listen and Read the Following Words

农	nóng	agriculture
你	nǐ	you
年	nián	year
内	nèi	inner
脑	nǎo	brain
奶奶	nǎinai	grandma
农奴	nóngnú	serf
男女	nánnǚ	male and female
牛年	niúnián	Year of the Ox
泥泞	nínìng	muddy

【提示】

“奶奶（nǎinai）”是轻声现象。

三 速读短语，注意加点字的声母 Read Phrases Quickly, Pay Attention to the Initials of the Characters Marked with Dots

拿主意	ná zhǔyi	make a decision
难为情	nánwéiqíng	to be embrassed; shame faced
弄假成真	nòng jiǎ chéng zhēn	what was make-believe has become reality
能说会道	néng shuō huì dào	have the gift of the gab; have a glib tongue

四 跟读绕口令和经典选文，注意句中加点字的声母 Read the Tongue Twister and the Adapted Classic Following the Teacher, Pay Attention to the Initials of the Characters Marked with Dots

1.

Yǒu jiā niúròu miàn pù mén cháo nán, mén shang guàzhe lánbù mián ménlián, xiānkāi lánbù mián ménlián, mǎnwū rén chī niúròu miàn.

有家牛肉面铺门朝南，门上挂着蓝布棉门帘，掀开蓝布棉门帘，满屋人吃牛肉面。

【提示】

牛肉面：俗称“牛肉拉面”，是兰州最具特色的大众化经济小吃。相传，牛肉面是清末光绪年间，一个叫马保子的回民厨师所创制的面食。

2.

Mèngzǐ yuē: “Xié Tàishān yǐ chāo Běihǎi, yǔ rén yuē: ‘wǒ bù néng’, shì chéng bù néng yě. Wéi zhǎngzhě zhézhī, yǔ rén yuē: ‘wǒ bù néng’, shì bù wéi yě, fēi bù néng yě.”

孟子曰：“挟泰山以超北海，语人曰：‘我不能’，是诚不能也。为长者折枝，语人曰：‘我不能’，是不为也，非不能也。”

选自《孟子·梁惠王上》

【提示】

挟：夹在胳膊下。

诚：真，确实。

长者：老人。

折枝：折一段树枝。

不为：不做。

语人曰：有人说。

全句以自问自答的方式揭示了在客观条件下做与不做的辩证关系。

五　听诵古诗，给诗中加点的字注上声母　Listen and Recite the Ancient Poem, Write the Initials for the Characters Marked with Dots

春日寄乡友

南朝·王僧孺

旅心已多恨，春至尚离群。
翠枝结斜影，绿水散回文。
戏鱼两相顾，游鸟半藏云。
何时不悯默，是日最思君。

【提示】

回文：水面上荡起的波纹向四面散开。

作者在春光明媚之时，触景生情，为怀念故乡友人而写下此诗。

王僧孺（465—522），南朝梁诗人、骈文家。他是当时的三大藏书家之一。

L l

一 语音视听 Audio-visual Pronunciation

1. 发音示意图 Diagrammatic Sketch of Pronunciation

2. 发音特点 Characteristics of Pronunciation

l [l] 舌尖中、浊、边音。发音时，舌尖抵上齿龈，气流振动声带从舌尖两边通过成音。

l [l] An alveolar, voiced, lateral sound. It is produced by raising the tip of the tongue against the upper teeth ridge and the airstream comes out by the two sides of the tongue with a vibration of the vocal cord.

二 听读词语 Listen and Read the Following Words

拉	lā	pull
兰	lán	orchid
老	lǎo	old
路	lù	road
落	luò	fall
姥姥	lǎolao	grandma
来路	láilù	origin
力量	lìliàng	strength
冷落	lěngluò	snub
理论	lǐlùn	theory

【提示】
"姥姥（lǎolao）" "力量（lìliang）"是轻声现象。

三 速读短语，注意加点字的声母 Read Phrases Quickly, Pay Attention to the Initials of the Characters Marked with Dots

拉肚子	lā dùzi	suffer from diarrhoea; have loose bowels
力不从心	lì bù cóng xīn	ability not equal to one' s ambition
连锁店	liánsuǒdiàn	chain shops
礼尚往来	lǐ shàng wǎng lái	reciprocal courtesy

四 跟读绕口令，注意句中加点字的声母 Read the Tongue Twister Following the Teacher, Pay Attention to the Initials of the Characters Marked with Dots

Lǎolóng nǎonù nào lǎonóng, lǎonóng nǎonù nào lǎolóng. Nóng nù lóng nǎo nóng gèng nù, lóng nǎo nóng nù lóng pà nóng.

老龙恼怒闹老农，老农恼怒闹老龙。农怒龙恼农更怒，龙恼农怒龙怕农。

五　听诵古诗，给诗中加点字注上学过的声母 Listen and Recite the Ancient Poem, Write the Initials for the Characters Marked with Dots

行路难

唐 · 李白

行路难，行路难，多歧路，今安在？

长风破浪会有时，直挂云帆济沧海。

【提示】

行路，泛指人生之路。

诗人在悲愤中想到，总有一天会乘风破浪，达到自己想要达到的目的。

六　听歌学汉语，注意加点字的声母 Learn Chinese by Listening to the Song, Pay Attention to the Initials Marked with Dots

康定情歌

1= F 2/4

四川民歌
王洛宾编

3	5	6	6 5	6·	3	2	3	5	6	6 5	6	3·
跑	马	溜	溜的	山		上，	一	朵	溜	溜的	云	哟，
李	家	溜	溜的	大		姐，	人	才	溜	溜的	好	哟，
一	来	溜	溜的	看		上，	人	才	溜	溜的	好	哟，
世	间	溜	溜的	女		子，	任	我	溜	溜的	爱	哟，

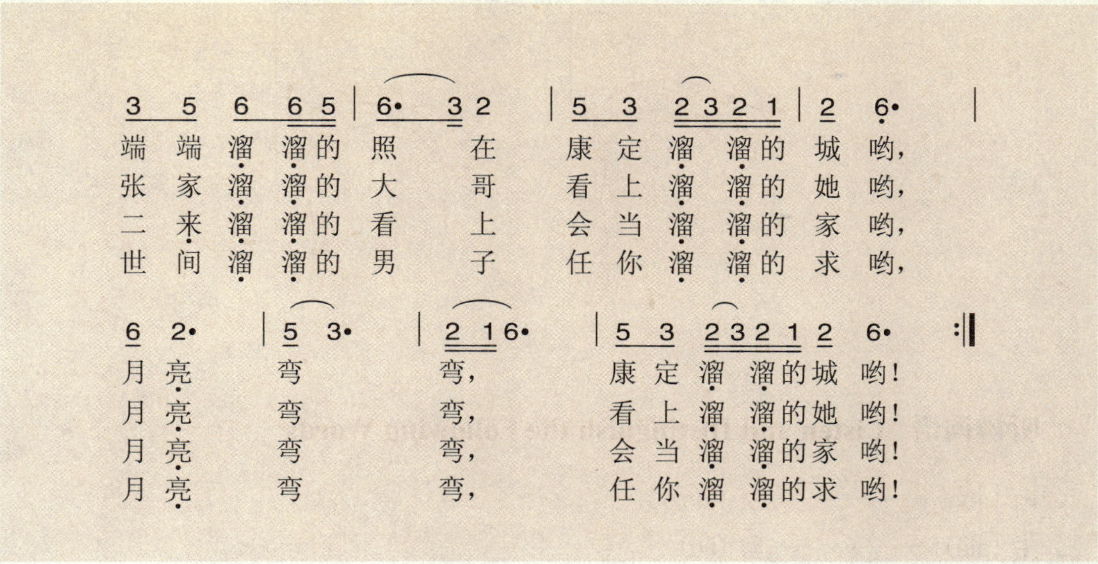

3 5	6 65	6• 32	5 3	2321	2	6•
端端	溜溜的	照在	康定	溜溜的	城	哟，
张家	溜溜的	大哥	看上	溜溜的	她	哟，
二来	溜溜的	看上	会当	溜溜的	家	哟，
世间	溜溜的	男子	任你	溜溜的	求	哟，

6 2•	5 3•	2 16•	5 3	23212	6•
月亮	弯	弯，	康定	溜溜的城	哟！
月亮	弯	弯，	看上	溜溜的她	哟！
月亮	弯	弯，	会当	溜溜的家	哟！
月亮	弯	弯，	任你	溜溜的求	哟！

复习一　分辨 n 和 l 声母
Revision 1　Distinguish n from l

在部分汉语方言中，普通话的鼻音 n 和边音 l 声母相混，发音时要区分两个声母的发音部位和方法。

In some dialects, people always mix up the nasal n and the lateral l. Therefore, we need to distinguish their places and manners of articulations.

n 和 l 都是舌尖抵住上齿龈发音的，它们的不同主要在于有无鼻音。n 是从鼻腔出气，而 l 是从舌头两边出气。

N and l are both alveolar. Their difference is whether the airstream passes through the nose. N is articulated with the tongue tip at the upper gum, and the air-steam breaks through the obstruction in the nasal tract. In the production of l the air-steam is obstructed along the centre of the oral tract, but both sides of the tongue are away from the roof of the mouth, so that the air can go through the mouth laterally.

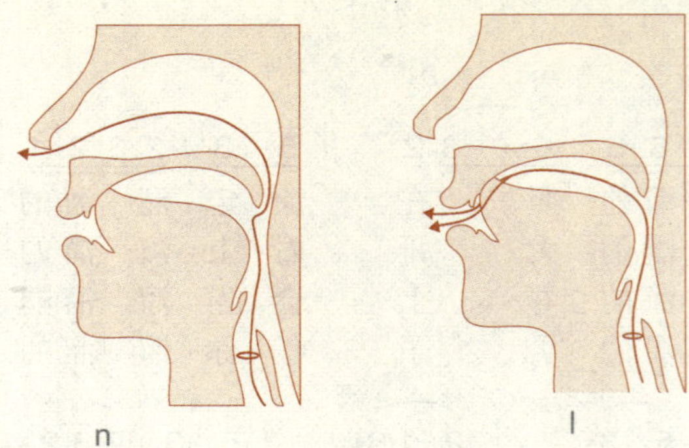

一 听辨词语 Listen and Distinguish the Following Words

南（nán）———— 兰（lán）

牛（niú）———— 留（liú）

努（nǔ）———— 鲁（lǔ）

女（nǚ）———— 吕（lǚ）

二 跟读绕口令，注意句中加点字的声母 Read the Tongue Twister Following the Teacher, Pay Attention to the Initials of the Characters Marked with Dots

1.

Niàn yi niàn,liàn yi liàn,n l liǎngyīn fāyīn yào fēnbiàn.n shì bíyīn shéjiān dí chǐ bí chūqì,l shì biānyīn shé dǐng chǐyín qì liǎngbiān. Nǐ lái liàn, wǒ lái niàn, bú pà lèi, bú pà nán, qí nǔlì,guò nánguān.

念一念，练一练，n、l两音发音要分辨。n是鼻音舌尖抵齿鼻出气，l是边音舌顶齿龈气两边。你来练，我来念，不怕累，不怕难，齐努力，过难关。

2.

Láo nǎinai yào chī dòufunǎo,dòufunǎo zuòde yòu là yòu lǎo wèi bùhǎo, làde láo nǎinai lèi liú mǎnmiàn yáo tóu huàng nǎo zhí fāxiào.

老奶奶要吃豆腐脑，豆腐脑做得又辣又老味不好，辣得老奶奶泪流满面摇头晃脑直发笑。

第四节 舌尖后音

Section IV Retroflexus

舌尖后音，由舌尖接触或接近硬腭前部构成阻碍而发出的音，有 zh, ch,sh, r 四个。

Retroflex is formed with the tongue curled back so that it touches (or almost touches) the hard part of the roof of the mouth. There are four retroflexus — zh, ch, sh and r.

zh zh

一 语音视听 Audio-visual Pronunciation

1. 发音示意图 Diagrammatic Sketch of Pronunciation

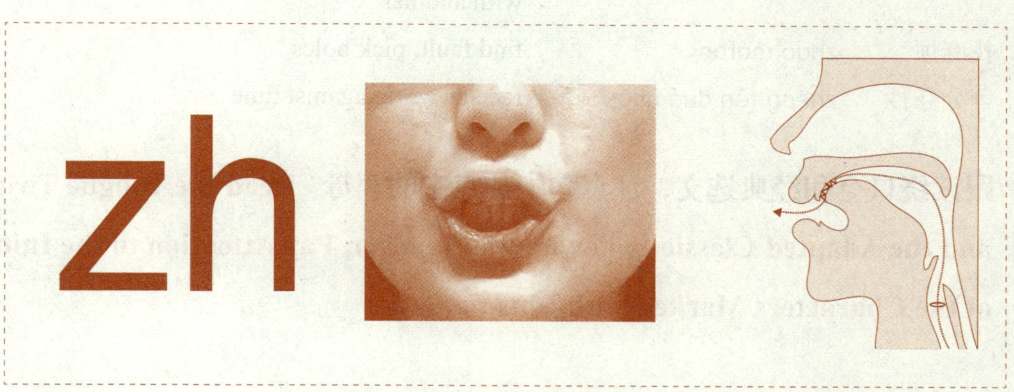

2. 发音特点 Characteristics of Pronunciation

zh [tʂ] 舌尖后、清、弱气流、塞擦音。发音时，舌尖翘起抵硬腭前部，弱气流冲开舌尖，先堵塞，后摩擦成音。

zh [tʂ] A retroflex, unvoiced, weak airstream, affricate sound. It is produced by turning up the tip of the tongue against the front part of the hard palate and the weak airstream bursts the tip of the tongue with friction.

二 听读词语 Listen and Read the Following Words

主	zhǔ	host
真	zhēn	true
宅	zhái	residence

纸	zhǐ	paper
壮	zhuàng	strong
正直	zhèngzhí	upright
住宅	zhùzhái	house
纸张	zhǐzhāng	papers
专注	zhuānzhù	absorbed
战争	zhànzhēng	war

三 速读短语，注意加点字的声母 Read Phrases Quickly, Pay Attention to the Initials of the Characters Marked with Dots

沾沾自喜	zhān zhān zì xǐ	feel complacent; be pleased with oneself
张冠李戴	Zhāng guān Lǐ dài	put Zhang's hat on Li's head; confuse one thing with another
找麻烦	zhǎo máfan	find fault; pick holes
争分夺秒	zhēng fēn duó miǎo	race or work, against time

四 跟读绕口令和经典选文，注意句中加点字的声母 Read the Tongue Twister and the Adapted Classic Following the Teacher, Pay Attention to the Initials of the Characters Marked with Dots

1.

Zǎo zhāozū, wǎn zhāozū. Zǒng zhǎo Zhōu Zhào Zhèng Zhāng Zhū.

早招租，晚招租。总找周赵郑张朱。

【提示】

中国人的名字分为姓和名两部分，姓在前，名在后。姓多为一个字，例如：周（Zhōu）、赵（Zhào）、郑（Zhèng）、张（Zhāng）、朱（Zhū）。名有两个字，也有一个字的。拼写时，姓和名要分写，姓和名的第一个字要大写。例如：周兵（Zhōu Bīn）。

2.

Zǐ yuē: "Wéi zhèng yǐ dé, pìrú běichén, jū qí suǒ ér zhòngxīng gǒng zhī."

子曰："为政以德，譬如北辰，居其所而众星共之。"

——《论语·为政》

【提示】

北辰：北极星。

居其所：一定的位置中。

众星共之：共，同“拱”。众星围绕着它。

3.

Zǐ yuē: “Zhīzhīzhě bùrú hàozhīzhě, hàozhīzhě bùrú lèzhīzhě.”

子曰：“知之者不如好之者，好之者不如乐之者。”

——《论语·雍也第六》

【提示】

之：代词，可作为学问或仁德去理解。

孔子说：“对于学问和仁德，知道它的人比不上爱好它的人，爱好它的人比不上乐在其中的人。”孔子对做学问或者仁德修养从“知之”“好之”“乐之”三个层面作了一层比一层高的分析比较。

五 听诵古诗，给诗中加点的字注上声母 Listen and Recite the Ancient Poem, Write the Initials for the Characters Marked with Dots

金缕衣

唐·杜秋娘

劝君莫惜金缕衣，
劝君惜取少年时。
有花堪折直须折，
莫待无花空折枝。

【提示】

金缕衣：以金线制成的华丽衣裳。

《金缕衣》：词牌名。此诗反复强调爱惜时光，莫要错过青春年华。是对青春和爱情的大胆歌唱，是热情奔放的坦诚流露。然而字面背后，仍是“爱惜时光”的主旨。

杜秋娘，即杜秋，唐代间州（今江苏镇江）人。善歌《金缕衣》曲。

ch ch

一 语音视听 Audio-visual Pronunciation

1. 发音示意图 Diagrammatic Sketch of Pronunciation

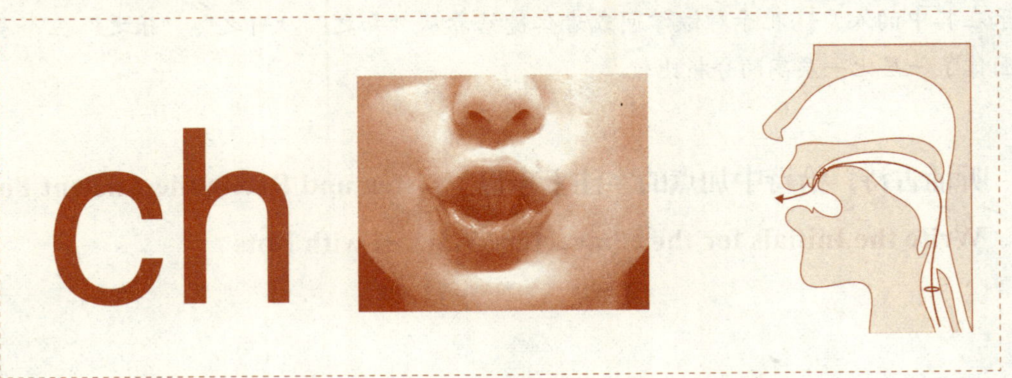

2. 发音特点 Characteristics of Pronunciation

ch [tʂʻ] 舌尖后、清、强气流、塞擦音。发音时，发音部位与 zh 相同，只是强气流冲开舌尖成音。

ch [tʂʻ] A retroflex, unvoiced, strong airstream, affricate sound. The place of its articulation is the same as the zh’ s except that ch is produced with the strong airstream.

二 听读词语 Listen and Read the Following Words

常	cháng	often
吵	chǎo	quarrel
串	chuàn	string
吃	chī	eat

臭	chòu	smelly
长城	Chángchéng	Great Wall
沉船	chén chuán	shipwreck
充斥	chōngchì	be packed with
长处	chángchù	advantage
超车	chāo chē	overtake

【提示】

长城（Chángchéng）是专有名词，专有名词在拼写时每个词的开头字母要大写。

zh 的气流弱，ch 的气流强。

三 速读短语，注意加点字的声母 Read Phrases Quickly, Pay Attention to the Initials of the Characters Marked with Dots

充其量	chōngqíliàng	at most, at best
持之以恒	chí zhī yǐ héng	to make unremitting effort; to persevere in doing sth.
成家立业	chéng jiā lì yè	get married and have a successful career
炒鱿鱼	chǎo yóuyú	be fired; be sacked

四 跟读绕口令，注意句中加点字的声母 Read the Tongue Twister Following the Teacher, Pay Attention to the Initials of the Characters Marked with Dots

Háishuǐ cháo zhāozhāo cháo zhāo cháo zhāo luò,
Fúyún zhǎng chángcháng zhǎng cháng zhǎng cháng xiāo.
海水潮朝朝潮朝潮朝落，
浮云涨长长涨长涨长消。

五 听诵词，给词中加点的字注上声母 Listen and Recite the *Ci* Poem, Write the Initials for the Characters Marked with Dots

踏莎行

宋·欧阳修

候馆梅残，溪桥柳细，草熏风暖摇征辔。离愁渐远渐无穷，迢迢不断如春水。寸寸柔肠，盈盈粉泪，楼高莫近危栏倚。平芜尽处是春山，行人更在春山外。

【提示】

候馆：驿站，旅馆，店。

草熏：春草味。

征：出行，行程。

辔：音 pèi，驾驭牲口的嚼环和缰绳等。

盈盈：满眼泪水。

平芜：平坦的草地。

行人：指恋人。

此词是欧阳修婉约词的代表作。它运用了三种艺术表现手法。一是托物兴怀，词的上片写残梅、细柳和薰草这些春天里的典型景物，点缀着候馆、溪桥和征途，表现出南方仲春融和的气氛，但对于离愁的行人来说，却倍增烦恼，更添愁思。二是比喻，化虚为实。“愁”是一种无可视感的情绪，将它比喻为迢迢不断的春水，既形象又贴切，这样化虚为实，可视可感。三是逐层深化，委曲尽情。“平芜尽处是春山，行人更在春山外”，更进一步说明行人离愁的无穷。全词悱恻幽回，情深意远。

欧阳修（1007—1072年），字永叔，号醉翁，晚年又号六一居士，吉州永丰（今江西永丰）人。是北宋诗文革新的领袖，一代文宗，散文名列“唐宋八大家”。

六 听歌学汉语，注意加点字的声母 Learn Chinese by Listening to the Song, Pay Attention to the Initials Marked with Dots

长城谣

潘孑农 词
刘雪庵 曲

1= F $\frac{4}{4}$

(5 3 5 6 1̇ 2̇ 3̇ 3̇ 2̇ 2̇ 1̇) :| 5 3 5 3 5 1̇· 6 5

万 里 长 城 万 里 长，
没 齿 难 忘 仇 和 恨，

5 6 i 3 5 3 2· 6 1 5 3 5 3 5 i· 6 5
长城外面是故乡，高粱肥大豆香，
日夜只想回故乡，大家拼命打回去，

5 5 6 i 3 2 1 0 2 1 2 1 2 5· 3 2
遍地黄金少灾殃。自从大难平地起，
哪怕贼禄逞豪强。万里长城万里长，

3 1 2 3 5 3 5 6 i· 6 i· 3 5 3 5 3 5 i· 6 5
奸淫掳掠苦难当。苦难当，奔他方，
长城外面是故乡。四万万同胞心一条，

5 5 6 i 3· 5 3 2 1 0 (2 1 2 1 2 5· 3 2
骨肉流散父母丧。
新的长城万里

3 1 2 3 5 3 5 6 i· 6 1) :| 1 0 |
长。

sh sh

一 语音视听 Audio-visual Pronunciation

1. 发音示意图 Diagrammatic Sketch of Pronunciation

2. 发音特点 Characteristics of Pronunciation

sh [ʂ] 舌尖后、清、擦音。发音时，舌尖翘起接近硬腭前部，留出窄缝，气流摩擦成音。

sh [ʂ] A retroflex, unvoiced, fricative sound. It is produced by turning the tip of the tongue close to the front of the hard palate to make a narrow passage and the airstream comes out through it with friction.

二 听读词语 Listen and Read the Following Words

沙	shā	sand
石	shí	stone
山	shān	mountain
神	shén	god
税	shuì	tax
上山	shàng shān	climb a hill
双数	shuāngshù	even numbers
硕士	shuòshì	master’s degree
叔叔	shūshu	uncle
婶婶	shěnshen	aunt

【提示】

叔叔（shūshu）、婶婶（shěnshen）是轻声现象。

三 速读短语，注意加点字的声母 Read Phrases Quickly, Pay Attention to the Initials of the Characters Marked with Dots

山穷水尽	shān qióng shuǐ jìn	where the hill and streams end; at the end of one’s rope, without resources
伤脑筋	shāng nǎojīn	knotty, troublesome, bothersome
伸懒腰	shēn lǎnyāo	stretch oneself; stretch one’ s limbs
顺手牵羊	shùn shǒu qiān yáng	walk off with sth.; pick up sth. on the sly

四 跟读经典选文，注意句中加点字的声母 Read the Adapted Classic Following the Teacher, Pay Attention to the Initials of the Characters Marked with Dots

Fēngshēng yǔshēng dúshū shēng, shēngshēng rù ěr.
Jiāshì guóshì tiānxià shì, shìshì guānxīn.
风声雨声读书声，声声入耳。
家事国事天下事，事事关心。

五 听诵词，给词中加点的字注上声母 Listen and Recite the *Ci* Poem, Write the Initials for the Characters Marked with Dots

声声慢

宋 · 李清照

寻寻觅觅，冷冷清清，凄凄惨惨戚戚。乍暖还寒时候，最难将息。

三杯两盏淡酒，怎敌他、晚来风急？雁过也，正伤心，却是旧时相识。

【提示】

《声声慢》：词牌名。这首词通过描写残秋所见、所闻、所感，抒发自己孤寂落寞、悲凉愁苦的心绪。词风深沉凝重、哀婉凄苦。

李清照（1084—1155），号易安居士，南宋杰出女文学家，山东济南人。主张“词，当别具一家也”，历史上与济南历城人辛弃疾并称“济南二安”。早年生活安定、优裕，词作多写相思之情；后遭国家巨变，词多感慨身世飘零。有《漱玉词》等。

r r

一 语音视听 Audio-visual Pronunciation

1. 发音示意图 Diagrammatic Sketch of Pronunciation

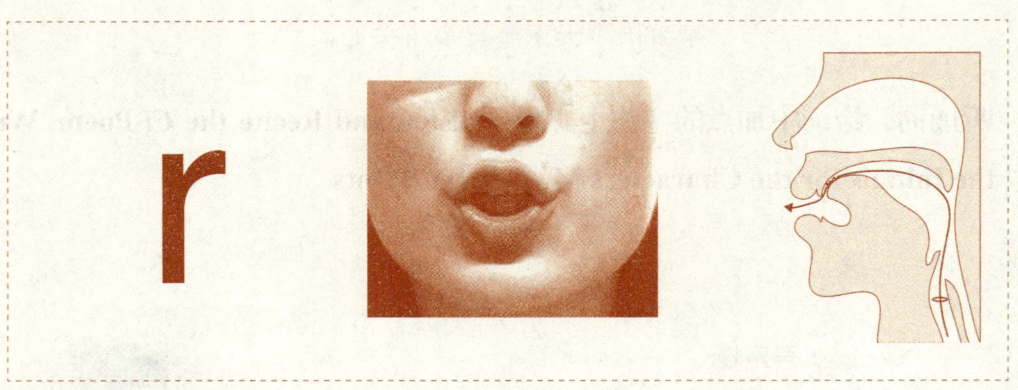

2. 发音特点 Characteristics of Pronunciation

r [ʐ] 舌尖后、浊、擦音。发音部位与 sh 相近，只是气流振动声带摩擦成音。

r [ʐ] A retroflex, voiced, fricative sound. The place of its articulation is the same as the sh's except that there is a vibration of the vocal cord in the r's articulation.

二 听读词语 Listen and Read the Following Words

扔	rēng	throw
如	rú	like
日	rì	sun
软	ruǎn	soft
肉	ròu	meat
忍让	rěnràng	forbearance
柔软	róuruǎn	tender
仍然	réngrán	still
容忍	róngrěn	tolerate
荣辱	róngrǔ	honour and disgrace

三 速读短语，注意加点字的声母 Read Phrases Quickly, Pay Attention to the Initials of the Characters Marked with Dots

绕弯子	rào wānzi	beat about the bush
惹是非	rě shìfēi	provoke a controversy;stir up trouble
燃眉之急	rán méi zhī jí	as pressing as a fire singeing one's eyebrows; emergency; urgent situation
如饥似渴	rú jī sì kě	as if thirsting or hungering for sth.;with great eagerness

四 跟读绕口令和经典选文，注意句中加点字的声母 Read the Tongue Twister and the Adapted Classic Following the Teacher, Pay Attention to the Initials of the Characters Marked with Dots

1.

Chūnrì yǒu rì tiān jiàn nuǎn, xiàrì wú rì rì yì rè.
Qiūrì tiān gāo yún fù dàn, dōngrì yǒu rì rì yì hán.
春日有日天渐暖，夏日无日日亦热。
秋日天高云复淡，冬日有日日亦寒。

2.

Mèngzǐ yuē: “Jūnzǐ yǐ rén cún xīn, yǐ lǐ cún xīn. Rénzhě ài rén, yǒulǐzhě jìng rén. Ài rénzhě, rén héng ài zhī; jìngrénzhě, rén héng jìng zhī.”

孟子曰：“君子以仁存心，以礼存心。仁者爱人，有礼者敬人。爱人者，人恒爱之；敬人者，人恒敬之。”

——《孟子·离娄下》

孟子（前372年—前289年）

【提示】

孟子指出：“君子和普通人不同，在于居心，因君子的心存仁、存礼，为此，就会有爱，有礼。”

3.

Gǔrén yún: “Yǔ shànrén jū, rú rù zhī lán zhī shì, jiǔ ér zì fāng yě; yǔ èrén jū,rú rù bào yú zhī sì, jiǔ ér zì chòu yě.”

古人云：“与善人居，如入芝兰之室，久而自芳也；与恶人居，如入鲍鱼之肆，久而自臭也。”

【提示】

鲍：鲍鱼。

肆：店、铺，此处泛指鱼市。以此喻臭、坏。

与好人在一起，时间长了就学好了；与坏人在一起，时间长了也就变坏了。

五　听诵古诗，给诗中加点的字注上声母 Listen and Recite the Ancient Poem, Write the Initials for the Characters Marked with Dots

望庐山瀑布

唐 · 李白

日照香炉生紫烟，遥看瀑布挂前川。

飞流直下三千尺，疑是银河落九天。

【提示】

庐山：地处江西省北部的鄱阳湖盆地，九江市以南，濒临鄱阳湖，雄峙长江南岸。庐山山体呈椭圆形，长约二十五公里，宽约十公里，以雄、奇、险、秀闻名于世，素有“匡庐奇秀甲天下”之美誉。是中国久负盛名的风景名胜区和避暑游览胜地。

香炉：指庐山香炉峰。

全诗描写庐山香炉瀑布的巨大壮观，语言奔放，历来为人们所传诵。

复习二　分辨 zh ch sh 和 z c s 声母

Revision 2 Distinguish zh ch and sh from z c and s

在部分汉语方言中，把普通话舌尖后声母 zh, ch, sh，读作普通话舌尖前声母 z, c, s。学习时要仔细分辨两组声母的发音部位和方法。

In some dialects, people mispronounce zh, ch and sh as z, c and s respectively. Therefore, we need to distinguish their places and manners of articulation.

发 zh，ch，sh 舌尖后音时，舌尖要翘起来，对准硬腭前部；而发 z，c，s 舌尖前音时，舌尖不翘，对准（抵住或接近）齿背。

When the retroflexus zh, ch, sh, are articulated, the tongue tip is raised up and is against the front part of the hard palate; however, when the dental sibilants z, c, s are articulated, the tongue tip is not raised up and is close to the upper front teeth.

一　听辨词语　Listen and Distinguish the Following Words

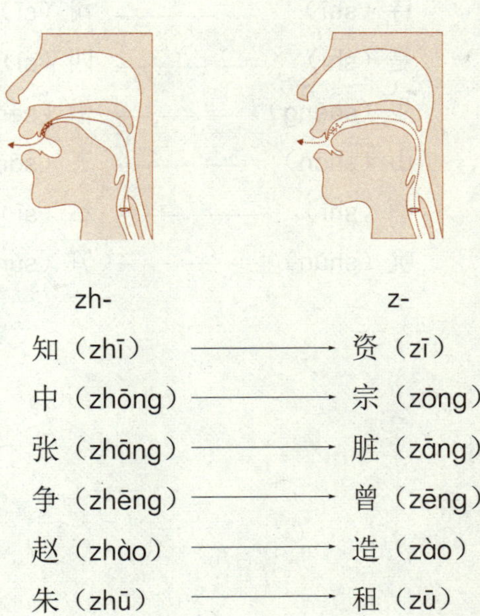

zh-		z-
知（zhī）	——→	资（zī）
中（zhōng）	——→	宗（zōng）
张（zhāng）	——→	脏（zāng）
争（zhēng）	——→	曾（zēng）
赵（zhào）	——→	造（zào）
朱（zhū）	——→	租（zū）

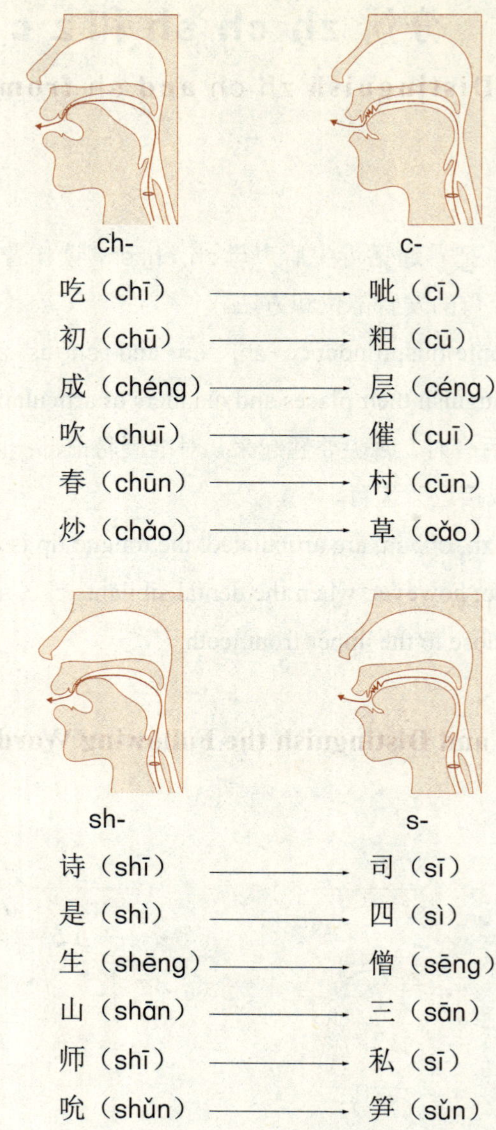

吃（chī）——→ 呲（cī）
初（chū）——→ 粗（cū）
成（chéng）——→ 层（céng）
吹（chuī）——→ 催（cuī）
春（chūn）——→ 村（cūn）
炒（chǎo）——→ 草（cǎo）

诗（shī）——→ 司（sī）
是（shì）——→ 四（sì）
生（shēng）——→ 僧（sēng）
山（shān）——→ 三（sān）
师（shī）——→ 私（sī）
吮（shǔn）——→ 笋（sǔn）

二 跟读绕口令和经典选文，注意句中加点字的声母 Read the Tongue Twister and the Adapted Classic Following the Teacher, Pay Attention to the Initials of the Characters Marked with Dots

1.

Sì shì sì, shí shì shí, sìshí shì sìshí, shísì shì shísì. Shuí néng shuōzhǔn sìshí, shísì, sìshísì, jiù lái shì yi shì. Shuí shuō shísì shì sìsì, jiù dǎ shuí shísì, shuí shuō sìshí shì xìxí, jiù dǎ shuí sìshí.

四是四，十是十，四十是四十，十四是十四。谁能说准四十、十四、四十四，就来试一试。谁说十四是四四，就打谁十四，谁说四十是细席，就打谁四十。

2.

Zǐ yuē: " Wú shí yǒu wǔ ér zhì yú xué, sānshí ér lì, sìshí ér búhuò, wǔshí ér zhī tiānmìng, liùshí ér ěr shùn, qīshí ér cóng xīn suǒ yù, bù yú jǔ."

子曰："吾十有五而志于学，三十而立，四十而不惑，五十而知天命，六十而耳顺，七十而从心所欲，不逾矩。"

——《论语 · 为政》

【提示】

学：学习，学问。　立：立身处世。　不惑：坚信不疑。

天命：世事的变化发展。　耳顺：对所闻所见能理解。

逾矩：不超越礼的规范。

此文是孔子对自己一生的经验总结，传诵迄今的千古名言。

第五节 舌面音
Section V Palatals

舌面音，由舌面前部接触或接近硬腭前部构成阻碍而发出的音，有 j, q, x 三个。

Palatal, which is formed with the front and middle of the tongue, close to or touch the roof of the mouth.There are j, q and x.

j j

一 语音视听 Audio-visual Pronunciation

1. 发音示意图 Diagrammatic Sketch of Pronunciation

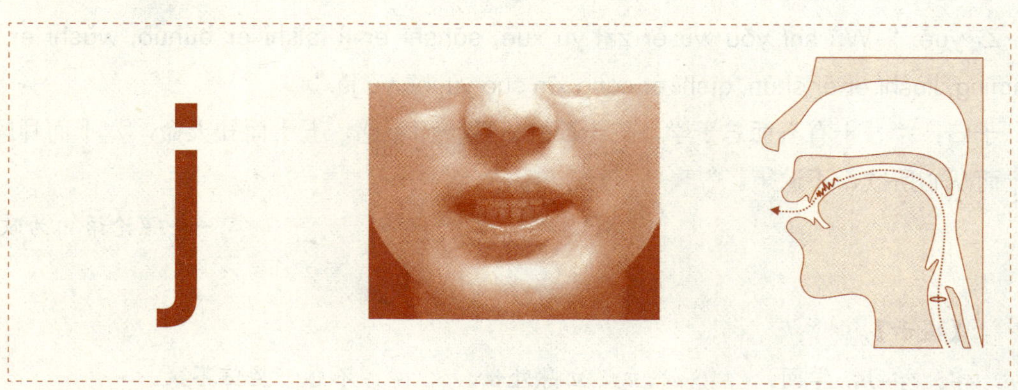

2. 发音特点 Characteristics of Pronunciation

j [tɕ] 舌面、清、弱气流、塞擦音。发音时，舌面贴硬腭，弱气流冲开舌面，先堵塞后摩擦成音。

j [tɕ] A dorsal, unvoiced, weak airstream, affricate sound. It is produced by raising the blade of the tongue against the hard palate and the weak airstream bursts the blade of the tongue with friction.

二 听读词语 Listen and Read the Following Words

鸡	jī	chicken
节	jié	festival
举	jǔ	hold
见	jiàn	meet

井	jǐng	well
积极	jījí	active
季节	jìjié	season
家具	jiājù	furniture
京剧	jīngjù	*Beijing* Opera
坚决	jiānjué	determined

三 速读短语，注意加点字的声母 Read Phrases Quickly, Pay Attention to the Initials of the Characters Marked with Dots

鸡飞蛋打	jī fēi dàn dǎ	the hen has flown away and the eggs in the basket are broken; all is lost
绝无仅有	jué wú jǐn yǒu	only one of its kind; unique
救死扶伤	jiù sǐ fú shāng	heal the wounded and rescue the dying
紧巴巴	jǐn bābā	tight; hard up; short of money

四 跟读绕口令，注意句中加点字的声母 Read the Tongue Twister Following the Teacher, Pay Attention to the Initials of the Characters Marked with Dots

Xiáoxiǎo jī, jī yǐ jí. Jǐ yìqǐ, děng mǔjī.
Mǔjī diāolái yì tiáo jì, xiǎojī kànjiàn jī jī jī.
小小鸡，饥已极。挤一起，等母鸡。
母鸡叼来一条鲫，小鸡看见叽叽叽。

【提示】
“一起（yìqǐ）”“一条（yì tiáo）”是“一”的变调现象。

五 听诵古诗，给诗中加点的字注上声母 Listen and Recite the Ancient Poem, Write the Initials for the Characters Marked with Dots

将进酒（节选）

唐 · 李白

君不见黄河之水天上来，奔流到海不复回。君不见高堂明镜悲白发，朝如青丝暮成雪。

【提示】

《将进酒》：词牌名。将，音 qiāng，意为请。这两句诗主要说时光飞逝，人生苦短。

黄河：是我国第二长河，源于青海巴颜喀拉山北麓，干流贯穿九个省、自治区，流经青海、四川、甘肃、宁夏、内蒙古、陕西、山西、河南、山东，全长 5 464 公里，流域面积 75 万平方公里，年径流量 574 亿立方米。是中华民族的母亲河。作为中华文明的发祥地，是中华民族的民族精神与民族情感的象征。

高堂：对父母的一种代称。古代父母居正屋，故用高堂指父母居处，或代称父母。

q q

一 语音视听 Audio-visual Pronunciation

1. 发音示意图 Diagrammatic Sketch of Pronunciation

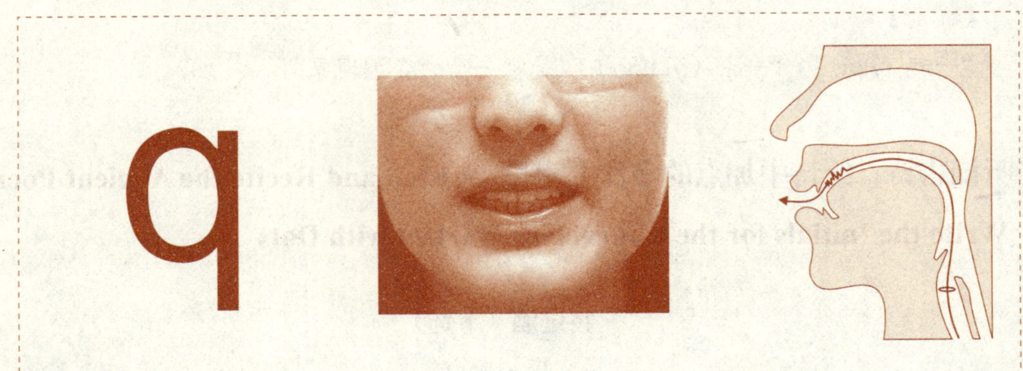

2. 发音特点 Characteristics of Pronunciation

q [tɕ‘] 舌面、清、强气流、塞擦音。发音部位与 j 相同，只是强气流冲开舌面，先堵塞后摩擦成音。

q [tɕ‘] A dorsal, unvoiced, strong airstream, affricate sound. The place of its articulation is the same as the j’s except that q is produced with the strong airstream.

二 听读词语 Listen and Read the Following Words

期	qī	period
劝	quàn	persuade
请	qǐng	please
前	qián	front
掐	qiā	pinch
亲戚	qīnqi	relative
欠钱	qiànqián	owe one’s money
气枪	qìqiāng	air gun
亲切	qīnqiè	kindness

【提示】

j 的气流弱，q 的气流强。

三 速读短语，注意加点字的声母 Read Phrases Quickly, Pay Attention to the Initials of the Characters Marked with Dots

七十二行	qīshí’ èr háng	all professions and trades; all walks of life
千方百计	qiān fāng bǎi jì	by hook or by crook; by every possible means
求之不得	qiú zhī bù dé	more than one could wish for; most welcome; rare even the most capable
全心全意	quán xīn quán yì	whole heartedly; heart and soul

四 听诵古诗，给诗中加点字注上学过的声母 Listen and Recite the Ancient Poem, Write the Initials for the Characters Marked with Dots

关雎

关关雎鸠，在河之洲。
窈窕淑女，君子好逑。
求之不得，寤寐思服。
悠哉悠哉，辗转反侧。

【提示】

本诗节选自《诗经·关雎》，是一首表现男女恋爱的民歌。

关关：鸟鸣声。

雎鸠：一种水鸟。

洲：水中小岛。

窈窕：文静、优雅、美丽的姑娘。

好逑：好配偶。

寤寐：梦中醒来都在想。

思服：思念。

悠哉：想啊。

辗转反侧：翻来覆去。

《诗经》是我国第一部诗歌总集，共收入自西周初期（公元前11世纪）至春秋中叶（公元前6世纪）约五百年间的诗歌，共305篇。

X x

一　语音视听　Audio-visual Pronunciation

1. 发音示意图　Diagrammatic Sketch of Pronunciation

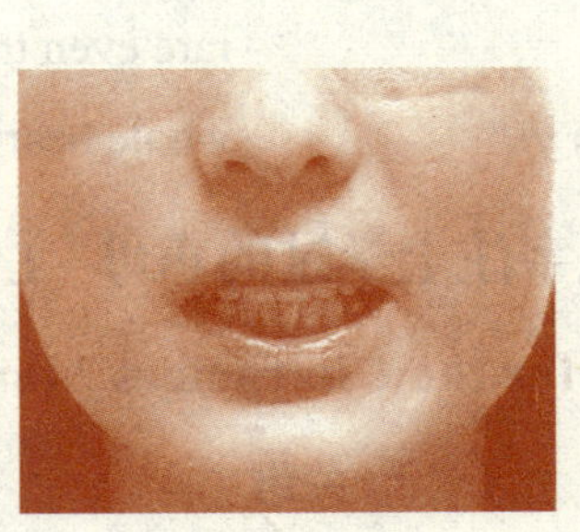

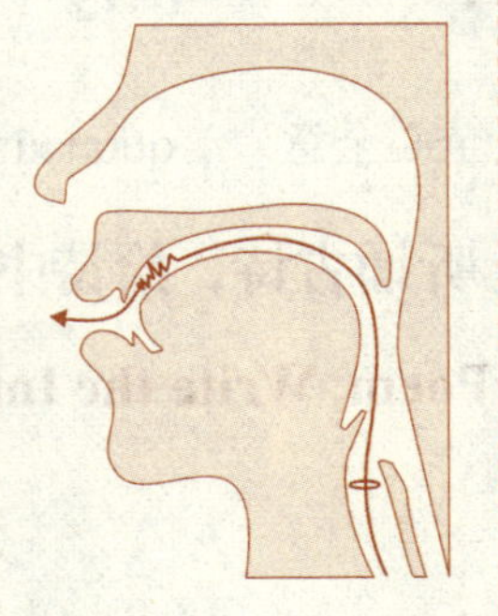

2. 发音特点 Characteristics of Pronunciation

x [ɕ] 舌面、清、擦音。发音时，舌面接近硬腭，中间留窄缝，气流从中摩擦成音。

x [ɕ] A dorsal, unvoiced, fricative sound. It is produced by raising the blade of the tongue close to the hard palate to make a narrow passage and the airstream comes out through it with friction.

二 听读词语 Listen and Read the Following Words

西	xī	west
仙	xiān	immortal
行	xíng	OK
响	xiǎng	loud
训	xùn	train
消息	xiāoxi	news
新鲜	xīnxiān	fresh
学习	xuéxí	study
相信	xiāngxìn	believe
学校	xuéxiào	school
休息	xiūxi	rest

三 速读短语，注意加点字的声母 Read Phrases Quickly, Pay Attention to the Initials of the Characters Marked with Dots

息息相关	xī xī xiāng guān	be closely interrelated
寻开心	xún kāixīn	make fun of; poke fun at
雪中送炭	xuě zhōng sòng tàn	provide timely help; provide material help to others in need
心平气和	xīn píng qì hé	calm, even-tempered and good humoured

四 跟读绕口令，注意句中加点字的声母 Read the Tongue Twister Following the Teacher, Pay Attention to the Initials of the Characters Marked with Dots

Qiánjiē yǒu gè yóuqī jiàng, hòuxiàng yǒu gè xītiě jiàng. Qiánjiē yóuqī jiàng qīle hòuxiàng xītiě jiàng de xī,hòuxiàng xītiě jiàng xiāole qiánjiē yóuqī jiàng de qī.

前街有个油漆匠，后巷有个锡铁匠。前街油漆匠漆了后巷锡铁匠的锡，后巷锡铁匠消了前街油漆匠的漆。

五　听诵古诗，给加点的字注上声母　Listen and Recite the Ancient Poem, Write the Initials for the Characters Marked with Dots

桑茶坑道中

南宋·杨万里

晴明风日雨干时，草满花堤水满溪。

童子柳阴眠正着，一牛吃过柳阴西。

【提示】

这首诗描写的是初春景物。河岸上，草绿花红，柳荫浓密。牧童酣睡、一牛悠然食草的情景，具有独特的生活情趣和原始朴素的美感。

杨万里（1127—1206），字廷秀，号诚斋。吉州吉水（今江西吉水县）人。南宋杰出的诗人。其诗风格淳朴，语言口语化，构思新巧，号为“诚斋体”。

第六节 舌根音
Section VI Velars

舌根音，由舌根接触或接近软腭构成阻碍而发出的音，有 g, k, h 三个。

Velar is formed with the back of the tongue close to touching the soft part of the roof of the mouth.There are g, k and h.

g g

一 语音视听 Audio-visual Pronunciation

1. 发音示意图 Diagrammatic Sketch of Pronunciation

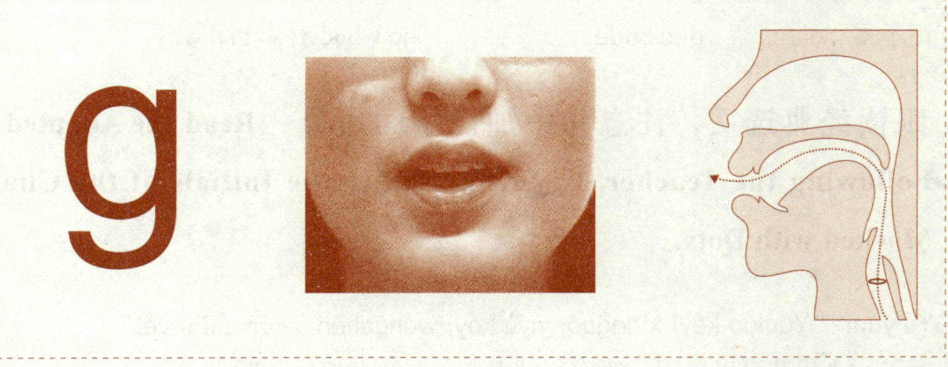

2. 发音特点 Characteristics of Pronunciation

g [k]舌根、清、弱气流、塞音。发音时，舌根抵硬腭，弱气流冲开舌根成音。

g [k] A velar, unvoiced, weak airstream, occlusive sound. It is produced by raising the back of the tongue against the soft palate and the weak airstream bursts the back of the tongue to form the sound.

二 听读词语 Listen and Read the Following Words

肝	gān	liver
古	gǔ	ancient
高	gāo	high
广	guǎng	broad

该	gāi	ought to
更改	gēnggǎi	correct
公告	gōnggào	announcement
古怪	gǔguài	odd
故宫	Gùgōng	the Imperial Palace
观光	guānguāng	tour

三 速读短语，注意加点字的声母 Read Phrases Quickly, Pay Attention to the Initials of the Characters Marked with Dots

干打雷，不下雨	gān dǎ léi, bú xià yǔ	all thunder but no rain — much noise but no action
各就各位	gè jiù gè wèi	man your posts; on your marks
给面子	gěi miànzi	do sb. a favour; save sb' s face
怪不得	guàibude	no wonder; so that why

四 跟读经典选文，注意句中加点字的声母 Read the Adapted Classic Following the Teacher, Pay Attention to the Initials of the Characters Marked with Dots

Yǔ yún: "Yōuláo kéyǐ xīngguó, yìyù kéyǐ wángshēn, zìrán zhī lǐ yě."

语云："忧劳可以兴国，逸豫可以亡身，自然之理也。"

选自欧阳修《五代史伶官传序》

【提示】

忧劳：忧愁，思虑。

逸豫：过度嬉戏玩乐。

可以（kěyǐ），读"kéyǐ"，是汉语中两个字都读三声且音连读时的变调现象，第一个字的音变读为二声。

五 听诵古诗，给诗中加点的字注上声母 Listen and Recite the Ancient Poem, Write the Initials for the Characters Marked with Dots

哥舒歌

唐·西鄙人

北斗七星高，哥舒夜带刀。

至今窥牧马，不敢过临洮。

【提示】

全诗赞扬守边将士坚强勇猛的战斗精神。

哥舒：即守边将军哥舒翰。

窥：远处偷看。

牧马：胡人的骑兵等。

k k

一 语音视听 Audio-visual Pronunciation

1. 发音示意图 Diagrammatic Sketch of Pronunciation

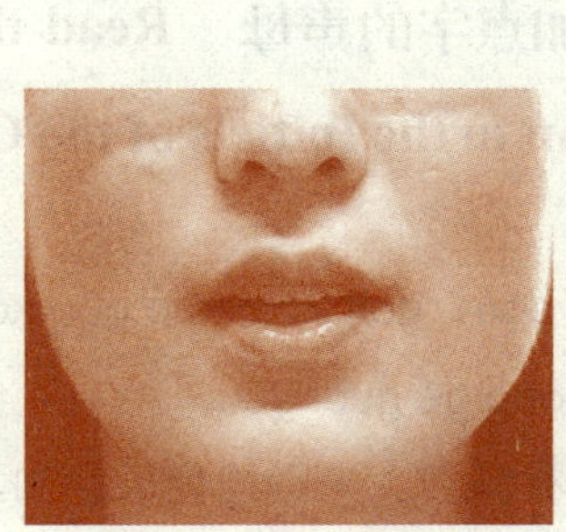

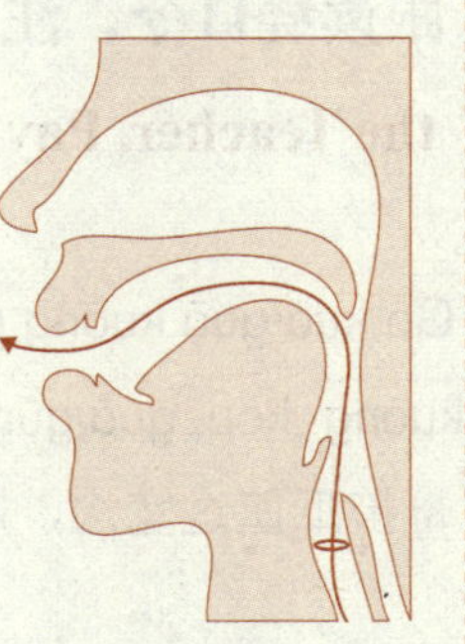

2. 发音特点 Characteristics of Pronunciation

k [k‘] 舌根、清、强气流、塞音。发音部位与 g 相同，只是强气流冲开舌根成音。

k [k‘] A velar, unvoiced, strong airstream, occlusive sound. The place of its articulation is the same as the g's except that k is produced with the strong airstream.

二 听读词语 Listen and Read the Following Words

开	kāi	open
口	kǒu	mouth
苦	kǔ	miserable
空	kōng	empty
哭	kū	cry
亏空	kuīkong	deficit
夸口	kuā kǒu	boast
困苦	kùnkǔ	hardship
可靠	kěkào	reliable
刻苦	kèkǔ	painstaking

三 速读短语，注意加点字的声母 Read Phrases Quickly, Pay Attention to the Initials of the Characters Marked with Dots

开门红	kāiménhóng	make a good beginning
看不起	kànbuqǐ	look down on; scorn; despise
苦尽甘来	kǔ jìn gān lái	After suffering comes happiness.
口口声声	kǒu kǒu shēng shēng	say again and again; keep on saying

四 跟读绕口令，注意句中加点字的声母 Read the Tongue Twister Following the Teacher, Pay Attention to the Initials of the Characters Marked with Dots

Gē kuà guā kuāng guò kuān gōu，gǎn kuài guò gōu kàn guài gǒu. Guāng kàn guài gǒu guā kuāng kòu, guā gǔn kuāng kōng gē guài gǒu.

哥挎瓜筐过宽沟，赶快过沟看怪狗。光看怪狗瓜筐扣，瓜滚筐空哥怪狗。

五 听诵古诗，给诗中加点的字注上声母 Listen and Recite the Ancient Poem, Write the Initials for the Characters Marked with Dots

蜀相

唐·杜甫

丞相祠堂何处寻，
锦官城外柏森森。
映阶碧草自春色，
隔叶黄鹂空好音。
三顾频烦天下计，
两朝开济老臣心。
出师未捷身先死，
长使英雄泪满襟。

【提示】

诸葛亮（181—234），字孔明，号卧龙。中国魏、蜀、吴三国时期任蜀国丞相，是杰出的政治家、军事家，历来为人民群众所敬仰。他定国安邦为两朝国事鞠躬尽瘁，壮志未酬，身先亡故，千古以来多少志士仁人为此仰首长叹，泪洒满怀啊！

h h

一　语音视听　Audio-visual Pronunciation

1. 发音示意图　Diagrammatic Sketch of Pronunciation

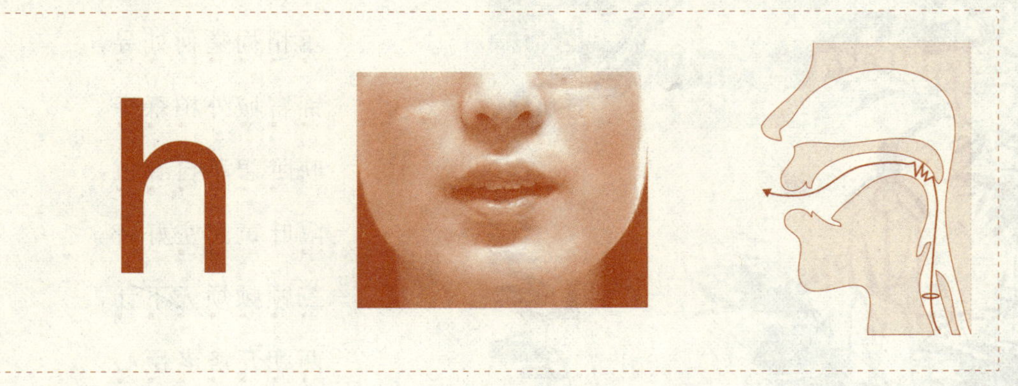

2. 发音特点　Characteristics of Pronunciation

h [x] 舌根、清、擦音。发音时舌根对软腭，中间留窄缝，气流从窄缝中摩擦成音。

h [x] A velar, unvoiced, fricative sound. It is produced by raising the back of the tongue against the soft palate to make a narrow passage and the airstream comes out through it with friction.

二　听读词语　Listen and Read the Following Words

虎	hǔ	tiger
后	hòu	back
花	huā	flower
红	hóng	red
火	huǒ	fire
好汉	hǎohàn	hero
会合	huìhé	assemble
火花	huǒhuā	spark
后悔	hòuhuǐ	regret
呼号	hūháo	howl
和好	héhǎo	reconcile

三 速读短语，注意加点字的声母 Read Phrases Quickly, Pay Attention to the Initials of the Characters Marked with Dots

海底捞针	hái dǐ lāo zhēn	fishing for a needle in the ocean; very difficult to find
合不来	hébulái	not get along well with; to be incompatible
旱鸭子	hànyāzi	duck raised on dry land; land lubbers
回头客	huítóukè	regular customer; frequenter

【提示】

海底捞针（hǎi dǐ lāo zhēn），读“hái dǐ lāo zhēn”。这是三声的变调现象。

四 跟读经典选文，注意句中加点字的声母 Read the Adapted Classic Following the Teacher, Pay Attention to the Initials of the Characters Marked with Dots

Jūnzǐ yuē: Xué bù kéyǐ yǐ. Qīng, qǔ zhī yú lán ér qīng yú lán; bīng, shuǐ wéi zhī ér hán yú shuǐ.

君子曰：学不可以已。青，取之于蓝而青于蓝；冰，水为之而寒于水。

——《荀子·劝学》

【提示】

已：停止。

青：比蓝青。

寒：比水还冰。

荀子（前313？—前238？），名况，字卿，也称孙卿，战国时期赵国猗氏（今山西安泽）人，著名思想家、文学家、政论家，儒家重要代表人物之一，对重整儒家典籍有很大的贡献。荀子提出了“礼”的思想，即需要由圣王及礼法的教化来使人格提高。

《荀子》：作者为荀子，文章论题鲜明，结构严谨，说理透彻，有很强的逻辑性。语言丰富多彩，善于比喻。文中排比句、对偶句很多，有荀子特有的风格。对后世说理文章有一定影响。

《劝学》：比较系统地讨论了学习的目的、意义、态度和方法。劝：劝勉，鼓励。

五 听诵古诗，给诗中加点的字注上声母 Listen and Recite the Ancient Poem, Write the Initials for the Characters Marked with Dots

从军行（节选）

唐·王昌龄

大漠风尘日色昏，红旗半卷出辕门。

前军夜战洮河北，已报生擒吐谷浑。

【提示】

吐谷浑，当时中国西部民族名称。全诗写了边防将士反击吐蕃入侵战斗告捷的场面。

复习三　分辨 f 和 h 声母
Revision 3　Distinguish f from h

部分方言中，把普通话中的唇齿音 f 读成舌根音 h 或 f，h 相混。发音时，要区分两个声母的发音部位和方法。f 是唇齿音，上齿轻接下唇，留有缝隙，气流擦缝隙通过成音。h 是舌根音，舌根隆起接近软腭留有缝隙，气流通过缝隙摩擦成音。

In some dialects, people mispronounce f as h or mix them up. Therefore, we need to distinguish their places and manners of articulation. f is a labio-dental sound with the upper teeth against the lower lip and there is a narrow passage between them. The air comes out through the passage. h is a velar sound with the back of the tongue rises near the soft palate. And the air comes out through the interstice between them.

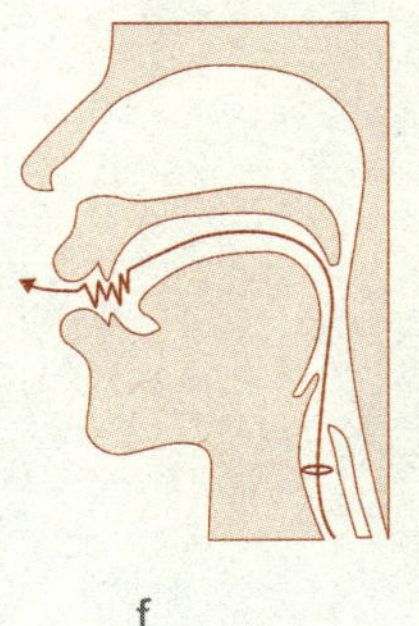

f

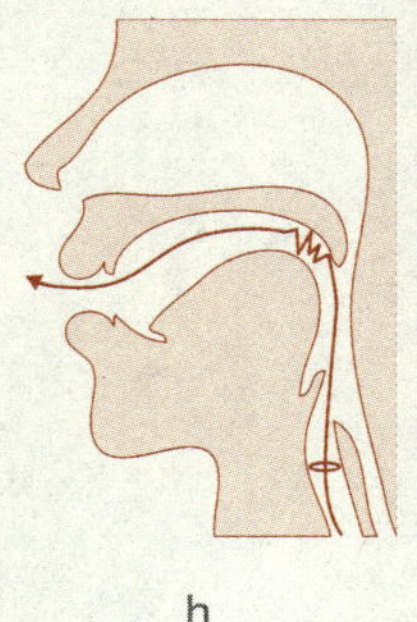

h

一　听辨词语　Listen and Distinguish the Following Words

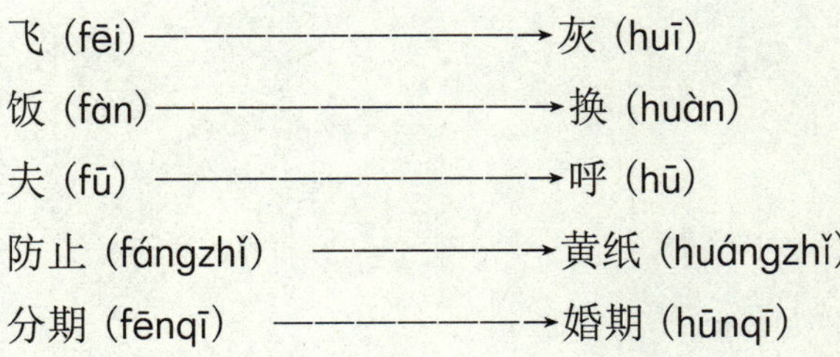

飞（fēi）——————————→灰（huī）

饭（fàn）——————————→换（huàn）

夫（fū）——————————→呼（hū）

防止（fángzhǐ）————————→黄纸（huángzhǐ）

分期（fēnqī）————————→婚期（hūnqī）

二　跟读绕口令，注意句中加点字的声母 Read the Tongue Twister Following the Teacher, Pay Attention to the Initials of the Characters Marked with Dots

Hóng fènghuáng,huáng fènghuáng, fěnhóng fènghuáng,huī fènghuáng,fēnfēn fēiluò zài fènghuáng táishang fěnhóng qiáng, fēnbuqīng nǎ shì fěnhóng fènghuáng,huáng fènghuáng, kànbuqīng nǎ shì fènghuáng táishang de fěnhóng qiáng hé fěnhóng fènghuán,huáng fènghuáng.

红凤凰，黄凤凰，粉红凤凰，灰凤凰，纷纷飞落在凤凰台上粉红墙，分不清哪是粉红凤凰，黄凤凰，看不清哪是凤凰台上的粉红墙和粉红凤凰，黄凤凰。

【提示】

凤凰：亦称为朱鸟、丹鸟、火鸟等，在西方神话里又叫火鸟、不死鸟，其形象一般为尾巴比较长的火烈鸟，周身是火。

第七节 零声母
Section VII Zero Consonants

汉语普通话中有的音节不以辅音开头，元音前头那个部分是零，习惯上叫“零声母”。

Some syllables in *Putonghua* may be without an initial. They are named by “Zero consonants”.

一 听读词语 Listen and Read the Following Words

爱	ài	love
鹅	é	goose
安	ān	calm; to be content; safe
雨	yǔ	rain
腰	yāo	waist
衣	yī	coat
屋	wū	house
温	wēn	warm
王	wáng	king

【提示】

汉语拼音字母 y 和 w 不是声母，而是起隔音作用的字母。它起避免音节界限发生混淆的作用。例如把“大衣”拼写称“dai”，就会以为是一个音节的“呆”，i 的前头加 y，写成“dayi”，音节界限就分明了。

i 行的韵母，前面没有声母时，i 改成 y，写成：

When there is not an initial in the front, the final i is changed into y , such as:

yi ya ye yao yan yin yang ying yong

u 行的韵母，前面没有声母时，u 改成 w，写成：

When there is not an initial in the front, the final u is changed into w , such as:

wu wa wo wai wei wen wang weng

ü 行的韵母，前面没有声母时，ü 改成 y，写成：

When there is not an initial in the front, the final ü is changed into w , such as:

yu yue yun

二 速读短语，注意加点字的声母 Read Phrases Quickly, Pay Attention to the Initials of the Characters Marked with Dots

安居乐业	ān jū lè yè	live and work in peace and contentment
奥运会	Àoyùnhuì	Olympic Games
玩意儿	wányìr	toy; thing
无奇不有	wúqíbùyǒu	there is no lack of strange things

【提示】

奥运会，音 Àoyùnhuì。汉语普通话语音拼写时，专有名词的第一个字母要大写。

玩意儿，音 wányìr，汉语普通话中的儿化音。

三 听诵古诗，给诗中加点的字注上声母 Listen and Recite the Ancient Poem, Write the Initials for the Characters Marked with Dots

竹枝词

唐 · 刘禹锡

杨柳青青江水平，闻郎江上踏歌声。
东边日出西边雨，道是无晴却有晴。

【提示】

《竹枝词》：词牌名。这首诗使用“晴”(qíng) 与“情”(qíng) 的谐音，“无晴”“有晴”即“无情”“有情”。在我国西南地区，民歌最为发达。男女的结合，往往开始于唱歌。在恋爱时，更是用唱歌来表情达意。

刘禹锡（772—842），字梦得，洛阳人。唐代中晚期诗人、哲学家，政治上主张革新。

四 听诵《太平歌》，给歌词注上声母 Listen and Recite *Tai Ping Ge,* Write the Initials for the Lyrics.

太平歌

子夜久难明，

喜报东方亮。

此日笙歌颂太平，

众口齐欢唱。

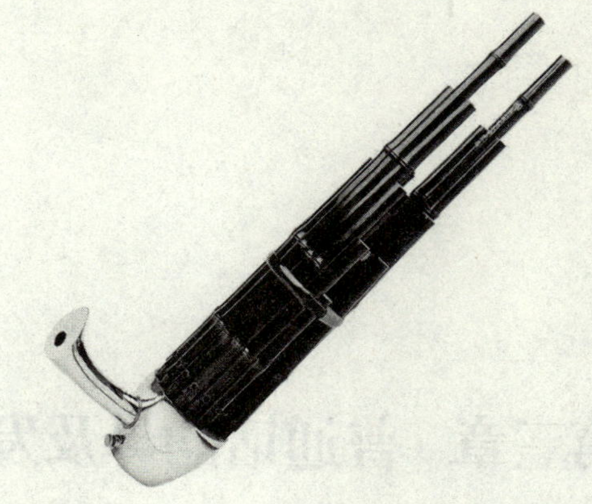

【提示】

子夜：夜间 11 点到 1 点。

笙：中国古老的簧管乐器。春秋战国时期，笙已经非常流行，在当时不仅是为声乐伴奏的主乐器，而且也有合奏、独奏的形式。

（注：这首诗涵盖了汉语拼音中的 21 个辅音声母和零声母。）

第三章　普通话韵母及发音

Chapter III　Finals and Their Pronunciation in *Putonghua*

★ 普通话韵母有39个。

★ 按内部成分不同，韵母可分为三大类：10个单元音韵母（7个舌面单元音，3个特殊单元音），13个复韵母和16个鼻韵母。

韵母就是一个音节中辅音声母后面的部分。如“Zhōnghuá”（中华）两个音节中的声母是“zh-”“h-”，它们后面的部分“ong”“uɑ”就是韵母。

Final is the syllable behind the consonantal initial. Taking Zhōnghuá as an example, zh- and h- are initials and the parts behind them, ong and uɑ, are finals.

普通话韵母总表
The Table of Finals in *Putonghua*

按口形分 / 韵母 / 按结构分	开口呼 Open Vowels	齐齿呼 Even Vowels	合口呼 Closed Vowels	撮口呼 Pursed Vowels
单韵母 Single Finals	-i [ɿ][ʅ]	i [i]	u [u]	ü [y]
	ɑ [A]	iɑ [iA]	uɑ [uA]	
	o [ɣ]		uo [uo]	
	e [ə]			
	ê [ɛ]	ie [iɛ]		üe [yɛ]
	er [ɚ]			
复韵母 Compound Finals	ɑi [ai]		uɑi [uai]	
	ei [ei]		uei [uei]	
	ɑo [ɑu]	iɑo [iɑu]		
	ou [ou]	iou [iou]		
鼻韵母 Nasal Finals	ɑn [an]	iɑn [iɛn]	uɑn [uan]	üɑn [yan]
	en [ən]	in [in]	uen [uən]	ün [yn]
	ɑng [ɑŋ]	iɑng [iɑŋ]	uɑng [uɑŋ]	
	eng [əŋ]	ing [iŋ]	ueng [uəŋ]	
			ong [uŋ]	iong [yŋ][①]

① ong [uŋ] 放在合口呼、iong [yŋ] 放在撮口呼，是按古今音韵系统排列的。

ong [uŋ] belongs to closed vowels, while iong [yŋ] is classified as a pursed vowel. Such classification is made according to the ancient and modern vowels and tone system.

普通话的韵母共39个，主要由元音或元音与鼻辅音构成，按结构分为单韵母、复韵母、鼻韵母三类，按起头元音发音口形分为开口呼、齐齿呼、合口呼、撮口呼四类（简称“四呼”）。所谓“四呼”就是：

There are thirty-nine finals in *Putonghua*, which consist of vowels or the combination of vowels and nasals. These finals can be classified by structure as single, compound and nasal finals, or by the degree of lip-rounding of the initial vowels as open, even, closed and pursed vowels, whose definitions are given in the following table:

开口呼　韵母不是 i，u，ü 或不以 i，u，ü 起头的韵母属于开口呼。

Open vowels refer to the finals whose initial vowels are not i, u and ü.

齐齿呼　i 或以 i 起头的韵母属于齐齿呼。

Even vowels refer to the final i or finals starting with i.

合口呼　u 或以 u 起头的韵母属于合口呼。

Closed vowels refer to the final u or finals starting with u.

撮口呼　ü 或以 ü 起头的韵母属于撮口呼。

Pursed vowels refer to the final ü or finals starting with ü.

我们已经学过声母（辅音），了解了辅音的形成及发音。下面请看元音的形成及发音。

Previously, we've learned the form and articulation of initials (consonants), and now let's come to the finals.

第一节　舌面单韵母
Section I Tongue Single Vowels

普通话有七个舌面单韵母，它们是 ɑ，o，e，ê，i，u，ü。

There are seven tongue single vowels in *Putonghua*: ɑ, o, e, ê, i, u, ü.

不同的元音是由口腔的开闭，舌头位置高低、前后、口形圆与不圆形成的。舌头由 ɑ 升到 i 是舌位的高低变化，舌头由 i 收缩到 u 是舌位的前后变化，口形由 o 成 e，是圆与不圆的变化。

The difference between different vowels lies in the opening or closing of mouth, the place of tongue (high or low, front or back) and the shape of lips (round or not). The place of tongue is raised from low to high when producing ɑ and i and held back from front to back when articulating i and u, while the shape of lips is altered from rounding to unrounding when pronouncing o and e.

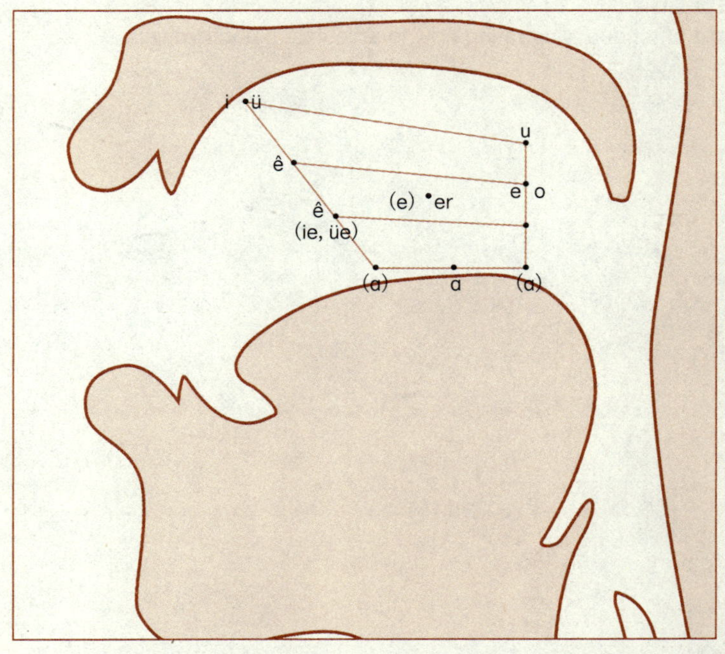

图 3-1　元音发音舌位变化示意简图
Figure 3-1 The varied places of tongue, illustrating how to articulate vowels

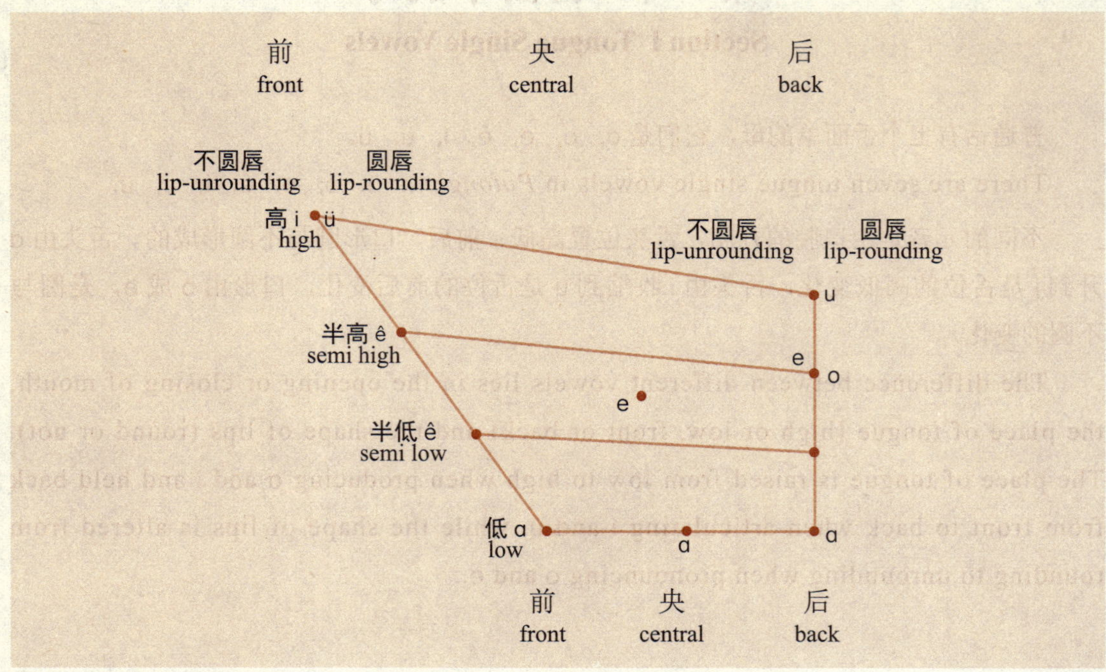

图 3-2 舌面元音舌位简图
Figure 3-2 The place of tongue, illustrating how to articulate palatal vowels

ɑ ɑ

一 语音视听 Audio-visual Pronunciation

1. 发音示意图 Diagrammatic Sketch of Pronunciation

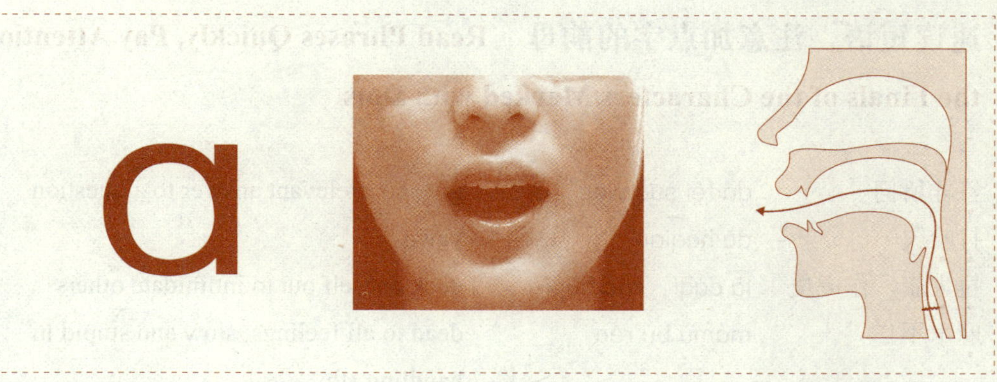

2. 发音特点 Characteristics of Pronunciation

ɑ [A] 舌面央、低、不圆唇元音。发音时，口大开，舌位低，舌居中，气流振动声带从口腔出，可自成音节。

ɑ [A] A palatal, low, lip-unrounding vowel. It is produced by wide opening the mouth and putting the tongue in central and its lowest position. The airstream comes out of the vibration of the vocal cords. It can stand alone as a syllable.

二 听读词语 Listen and Read the Following Words

阿	ā	an initial partical
啊	á	ah
巴	bā	bar
拿	ná	take
马	mǎ	horse
拉	lā	pull
杂	zá	complex
大厦	dàshà	building
喇叭	lǎba	horn

发达	fādá	developed
打靶	dá bǎ	target practice

【提示】

喇叭（lǎbā），读“lǎba”，第二个汉字“叭”是轻声，不标注声调符号。

打靶（dǎ bǎ），读“dá bǎ”，是三声的变调现象。

三　速读短语，注意加点字的韵母　Read Phrases Quickly, Pay Attention to the Finals of the Characters Marked with Dots

答非所问	dá fēi suǒ wèn	give an irrelevant answer to a question
打哈欠	dǎ hāqian	yawn
拉大旗，作虎皮	lā dàqí，zuò hǔpí	deck oneself out to intimidate others
麻木不仁	mámù bù rén	dead to all feelings; slow and stupid in handling sth.
马大哈	mǎdàhā	careless; unmindful

四　跟读绕口令，注意句中加点字的韵母　Read the Tongue Twister Following the Teacher, Pay Attention to the Finals of the Characters Marked with Dots

Māma zhòng má,wǒ qù fàng mǎ. Mǎ chīle má, māma mà mǎ.

妈妈种麻，我去放马。马吃了麻，妈妈骂马。

五　听诵古诗，给全诗注上声母并给加点的字注上韵母　Listen and Recite the Ancient Poem, Write the Initials for the Poem and the Finals for the Characters Marked with Dots

蒙学诗

宋·邵雍

一去二三里，烟村四五家，

青苔六七点，八九十枝花。

【提示】

该诗语言优美，形式新颖，巧妙运用十个数字描绘了乡村景色，开“十字诗”之先河。它是儿童学习一到十计数的启蒙诗，是最早的数学方面的科普诗歌。

邵雍（1011—1077），北宋哲学家，理学家，字尧夫，谥（音 shì）康节，先为范阳人，后随父迁至共城（今河南辉县），擅长占卜，后人称他百源先生。著有《皇极经世》《伊川击壤集》等。

六 听京剧学汉语，注意加点字的韵母 Learn Chinese by Listening to the *Beijing* Opera

夸铁梅

提篮叫卖拾煤渣，担水劈柴也靠她。
里里外外一把手，穷人的孩子早当家。
栽什么树苗结什么果，撒什么种子开什么花。

——《红灯记》

【提示】

《红灯记》：该故事取材于电影《自有后来人》，原创作者为黄泳江，后由哈尔滨京剧院率先搬上京剧舞台。

O o

一 语音视听 Audio-visual Pronunciation

1. 发音示意图 Diagrammatic Sketch of Pronunciation

2. 发音特点 Characteristics of Pronunciation

o [o] 舌面后、半高、圆唇元音。发音时，口拢圆，舌头后缩，气流振动声带从口腔出。

o [o] A velar, mid-high, lip-rounding vowel. It is produced by rounding the mouth and holding back the tongue. The air comes out of the vibration of the vocal cords.

二 听读词语 Listen and Read the Following Words

1.

磨	mó	grind
抹	mǒ	mop up
莫	mò	do not
拨	bō	dial
破	pò	broken
迫	pò	force
玻	bō	glass
婆婆	pópo	mother-in-law
伯伯	bóbo	father's elder brother
薄膜	bómó	film
磨破	mópò	wear through

【提示】

婆婆（pópo）和伯伯（bóbo）是轻声词。

2.

搏斗	bódòu	fight; engage in hand-to-hand combat
拨款	bōkuǎn	appropriate funds; allocate funds
活泼	huópō	active; lively
湖泊	húpō	lakes
博学	bóxué	erudition
玻璃	bōli	glass
婆娑	pósuō	uhirling; dancing
播种	bōzhǒng	to sow seeds
佛像	fóxiàng	joss; figure of Buddha
魄力	pòlì	daring and resolution
默默	mòmò	silently; quietly; mute
破坏	pòhuài	destroy; ruin; damage

三　速读短语，注意加点字的韵母 Read Phrases Quickly, Pay Attention to the Finals of the Characters Marked with Dots

伯仲叔季	bó zhòng shū jì	eldest, second, third and yongest of brothers
泼冷水	pō léngshuǐ	dampen one' s enthusiasm for
磨工夫	mó gōngfu	consume time
抹一鼻子灰	mǒ yì bízi huī	try to please someone but get a snub

【提示】

泼冷水（pō lěngshuǐ），读“pō léngshuǐ”，是三声的变调现象。

四　跟读经典选文，注意加点字的韵母 Read the Adapted Classic Following the Teacher, Pay attention to the Finals of the Characters Marked with Dots

Hé bào zhī mù,shēng yú háo mò; jiǔ céng zhī tái, qǐ yú lěi tǔ; qiānlǐ zhī xíng shǐ yú zúxià.

合抱之木，生于毫末；九层之台，起于垒土；千里之行，始于足下。

——《老子》

【提示】

垒土（lěi tǔ），读“léi tǔ”，是三声的变调现象。

这句话的意思是合抱的粗木，是从细如针毫时长起来的；九层的高台，是一筐土一筐土筑起来的；千里的行程，是一步一步迈出来的。说明万事起于忽微，量变引起质变。

《老子》：道教经书，是春秋战国时期道教创始人李聃（字伯阳，又名老聃 dān 或老子）撰写的，共五千字。

五　听诵古诗，给全诗注上声母并给加点的字注上韵母 Listen and Recite the Poem, Write the Initials for the Poem and the Finals for the Characters Marked with Dots

鹅

唐 · 骆宾王

鹅！鹅！鹅！曲项向天歌。

白毛浮绿水，红掌拨青波。

【提示】

该诗是骆宾王 7 岁时所做，短短 18 个字，把一群白鹅戏水的神态惟妙惟肖地表现了出来。

骆宾王（约 640—684），唐朝初期诗人。字观光，婺州义乌（今浙江义乌）人，与王勃、杨炯、卢照邻合称初唐四杰。有《骆宾王文集》传世。

e e

一 语音视听 Audio-visual Pronunciation

1. 发音示意图 Diagrammatic Sketch of Pronunciation

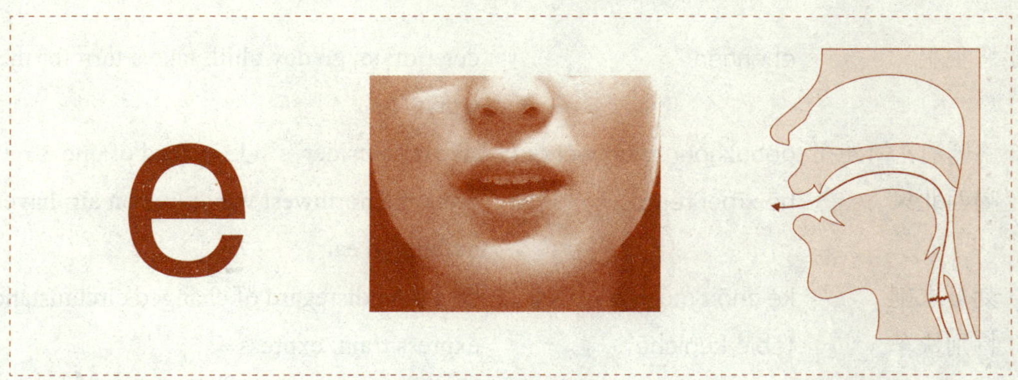

2. 发音特点 Characteristics of Pronunciation

e [ɣ] 舌面后、半高、不圆唇元音。发音时，口半开、舌稍后缩，气流振动声带从口腔出，可自成音节。

e [ɣ] A velar, mid-unrounding vowel. It is produced by half opening the mouth and holding back the tongue a little. The air comes out of the vibration of the vocal cords. It can stand alone as a syllable.

二 听读词语 Listen and Read the Following Words

阿	ē	play up to
俄	é	Russia
鹅	é	goose
恶	è	evil
厄	è	hardship
合格	hégé	qualified
特色	tèsè	feature
客车	kèchē	coach
乐得	lède	happy

【提示】

乐得（lède）中的“得”读轻声，汉语普通话中助词“的、地、得”读轻声。

三　速读短语，注意加点字的韵母 Read Phrases Quickly, Pay Attention to the Finals of the Characters Marked with Dots

恶狠狠	èhěnhěn	deteriorate; go downhill; take a turn for the worse
胳膊肘儿朝外拐	gēbozhǒur cháo wài guǎi	take on outsider' s side instead of one' s own
喝西北风	hē xīběi fēng	drink the northwest wind; live on air; have nothing to eat
刻舟求剑	kè zhōu qiú jiàn	do sth. in disregard of changed circumstances
特别快车	tèbié kuàichē	express train; express

四　跟读绕口令，注意句中加点字的韵母 Read the Tongue Twister Following the Teacher, Pay Attention to the Finals of the Characters Marked with Dots

Pō shang lìzhe yì zhī é, pō xia liúzhe yì tiáo hé. Kuānkuān de hé, féiféi de é, é yào guò hé, hé yào dù é, bùzhī é guò hé háishì hé dù é.

坡上立着一只鹅，坡下流着一条河。宽宽的河，肥肥的鹅，鹅要过河，河要渡鹅，不知鹅过河还是河渡鹅。

五　听诵古诗，给全诗注上声母并给加点的字注上韵母 Listen and Recite the Poem, Write the Initials for the Poem and the Finals for the Characters Marked with Dots

拟咏怀（其五）

北周 · 庾信

萧条亭障远，凄惨风尘多。
关门临白狄，城影如黄河。
秋风苏武别，寒水送荆轲。
谁言气盖世，晨起帐中歌。

【提示】

此诗以李陵、荆轲、项羽作比况，抒发作者流落异地后，归国无望、无所作为的痛苦感情。

亭障：岗亭和城堡，泛指防御工事。

白狄：北方部族狄族中的另一族。

关门：关口、面临。

苏武别：李陵别苏武的典故。

送荆轲：荆轲离开易水的典故。

帐中歌：项羽在帐中舞剑唱歌的典故。

庾信（513—581），字子山，小字兰成。他是南北朝文学的集大成者。

复习一　分辨 o 和 e 韵母

Revision 1　Distinguish o from e

在教学单元音韵母时，必须分清 o 和 e 的区别。o 是后半高圆唇元音，e 是后半高不圆唇元音，口形不同。但在现实教学中，两者常易混淆。如与 b, p, m 声母相拼时，把圆唇 o 读成不圆唇 e；在 ɑ, o, e 三个单元音韵母连读时，由于受前后音的影响，往往将圆唇元音 o 读成不圆唇元音 e。这些都是不正确的。例如：

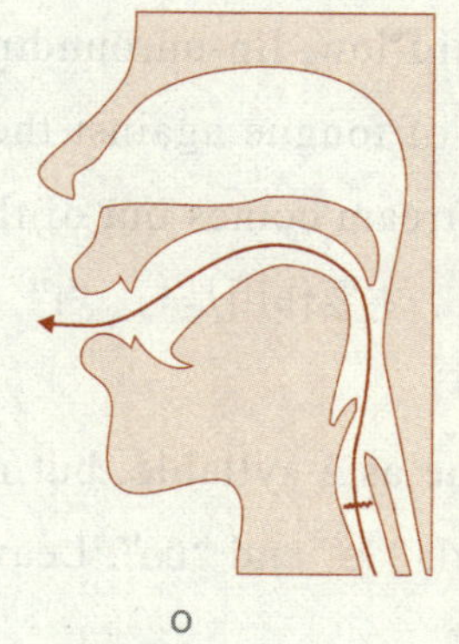

o

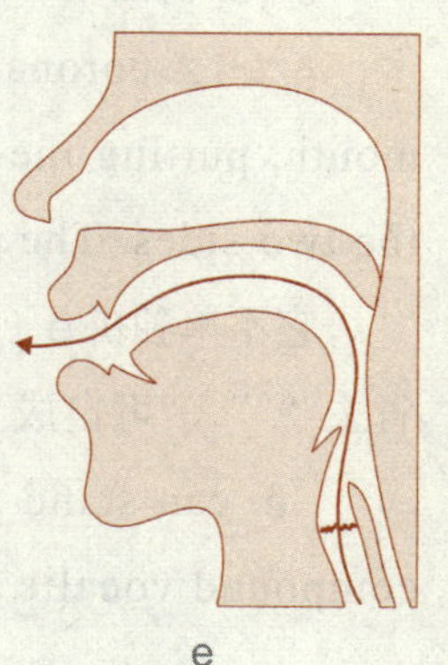

e

When learning single vocalic finals, students have to tell o from e. Above all, they are pronounced in different shape of mouth—o is velar, mid-high, lip-rounding vowel, while e is velar, mid-high, lip-unrounding vowel. However, in fact these two are easily mixed up. For example, lip-rounding o is pronouced as lip-unrounding e when they combine with initials b, p, m, or in the case of ɑ, o, e articulated in a row, it is likely to confuse o with e due to the influence of lip-unrounding ɑ and e. These are all incorrect. For example:

破格（pògé）　墨盒（mòhé）　隔膜（gémó）　薄荷（bòhe）

ê ê

一 语音视听 Audio-visual Pronunciation

1. 发音示意图 Diagrammatic Sketch of Pronunciation

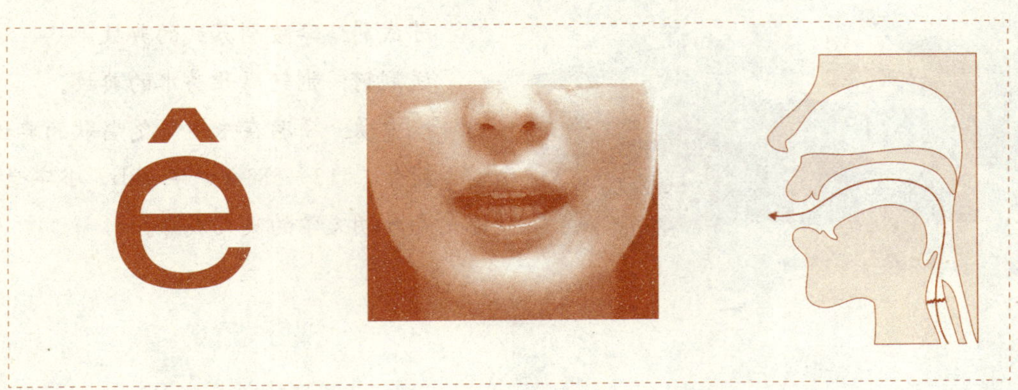

2. 发音特点 Characteristics of Pronunciation

ê [ε] 舌面前、半低、不圆唇元音。发音时，口半开，舌尖抵下齿背，气流振动声带从口出。

ê [ε] A coronal, mid-low, lip-unrounding vowel. It is produced by half opening the mouth, putting the tip of tongue against the lower gum and spreading the lips towards the two sides. The airstream comes out of the vibration of the vocal cords.

它不单独拼 ê（欸），主要作用是与 “i” “ü” 组合成复元音韵母 “ie” “üe”，书写时省去 “^”，可自成音节。

ê can stand alone as a syllable, but mostly it combines with “i” and “ü” to form compound vocalic finals “ie” and “üe”. Leave out “^” in written form.

二 听读词语 Listen and Read the Following Words

爷	yé	grandpa
也	yě	also
且	qiě	in addition
迭	dié	alternate
约	yuē	about
雪	xuě	snow

解决	jiějué	solve
雪夜	xuěyè	a snowy night
贴切	tiēqiè	approximate
节约	jiéyuē	save

三 速读短语，注意加点字的韵母 Read Phrases Quickly, Pay Attention to the Finals of the Characters Marked with Dots

跌眼镜	diē yǎnjìng	to one's surprise;amaze
皆大欢喜	jiē dà huānxǐ	everyone is happy;to the happiness of all
绝无仅有	jué wú jǐn yǒu	only one of its kind;unique
雪中送炭	xuě zhōng sòng tàn	provide timely help; provide material help to others in need

四 跟读绕口令，注意句中加点字的韵母 Read the Tongue Twister Following the Teacher, Pay Attention to the Finals of the Characters Marked with Dots

Jiějie duānzhe pánzi, pánzi li bǎizhe diézi, diézi li chéngzhe qiézi, shàng táijiē dǎle gè bànzi. Diēfānle pánzi suì le diézi, sǎle qiézi, qìde jiějie zhí cǎi qiézi.

姐姐端着盘子，盘子里摆着碟子，碟子里盛着茄子，上台阶打了个绊子。跌翻了盘子碎了碟子，撒了茄子，气得姐姐直踩茄子。

【提示】
绊：走动时或跑步时被物件绊了一下而摔倒。

五 听诵古诗，给全诗注上声母并给加点的字注上韵母 Listen and Recite the Poem, Write the Initials for the Poem and the Finals for the Characters Marked with Dots

江雪

唐·柳宗元

千山鸟飞绝，万径人踪灭。
孤舟蓑笠翁，独钓寒江雪。

【提示】

蓑笠：音 suōlì，意思为蓑衣和斗笠。

此诗是柳宗元被贬永州后写的一首诗。全诗立意高远，通过写雪景来赞美老翁“独钓寒江”的精神，表达了诗人自己孤独郁闷的心情。

柳宗元（773—819），字子厚，唐代文学家、哲学家，“唐宋八大家”之一，祖籍河东（今山西省永济市），与韩愈共同倡导唐代“古文运动”，并称“韩柳”。因为他是河东人，又在柳州刺史任上，所以人称“柳河东”或“柳柳州”。

I i

一 语音视听 Audio-visual Pronunciation

1. 发音示意图 Diagrammatic Sketch of Pronunciation

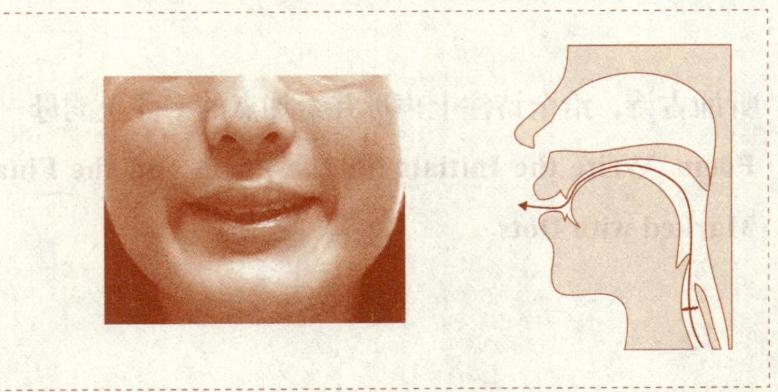

2. 发音特点 Characteristics of Pronunciation

i [i] 舌面前、高、不圆唇元音。口扁平开，舌尖前伸，抵下齿背，舌面隆起与硬腭接近，气流振动声带从口腔出，可自成音节。

i [i] A coronal, high, lip-unrounding vowel. It is produced by narrowly opening the mouth, spreading the lips towards the two sides into a flat position, pushing forward the tip of tongue against the lower gum and raising the tongue close to the hard palate. The airstream comes out of the vibration of the vocal cords. It can stand alone as a syllable.

二 听读词语 Listen and Read the Following Words

衣	yī	clothes
移	yí	move
椅	yǐ	chair
义	yì	righteous
笛	dí	flute
尼	ní	Buddhist nun
李	lǐ	a surname
气	qì	gas
皮衣	píyī	fur clothing
米粒	mǐlì	rice grains
机器	jīqì	machine
集体	jítǐ	group
第一	dìyī	the first
笔记	bǐjì	note
起立	qǐlì	stand up

【提示】

i 单独成音节，在 i 前加上隔音字母 y。如衣（yī）、移（yí）、椅（yǐ）、义（yì）。

三 速读短语，注意加点字的韵母 Read Phrases Quickly, Pay Attention to the Finals of the Characters Marked with Dots

一技之长	yí jì zhī cháng	proficiency in a particular line (or field); professional skill
立竿见影	lì gān jiàn yǐng	get instant results
鸡蛋里挑骨头	jīdàn li tiāo gǔtou	look for a bone in an egg; nitpick
起早贪黑	qí zǎo tān hēi	(of a diligent person) start work early and knock off late
喜气洋洋	xǐqì yángyáng	jubilant; joyful; full of joy

【提示】

一技之长（yī jì zhī cháng），读"yí jì zhī cháng"。这是"一"的变调现象。

起早贪黑（qǐ zǎo tān hēi），读"qí zǎo tān hēi"。这是三声的变调现象。

四 跟读绕口令和经典选文，注意加点字的韵母 Read the Tongue Twister and Adapted Classic Following the Teacher, Pay Attention to the Finals of the Characters Marked with Dots

1.

Yī èr sān, sān èr yī, yī èr sān sì wǔ liù qī.

Qī gè āyí lái zhāi lí, qī gè lán ér shǒu zhōng tí. Dàlí, xiǎolí jǐ yìqǐ.

一二三，三二一，一二三四五六七。

七个阿姨来摘梨，七个篮儿手中提。大梨、小梨挤一起。

【提示】

一起（yīqǐ），读"yìqǐ"，这是"一"的变调现象。

2.

Sān Zì Jīng (Jié Xuǎn)

Yù bù zhuó,bù chéng qì. Rén bù xué, bù zhī yì.

Wéi rén zǐ,fāng shào shí. Qīn shī yǒu, xí lǐ yí.

三字经（节选）

玉不琢，不成器。人不学，不知义。
为人子，方少时。亲师友，习礼仪。

【提示】

琢：雕刻。

《三字经》：世传由王应麟所撰。全书具有识字、增长见闻和灌输伦理道德观念等作用。仅用三百多字便概括了中华五千年的历史变迁，历来备受赞誉。与《百家姓》《千字文》一起俗称“三百千”。在中国古代蒙书教材中，它是影响最大、最有代表性的书。

王应麟（1223—1296），南宋学者，字伯厚，号深宁居士，祖籍河南开封，后迁居庆元府鄞县（今浙江鄞县），位至吏部尚书。他一生著述甚多。

《百家姓》：是我国流行最长、最广的一种蒙学教材。成书和普及要早于《三字经》，自公元十世纪起在中国广为流传，本是北宋初年钱塘（杭州）一书生所编撰的蒙学读物。他将常见的姓氏编成四字一句的韵文，很像一首四言诗，读来顺口，易学好记。

《千字文》：该书成书于南朝梁武帝在位时期，其编者是梁朝周兴嗣，因全书每四字一句，共二百五十句，一千个字，故称千字文。

3.

Bù jī kuǐ bù,wú yǐ zhì qiānlǐ;bù jī xiǎo liú,wú yǐ chéng jiāng hé.
不积跬步，无以至千里；不积小流，无以成江河。

——《荀子·劝学》

【提示】

跬：半步。古时称人行走，举足一次为跬，举足两次为步，故半步叫“跬”。
江河：古代许多文章中专指长江、黄河。

五 听诵古诗，给全诗注上声母并给加点的字注上韵母 Listen and Recite the Poem, Write the Initials for the Poem and the Finals for the Characters Marked with Dots

七步诗

魏 · 曹植

煮豆燃豆萁，豆在釜中泣。
本是同根生，相煎何太急。

【提示】

其：豆茎。

作者曹植才华出众，很受父亲曹操的疼爱。曹操死后，其兄曹丕继位称帝。他担心弟弟会威胁自己的皇位，就想害死他。一天，曹丕让曹植当场在七步之内作出一首诗，以证明他写诗的才华。如果他写不出，就等于是在欺骗皇上，要把他处死。曹植知道哥哥存心要害他，既伤心又愤怒。他强忍心中悲痛，在七步之内作出了这首诗。

曹植（192—232），三国时魏国（今安徽省亳州市）诗人，字子建，曹操第三子，卒于封地陈郡，谥思，故后人称之为“陈王”或“陈思王”。今存诗歌八十余首。

U u

一 语音视听 Audio-visual Pronunciation

1. 发音示意图 Diagrammatic Sketch of Pronunciation

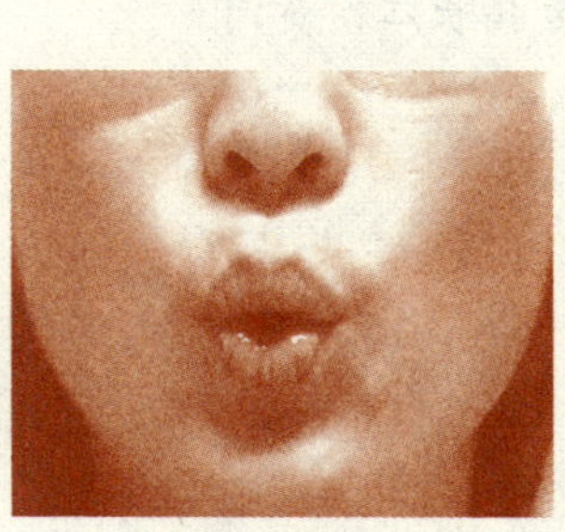

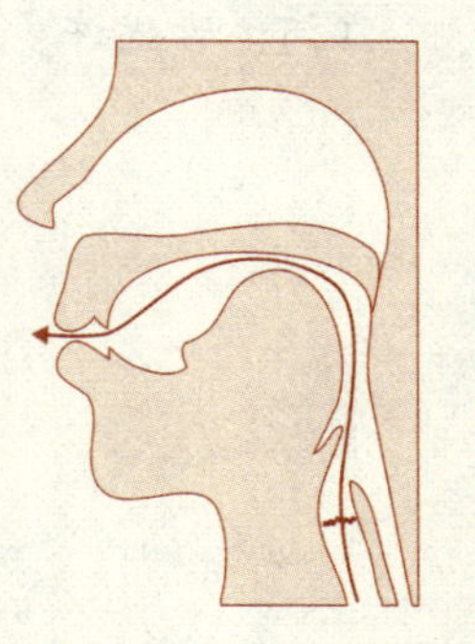

2. 发音特点 Characteristics of Pronunciation

u [u] 舌面后、高、圆唇元音。发音时，口拢圆，舌后缩隆起，舌根接近软腭，气流振动声带从口腔出，可自成音节。

u [u] A velar, high, lip-rounding vowel. It is produced by rounding the mouth and holding back the tongue with its back raised close to the soft palate. The airstream comes out of the vibration of the vocal cords. It can stand alone as a syllable.

二 听读词语 Listen and Read the Following Words

乌	wū	crow
吴	Wú	a kind of surname
五	wǔ	five
务	wù	business
部署	bùshǔ	arrange
木梳	mùshū	wooden comb
富庶	fùshù	wealthy
都督	dūdu	a military governor
路途	lùtú	journey
祖父	zǔfù	grandpa
奴仆	núpú	servant
粗布	cū bù	coarse cloth
主妇	zhǔfù	housewife
舒服	shūfu	comfortable
苦楚	kúchǔ	bitterness
互助	hùzhù	help each other

【提示】

“u”单独成音节，在“u”前加上隔音字母“w”。如乌（wū）、吴（Wú）、五（wǔ）。

舒服（shūfú），读“shūfu”，是轻声词。

苦楚（kǔchǔ），读“kúchǔ”，两个三声字连读，第一字应读二声。

三 速读短语，注意加点字的韵母 Read Phrases Quickly, Pay Attention to the Finals of the Characters Marked with Dots

不足为奇	bù zú wéi qí	not at all surprising; nothing to be taken as authoritative
出其不意	chū qí bú yì	take the opponent by surprise
胡说八道	hú shuō bā dào	talk nonsense or drivel; nonsense; drivel
目不识丁	mù bù shí dīng	illiterate

【提示】

出其不意（chū qí bù yì），读“chū qí bú yì”。这是“不”的变调现象。

四 跟读绕口令和经典选文，注意加点字的韵母 Read the Tongue Twister and the Adapted Classic Following the Teacher, Pay Attention to the Finals Marked with Dots

1.

Gǔ shang huà zhī hǔ, pòle ná bù bǔ. Bùzhī bù bú gǔ, háishì bù bú hǔ.

鼓上画只虎，破了拿布补。不知布补鼓，还是布补虎。

2.

Yìnián zhī jì,mò rú shù gǔ; shínián zhī jì, mò rú shù mù; zhōngshēn zhī jì, mò rú shù rén.

一年之计，莫如树谷；十年之计，莫如树木；终身之计，莫如树人。

——《管子·权修》

【提示】

做一年的打算没有赶得上种植一年的庄稼的；做十年的打算，没有赶得上种植树木的；做一生的打算，没有比得上培养人才的。说明培养人才的重要性。

《管子》：春秋时期（前722—前481），齐国政治家、思想家管仲及管仲学派的著述总集，大约成书于战国时代。共24卷，85篇，今存76篇。

管仲（?—前645），名夷吾，又名敬仲，字仲，春秋时期齐国著名的政治家，颍上（今安徽颍上）人，被称为“春秋第一相”，辅佐齐桓公成为春秋时期的第一霸主。

管仲注重经济，反对空谈主义，主张改革以富国强兵，他说：“国多财则远者来，地辟举则民留处，仓廪实而知礼节，衣食足而知荣辱。”齐桓公尊管仲为“仲父”，授权让他主持一系列政治和经济改革。

五 听诵古诗，给全诗注上声母并给加点的字注上韵母 Listen and Recite the Poem, Write the Initials for the Poem and the Finals for the Characters Marked with Dots

悯农

唐 · 李绅

锄禾日当午，汗滴禾下土。

谁知盘中餐，粒粒皆辛苦。

【提示】

该诗写劳动的艰辛，说明劳动成果来之不易。提醒世人珍惜粮食。

李绅（772—846），唐代诗人，字公垂，祖籍安徽亳州。其作品流传至今的有《追昔游诗》三卷、《杂诗》一卷，收录于《全唐诗》。另有《莺莺歌》，保存在《西厢记诸宫调》中。

《全唐诗》：共九百卷，清曹寅、彭定求等奉敕编纂，共收诗49 403首，句1 555条，作者2 873人。

ü ü

一 语音视听 Audio-visual Pronunciation

1. 发音示意图 Diagrammatic Sketch of Pronunciation

2. 发音特点 Characteristics of Pronunciation

ü [y] 舌面前、高、圆唇元音。发音时，口形拢圆，舌尖抵下齿背，舌面隆起与硬腭接近，气流振动声带从口腔出，可自成音节。

ü [y] A coronal, high, lip-rounding vowel. It is produced by rounding the mouth, pushing forward the tip of tongue against the lower gum and raising the tongue close to the hard palate. The airstream comes out of the vibration of the vocal cords. It can stand alone as a syllable.

二 听读词语 Listen and Read the Following Words

淤	yū	silt
鱼	yú	fish
雨	yǔ	rain
玉	yù	jade
语句	yǔjù	sentence
屈居	qūjū	inferior to…
区域	qūyù	district
女婿	nǚxu	son-in-law
玉律	yùlǜ	golden rule

雨具	yǔjù	rain gear
须臾	xūyú	in a short time
区区	qūqū	trifling

【提示】

“ü”单独成音节，在“ü”之前加上隔音字母“y”，同时“ü”上两点省写，如“淤（yū）”“鱼（yú）”“雨（yǔ）”“玉（yù）”。

“ü”跟n, l以外的声母相拼时都省写两点。如“屈居（qūjū）”。

女婿（nǚxu）是轻声词。

三　速读短语，注意加点字的韵母　Read Phrases Quickly, Pay Attention to the Finals of the Characters Marked with Dots

鱼目混珠	yú mù hùn zhū	pass off fish eyes as pearls; pass off sth. pass off sham as genuine
愚公移山	Yúgōng yí shān	do sth. with dogged perseverance and fear no difficulty
语重心长	yǔ zhòng xīn cháng	sincere words and earnest wishes
玉石俱焚	yù shí jù fén	destroy the good and the bad together; total destruction
欲速则不达	yù sù zé bù dá	desire to have things done quickly prevents them from be done thoroughly; haste does not bring success

四　跟读经典选文，注意加点字的韵母　Read the Adapted Classic Following the Teacher, Pay attention to the Finals of the Characters Marked with Dots

Zǐyuē: “Shǐ wú yú rén yě, tīng qí yán ér xìn qí xíng; jīn wú yú rén yě, tīng qí yán ér guān qí xíng.”

子曰：“始吾于人也，听其言而信其行；今吾于人也，听其言而观其行。”

——《论语·公冶长》

【提示】

孔子说：“开始我对于别人，是听到他的话就相信他的行为；现在我对于别人，听了他的话，还要看他的行为。”全句指不要只听言论，还要看实际行动。

五　听歌学汉语，注意加点字的韵母 Learn Chinese by Listening to the Song, Pay Attention to the Finals Marked with Dots

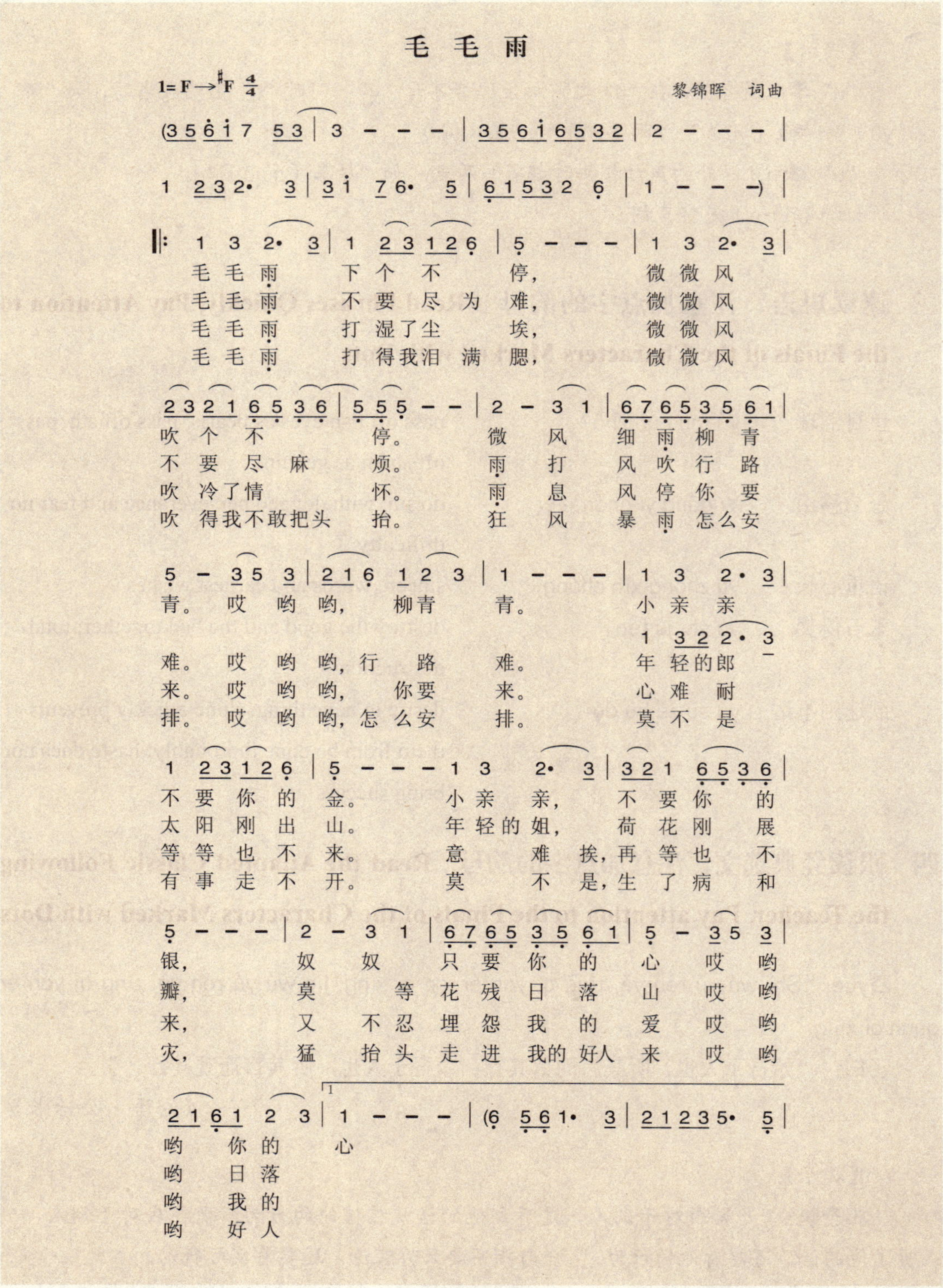

毛 毛 雨

1= F → #F 4/4　　　　　　　　黎锦晖　词曲

(3 5 6 1 7 5 3 | 3 - - - | 3 5 6 1 6 5 3 2 | 2 - - - |
1 2 3 2· 3 | 3 1 7 6· 5 | 6 1 5 3 2 6 | 1 - - -) |

‖: 1 3 2· 3 | 1 2 3 1 2 6 | 5 - - - | 1 3 2· 3 |
毛 毛 雨 下 个 不 停， 微 微 风
毛 毛 雨 不 要 尽 为 难， 微 微 风
毛 毛 雨 打 湿 了 尘 埃， 微 微 风
毛 毛 雨 打 得 我 泪 满 腮， 微 微 风

2 3 2 1 6 5 3 6 | 5 5 5 - - | 2 - 3 1 | 6 7 6 5 3 5 6 1 |
吹 个 不 停。 微 风 细 雨 柳 青
不 要 尽 麻 烦。 雨 打 风 吹 行 路
吹 冷 了 情 怀。 雨 息 风 停 你 要
吹 得 我 不 敢 把 头 抬。 狂 风 暴 雨 怎 么 安

5 - 3 5 3 | 2 1 6 1 2 3 | 1 - - - | 1 3 2· 3 |
青。 哎 哟 哟， 柳 青 青。 小 亲 亲
1 3 2 2· 3
难。 哎 哟 哟， 行 路 难。 年 轻 的 郎
来。 哎 哟 哟， 你 要 来。 心 难 耐
排。 哎 哟 哟， 怎 么 安 排。 莫 不 是

1 2 3 1 2 6 | 5 - - - 1 3 2· 3 | 3 2 1 6 5 3 6 |
不 要 你 的 金。 小 亲 亲， 不 要 你 的
太 阳 刚 出 山。 年 轻 的 姐， 荷 花 刚 展
等 等 也 不 来。 意 难 挨， 再 等 也 不
有 事 走 不 开。 莫 不 是， 生 了 病 和

5 - - - | 2 - 3 1 | 6 7 6 5 3 5 6 1 | 5 - 3 5 3 |
银， 奴 奴 只 要 你 的 心 哎 哟
瓣， 莫 等 花 残 日 落 山 哎 哟
来， 又 不 忍 埋 怨 我 的 爱 哎 哟
灾， 猛 抬 头 走 进 我 的 好 人 来 哎 哟

2 1 6 1 2 3 | [1. 1 - - - | (6 5 6 1· 3 | 2 1 2 3 5· 5 |
哟 你 的 心
哟 日 落
哟 我 的
哟 好 人

1=♯F

6 1 5 3 2 6 | 1 - - -) :‖ [2] 1 - - (5 | 1 2 3 2· 3 |
山

3 i 7 6· 5 | 6 1 5 3 2 6 | 1 - - -) :‖ [3] 1 - - - |
爱

(6 5 6 1· 3 | 2 1 2 3 5· 5 | 6 1 5 3 2 6 | 1 - - -) :‖

[4] 1 - - - | (0 5 i 3 5 i 3 5 | i 0 1 - | 1 - - -) ‖
来

六 听诵古诗，给全诗注上声母并给加点的字注上韵母 Listen and Recite the Poem, Write the Initials for the Poem and the Finals for the Characters Marked with Dots

迢迢牵牛星

汉·《西汉乐府·古诗》

迢迢牵牛星，皎皎河汉女。
纤纤擢素手，札札弄机杼。
终日不成章，泣涕零如雨。
河汉清且浅，相去复几许。
盈盈一水间，脉脉不得语。

【提示】

这首诗选自汉乐府《古诗十九首》。它描述了织女的相思之苦，借喻有情男女咫尺天涯的哀怨之情。

乐府是西汉汉武帝设置的礼乐机构，由李延年为都尉，专门搜集流传于民间的民歌、俗曲（古诗）等，一直延续到东汉末年。

迢迢：遥远。　牵牛星：银河南。　河汉：银河。　皎皎：洁白。

河汉女：指织女星，在银河北，与牵牛星隔河相对。　纤纤：细小。

擢：织布时用梭子的动作。　杼：织布时放纬线的梭子。

章：织布时经纬线搭配的纹理规格。　零：流落。　几许：多少。

盈盈：指水光轻盈。　脉脉：双目含情相视。

第二节 特殊单元音韵母
Section II Special Vocalic Finals

普通话中有三个特殊韵母“-i[ɿ]”“-i[ʅ]”“er”，它们虽属于单元音韵母，但其发音状况却不同于其他单元音韵母。

There are three special vocalic finals in *Putonghua*: -i[ɿ], -i[ʅ], er. Though they fall into the group of single vocalic finals, their pronunciation is different from others.

-i [ɿ]

一 语音视听 Audio-visual Pronunciation

1. 发音示意图 Diagrammatic Sketch of Pronunciation

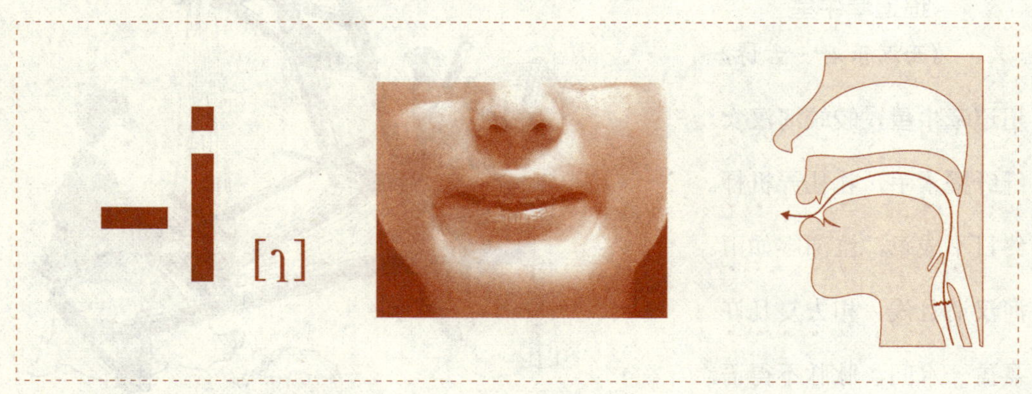

2. 发音特点 Characteristics of Pronunciation

-i [ɿ] 舌尖前、高、不圆唇元音。发音时，舌前伸、舌尖抵下齿背，气流振动声带从中通过，发出 z-, c-, s-, 将音略为延长一点，后面延长部分就是 -i[ɿ] 的音。

-i [ɿ] A supra-dental, high, lip-unrounding vowel. It is produced by pushing forward the tip of tongue against the lower gum, pronouncing z-, c-, s- and prolonging them a little. The extended part is the sound -i[ɿ]. The air comes out of the vibration of the vocal cords.

zi（资）, ci（词）, si（私）的韵母，只拼 z, c, s，不自成音节，也不能读成前、高、不圆唇元音 i。普通话中 z, c, s 永远不拼 i，故以 -i[ɿ] 代替。

The finals of zi(资), ci(词), si(私), different from [i] — the alveolo-palatal, high, unrounding vowel, cannot stand alone as a syllable. -i[ɿ] can only combine with initials of z, c, s, since those initials in *Putonghua* are never used together with [i]. Hence, -i[ɿ] is chosen instead.

二 听读词语 Listen and Read the Following Words

资	zī	capital
此	cǐ	this
四	sì	four
字	zì	character
词	cí	word
此次	cǐ cì	this time
自私	zìsī	selfish

三 速读短语，注意加点字的韵母 Read Phrases Quickly, Pay Attention to the Finals of the Characters Marked with Dots

自卖自夸	zì mài zì kuā	praise the goods one sells; blow one's own trumpet indulge in self-glorification
此起彼伏	cí qǐ bǐ fú	as one falls another rises
丝丝入扣	sī sī rù kòu	all threads neatly tied up; mostly of writings or artistic performances done with meticulous care and flawless artistry
四面八方	sì miàn bā fāng	all directions; all around; far and near

【提示】

此起彼伏（cǐ qǐ bǐ fú），读“cí qǐ bǐ fú”。这是三声的变调现象。

四 跟读绕口令，注意句中加点字的韵母 Read the Tongue Twister Following the Teacher, Pay Attention to the Finals of the Characters Marked with Dots

Yáng Lǎotóuzi

Dīng Lì

Yáng lǎotóuzi,
Mánzuǐ hēi húzi,

Zuò zài jiā li cuō shéngzi,
Míngtiān hǎo qù tái jiàozi,
Zhuànqián yǎnghuó yìjiāzi,
Hūrán láile gè xiǎo pàngzi,
Shǒu shang ná gēn zhú gùnzi,
Zǒujìn mén, xiàng fēngzi,
Luàn hǒu luàn nào xiàng gǒuzi,
Shuō shì zhèn shang yào fūzi,
Méiyǒu fūzi yào piàozi,
Méiyǒu piàozi,
Jǐgùn dǎ de jiào niáng jiào lǎozi,
Hái yào nòng qù táng pàozi,
Zhè jiào qióngrén zěnme guò rìzi ?

杨老头子

丁力

杨老头子，
满嘴黑胡子，
坐在家里搓绳子，
明天好去抬轿子，
赚钱养活一家子。
忽然来了个小胖子，
手上拿根竹棍子，
走进门，像疯子，
乱吼乱闹像狗子，
说是镇上要伕子，
没有伕子要票子，
没有票子，
几棍打得叫娘叫老子，
还要弄去搪炮子，
这叫穷人怎么过日子？

——《新诗选》，1948 年3月版

【提示】

子（zi），构词后缀。加在名词后。如：房子（fángzi）、车子（chēzi）；加在动词或形容词词素后。如：胖子（pàngzi）、瘦子（shòuzi）、垫子（diànzi）。

伕子（fūzi）：临时受雇供人役使的人，这里指被抓去当差的老百姓。

轿子（jiàozi）：一种靠人或畜扛、载而行，供人乘坐的交通工具。现代人所熟悉的轿子多系明、清以来沿袭使用的暖轿，又称帷轿。木制长方形框架，中部固定在两根具有韧性的细圆木轿杆上。轿底用木板封闭，上放可坐单人或双人的靠背坐箱。前设可掀动的轿帘，两侧多留小窗，另备窗帘。民间用的轿子分素帷小轿和花轿两种。前者为一般妇女出门所用，后者专用于婚嫁迎娶。

搪：抵挡。

五 听诵古诗，给全诗注上声母并给加点的字注上韵母 Listen and Recite the Poem, Write the Initials for the Poem and the Finals for the Characters Marked with Dots

望月怀远

唐·张九龄

海上生明月，天涯共此时。
情人怨遥夜，竟夕起相思。
灭烛怜光满，披衣觉露滋。
不堪盈手赠，还寝梦佳期。

【提示】

这首诗是作者在离乡时，望月而思念远方亲人及妻子而写的。全诗通过主人公望月时思潮起伏的描写，来表达诗人对远方亲人殷切怀念的情思。诗的前两句成为思念亲人的千古名句。

生：升起。

遥夜：夜太长。

竟夕：整一个晚上。

怜：怜惜。

露滋：露水湿衣。

不堪：不能。

盈：满、全。

张九龄(678—740)，唐开元尚书丞相，诗人。汉族，韶州曲江（今广东韶关市）人。诗风清淡。有《曲江集》。他是一位有胆识、有远见的著名政治家，文学家，诗人，名相。他的五言古诗，以素练质朴的语言，寄托深远的人生慨望，对扫除唐初所沿袭的六朝绮靡诗风，贡献尤大，誉为“岭南第一人”。

-i [ʅ]

一　语音视听　Audio-visual Pronunciation

1. 发音示意图　Diagrammatic Sketch of Pronunciation

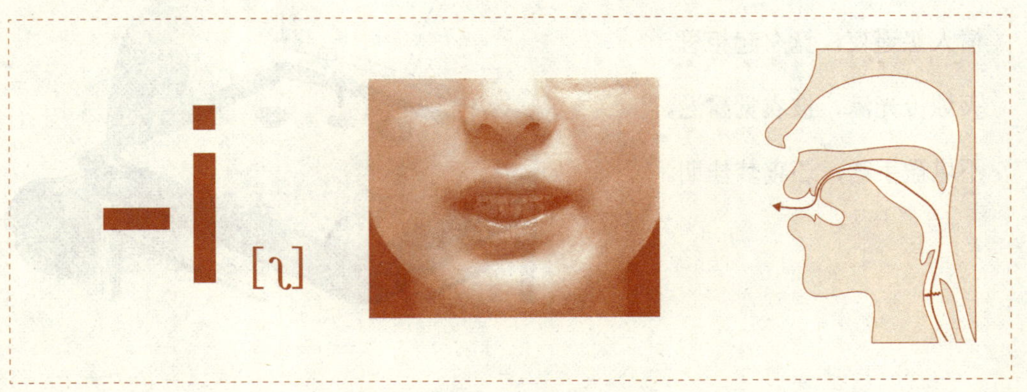

2. 发音特点 Characteristics of Pronunciation

-i [ʅ] 舌尖后、高、不圆唇元音。发音时，把 zh-, ch-, sh-, r- 的音略微延长一点，后面延长的部分就是 -i[ʅ] 的音。

-i [ʅ] A retroflex, high, lip-unrounding vowel. It is produced by prolonging the sounds zh-, ch-, sh-, r- a little, and the extended part is the sound -i[ʅ].

zhi（知），chi（池），shi（史），ri（日）的韵母，它只拼 zh，ch，sh，r，不自成音节，也不能读成前、高、不圆唇元音 i。普通话中 zh，ch，sh，r 声母永远不拼 i，故用 -i[ʅ] 代替。

The finals of zhi(知), chi(池), shi(史), ri(日), also different from [i]—the alveolo-palatal, high, unrounding vowel, cannot stand alone as a syllable. -i[ʅ] can only combine with initials of zh, ch, sh and r, since those initials in *Putonghua* are never used together with [i]. Hence, -i[ʅ] is chosen instead.

二 听读词语 Listen and Read the Following Words

之	zhī	possessive particle
值	zhí	worth
指	zhǐ	finger
至	zhì	arrive
知识	zhīshi	knowledge
指示	zhǐshì	instruction
志士	zhìshì	person of ideals and integrity
适时	shìshí	timely
誓师	shìshī	to vow before one's troops

【提示】

知识（zhīshi）是轻声词。

三 速读短语，注意加点字的韵母 Read Phrases Quickly, Pay Attention to the Finals of the Characters Marked with Dots

知己知彼	zhī jǐ zhī bǐ	know one's own situation and that of one's opponent
直肠子	zhí chángzi	straight forward person

指不定	zhǐ budìng	there is no telling; not sure
拾金不昧	shí jīn bú mèi	not pocket the money one picks up
十全十美	shí quán shí měi	be perfect in every way

【提示】

指不定（zhǐ bùdìng），读“zhǐ budìng”；拾金不昧（shí jīn bù mèi），读“shí jīn bú mèi”，这些都是“不”的变调现象。

四 跟读绕口令和经典选文，注意加点字的韵母 Read the Tongue Twister and the Adapted Classic Following the Teacher, Pay Attention to the Finals of the Characters Marked with Dots

1.

Zhī zhī wéi zhī zhī, bù zhī wéi bù zhī. Shì zhī yě.
知之为知之，不知为不知。是知也。

——《论语·为政》

2.

Zǐ yuē: “Bú huàn rén zhī bù jǐ zhī, huàn bù zhī rén yě.”
子曰：“不患人之不已知，患不知人也。”

——《论语·学而》

3.

Yuē Láng Yuè shàng Shí

Yuē láng yuē zài yuè shàng shí,
Děng láng děng zài yuè xié xī.
Bùzhī shì nóng chù shān dī yuè shàng zǎo,
Háishì láng chù shān gāo yuè shàng chí?

约郎月上时

约郎约在月上时，
等郎等在月斜西。
不知是侬处山低月上早，
还是郎处山高月上迟？

——《江苏传统歌谣》

【提示】

侬：代词。我、你。侬处：我这边。

中国各族人民的歌谣，十分丰富。古人说："诗言志，歌咏言。"歌谣是群众抒情言志的口头诗歌。每一个民族几乎都有自己独特的民歌形式和曲调。因为不识字的劳动者或根本没有文字的民族，无不习惯于以本民族、本地区群众喜闻乐见的歌谣形式，来描述自己的生活处境，记事抒怀，有的还以对歌为社交手段和交流感情的纽带。歌谣从来是人民心声的自然流露，也是一个民族的社会历史、时代生活和风土人情的一面镜子。从各民族的歌谣中可以看到民众不断用他们的诗歌创作描绘了一幅幅真实生动的历史画卷。它们是中国各族人民以自己的艺术天才和集体智慧创造出来的一份极其珍贵的文化财富。

五 听诵古诗，给全诗注上声母并给加点的字注上韵母 Listen and Recite the Poem, Write the Initials for the Poem and the Finals for the Characters Marked with Dots

夜雨寄北

唐·李商隐

君问归期未有期，巴山夜雨涨秋池。
何当共剪西窗烛，却话巴山夜雨时。

【提示】

君：你

巴山：在今四川省南江县以北。

秋池：秋天的池塘。

何当：哪一天？

共剪西窗烛：在西窗下共剪烛芯。

却话：从头谈起。

这首诗所寄何许人，有友人和妻子两说。前者认为李商隐居巴蜀期间，正是在他三十九岁至四十三岁做东川节度使柳仲郢幕僚时，而在此之前，其妻王氏已亡。有人认为在此之前李商隐已有过巴蜀之游。也有人认为它是寄给“眷属或友人”的。从诗中所表现出热烈的思念和缠绵的情感来看，似乎寄给妻子更为贴切。这首诗表现了李商隐诗的另一种风格：质朴、自然，却同样具有“寄托深而措辞婉”的艺术特色。

李商隐（813—858年），字义山，号玉溪生，怀州河内（今河南沁阳）人，晚唐著名诗人。擅长骈文写作，诗作文学价值也很高，他和杜牧合称“小李杜”，与温庭筠合称为“温李”，其诗构思新奇，风格浓丽，尤其是一些爱情诗写得缠绵悱恻，历来为人们所传诵。但过于隐晦迷离，难于索解，以至于有“诗家总爱西昆好，独恨无人作郑笺”之说。

er

一 语音视听 Audio-visual Pronunciation

1. 发音示意图 Diagrammatic Sketch of Pronunciation

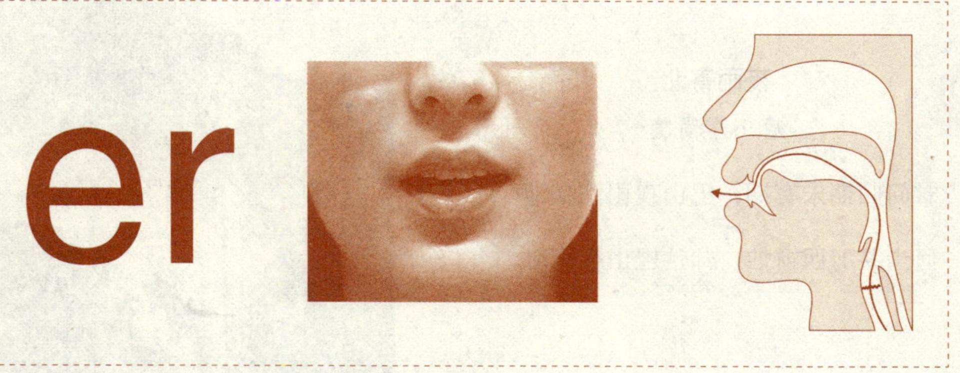

2. 发音特点　Characteristics of Pronunciation

er [ɚ] 卷舌、央、中、不圆唇元音。发音时，口半开，在发e时，舌尖同时卷起对硬腭，气流振动声带从口腔出。它可以自成音节。例如：

er [ɚ] A retroflex, central, lip-unrounding vowel. It is produced by half openning the mouth and raising the tongue of tip close to the hard palate when e is made. The air comes out of the vibration of the vocal cords. It can stand alone as a syllable. For example:

儿	ér	son
耳	ěr	ear
二	èr	two

此外，er中的r只是表示卷舌动作的符号，不是音素，虽是两个字母标写，仍是单元音韵母。它还可以结合在其他音节后面，使那个音节的韵母发生变化，韵尾加上表示卷舌动作的符号r，成“儿化韵”。

In addition, the r in er is just a symbol representing the action of curling back the tongue. It is not a phoneme. Though it is transcribed with two letters, er is still a final with one single vowel. It can also be put behind other syllable to form a retroflex ending by adding the symbol r and turn the syllable into retroflex final.

儿化在语义的表达上也有一定的作用。

Retroflexion affects the semantic meanings to some extent.

(1) 表示喜爱的心情。例如：

To show somebody's affection. For example,

好玩儿	hǎowánr	amusing
宝贝儿	bǎobèir	darling
男孩儿	nánháir	boy

(2) 表示“小”或“少”的意思。例如：

To mean “small” or “little”. For example,

一会儿	yíhuìr	a while
小孩儿	xiǎoháir	a little child
小鸟儿	xiáoniǎor	a little bird

(3) 区别词义。例如：

To distinguish the word meanings. For example,

块	kuài	for sth. shaped like chunks or lumps
块儿	kuàir	piece; lump; chunk

信	xìn	letter
信儿	xìnr	news
头	tóu	head
头儿	tóur	boss

(4) 区别词性。例如：

To distinguish the word classes. For example:

盖	gài	to cover
盖儿	gàir	lid
画	huà	to paint
画儿	huàr	painting
尖	jiān	sharp
尖儿	jiānr	sharp point

二 听读词语 Listen and Read the Following Words

1.

门儿	ménr	door
花儿	huār	flower
没准儿	méizhǔnr	maybe
小猫儿	xiǎomāor	kitten
肉馅儿	ròuxiànr	minced meat
树枝儿	shùzhīr	branch
笔尖儿	bǐjiānr	pen point
书本儿	shūběnr	book

2.

宝贝儿	bǎobèir	treasure; treasured object; baby
麦穗儿	màisuìr	ear of wheat
小孩儿	xiǎoháir	child; kid
老头儿	lǎotóur	old man
背心儿	bèixīnr	underwaist
一点儿	yìdiǎnr	a bit; a little
一块儿	yíkuàir	together
花瓶儿	huāpíngr	vase
画儿	huàr	picture

小曲儿	xiáoqǔr	ditty; bagatelle
小鸟儿	xiáoniǎor	bird
豆芽儿	dòuyár	bean sprout

【提示】

一点儿（yīdiǎnr），读“yìdiǎnr”；一块儿（yīkuàir），读“yíkuàir”。这是“一”的变调现象。小曲儿（xiǎoqǔr），读“xiáoqǔr”；小鸟儿（xiǎoniǎor），读“xiáoniǎor”。这是三声的变调现象。

三　速读短语，注意加点字的韵母　Read Phrases Quickly, Pay Attention to the Finals of the Characters Marked with Dots

耳目一新	ěr mù yì xīn	find everything fresh and new
二百五	èrbáiwǔ	(ironic) person who is a bit stupid and acts rudely
而立之年	ér lì zhī nián	one has made some achievements at the age of thirty
儿媳妇儿	érxífur	daughter-in-law

【提示】

二百五（èrbǎiwǔ），读“èrbáiwǔ”。这是三声的变调现象。

四　跟读绕口令，注意句中加点字的韵母　Read the Tongue Twister Following the Teacher, Pay Attention to the Finals of the Characters Marked with Dots

Yào shuō “ěr”, jiù shuō “ěr”, Máěrdàifū, Kābùěr, Āěrbāníyà, Zhāyīěr,Kǎdáěr, Níbóěr. Bèi’ ěrgéláidé, Āndàoěr. Sàérwǎduō,Bóníěr. Èguāduōěr, Sàishéěr.

要说“尔”，就说“尔”，马尔代夫，喀布尔。阿尔巴尼亚，扎伊尔。卡达尔，尼泊尔。贝尔格莱德，安道尔。萨尔瓦多，伯尼尔。厄瓜多尔，塞舌尔。

五 听诵民歌，给歌词注上声母并给加点的字注上韵母 Listen and Recite the Ballad, Write the Initials for the Ballad and the Finals for the Characters Marked with Dots.

人儿人儿今何在（寄生草）

清代民歌

人儿人儿今何在？花儿花儿为谁开？雁儿雁儿因何不把书带来？心儿心儿从今又把相思害，泪儿泪儿滚将下来。天吓天吓，无限的凄凉，教奴怎么耐？

【提示】

此歌极写相思之苦。选自《中国俗文学史》（下册）清代民歌总集《时尚南北雅调万花小曲》中《霓裳续谱》的一首曲调。

寄生草：曲调名称。

吓：叹词，音 e。

第三节 复韵母
Section III Compound Finals

普通话的复韵母是由复元音构成的，共有 13 个：ai, ei, ao, ou, ia, ie, ua, uo, üe, iao, iou, uai, uei，又叫复元音韵母。

Compound finals in *Putonghua*, thirteen in total, consists of compound vowels, also called compound vocalic finals.

复元音韵母发音时，其中由两个元音组成的，由前一个元音过渡到后一个元音；由三个元音组成的，则由第一个元音过渡到第二个元音，再过渡到第三个元音。过渡中，舌位的高低前后、口腔的开闭、唇形的圆展都会发生变化，不能跳动，气流更不能中断，要一气完成一个复元音韵母的整体。

During the pronunciation of compound vocalic finals, those with two vowels change quality from the first articulation to another, and those made up of three vowels glides quickly with a smooth movement of the tongue following in sequence. In the process of gliding, the place of tongue, the opening or closing of mouth and the degree of lip-rounding will all change and accomplish at one stretch without any jumping between the sounds or even break of the air.

复元音韵母可分为前响复元音韵母、中响元音复韵母和后响元音复韵母。前响复元音韵母有 ai, ei, ao, ou，它们成音时，前音响亮，后音模糊。中响复元音韵母有 iao, iou, uai, uei，它们成音时，中间的元音清晰响亮，前面的元音较短，后面的元音含混，只表方向。后响复元音韵母有 ia, ie, ua, uo, üe，它们成音时都是前音短弱，后音响亮。

According to the different place of stress, compound vocalic finals can be classified as front, central and back stressed. ai, ei, ao and ou belong to front-stressed compound vocalic finals, since the first vowel is loud and the second is vague when articulating. And iao, iou, uai, uei are central-stressed with a clear and loud vowel in the middle, short in front, blurred of the last which only stands for the size of the opening mouth. Back-stressed compound vocalic finals include ia, ie, ua, uo, üe, and their first vowels are short and soft, but the second clear and loud.

ai

一 语音视听 Audio-visual Pronunciation

1. 发音示意图 Diagrammatic Sketch of Pronunciation

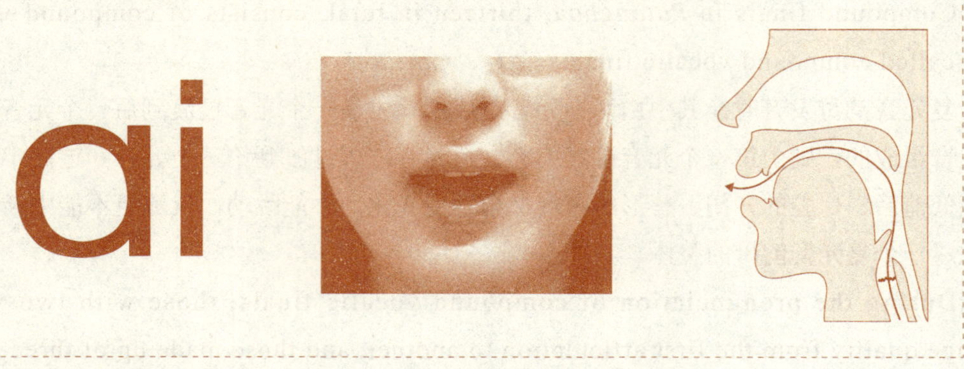

2. 发音特点 Characteristics of Pronunciation

ai [ai] 发音时，由 a 过渡到 i。

ai [ai] When ai is pronounced, the sound glides from a to i.

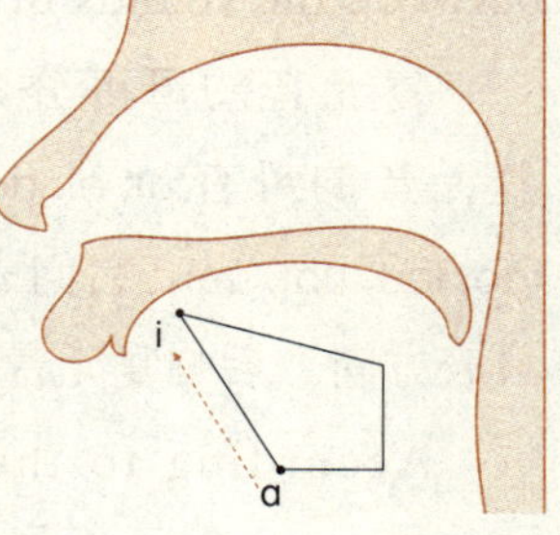

图 3-3 元音 ai 的发音舌位变化示意简图

Figure 3-3 The varied places of tongue, illustrating how to articulate vowel ai

二 听读词语 Listen and Read the Following Words

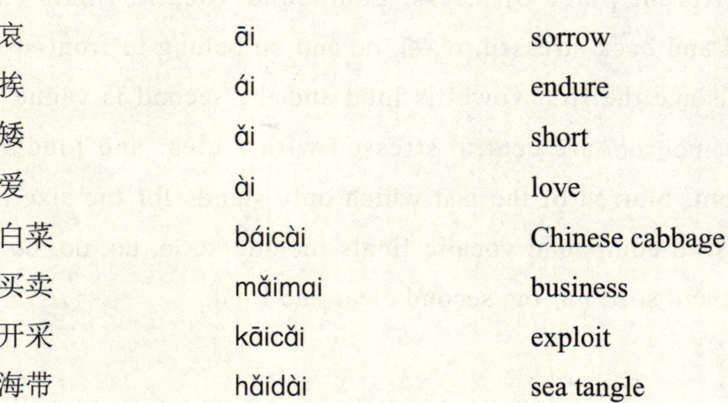

哀	āi	sorrow
挨	ái	endure
矮	ǎi	short
爱	ài	love
白菜	báicài	Chinese cabbage
买卖	mǎimai	business
开采	kāicǎi	exploit
海带	hǎidài	sea tangle

【提示】

买卖（mǎimai）是轻声词。

三 速读短语，注意加点字的韵母 Read Phrases Quickly, Pay Attention to the Finals of the Characters Marked with Dots

唉声叹气	āi shēng tàn qì	moan and groan; have deep sighs of grief, worry or anguish
爱不释手	ài bú shì shǒu	be so found of sth. as not to let go of it
白日做梦	báirì zuò mèng	spin day dreams; indulge in wishful thinking
待人接物	dài rén jiē wù	manner of dealing with people

【提示】

爱不释手（ài bù shì shǒu），读“ài bú shì shǒu”。这是“不”的变调现象。

四 跟读绕口令，注意句中加点字的韵母 Read the Tongue Twister Following the Teacher, Pay Attention to the Finals of the Characters Marked with Dots

Mǎi báicài, dā hǎidài,bù mǎi hǎidài báicài yě bú mài.
Mǎimai gǎi, bù dā mài, bù mǎi háidài yě kě mǎi báicài.
买白菜，搭海带，不买海带白菜也不卖。
买卖改，不搭卖，不买海带也可买白菜。

五 听诵古诗，给全诗注上声母并给加点的字注上韵母 Listen and Recite the Poem, Write the Initials for the Poem and the Finals for the Characters Marked with Dots

十一月四日风雨大作

宋 · 陆游

僵卧孤村不自哀，尚思为国戍轮台。
夜阑卧听风吹雨，铁马冰河入梦来。

【提示】

戍：守卫。

轮台：地名，今新疆轮台县。泛指边疆。

夜阑：深夜。

该诗是年近七旬的陆游在一个风雨交加的寒夜，支撑着衰老的身体，躺在冰凉的被子里，写下的一首热血沸腾的爱国主义诗篇。

陆游（1125—1210），南宋爱国诗人，字务观，号放翁，越州山阴（今浙江绍兴）人。一生著述丰富，今存诗九千三百余首。其中多抒写了抗金杀敌的豪情和对敌人、卖国贼的仇恨，风格雄奇奔放，沉郁悲壮，洋溢着强烈的爱国主义激情，生前有“小李白”之称，成为南宋一代诗坛领袖。

ei

一 语音视听 Audio-visual Pronunciation

1. 发音示意图 Diagrammatic Sketch of Pronunciation

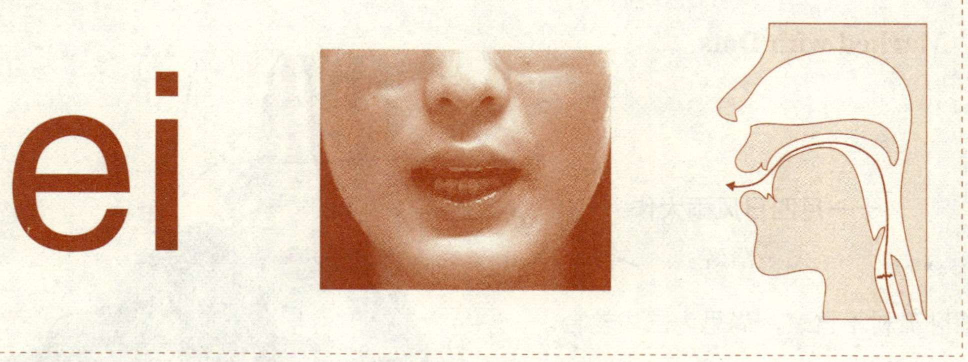

2. 发音特点　Characteristics of Pronunciation

ei [ei] 发音时，由 ê 过渡到 i。

ei [ei] When ei is pronounced, the sound glides from ê to i.

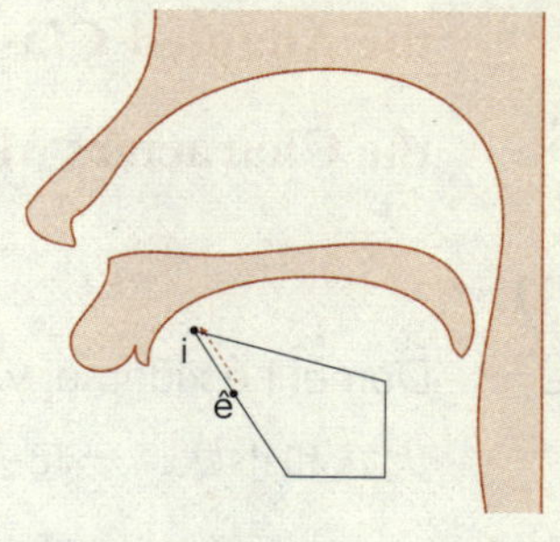

图 3-4 元音 ei 的发音舌位变化示意简图

Figure 3-4 The varied places of tongue, illustrating how to articulate vowel ei

二 听读词语　Listen and Read the Following Words

胚	pēi	fetus
雷	léi	thunder
给	gěi	give
费	fèi	fee
配备	pèibèi	equipment
背煤	bēi méi	carry the coal
蓓蕾	bèilěi	bud
肥美	féiměi	fertile

三 速读短语，注意加点字的韵母　Read Phrases Quickly, Pay Attention to the Finals of the Characters Marked with Dots

背包袱	bēi bāofu	have a weight or load on one' s mind; take on a mental burden
飞来横祸	fēi lái hènghuò	unexpected disaster (that has flown in from nowhere)
黑社会	hēishèhuì	underworld; social sphere beneath the level of ordinary life
雷打不动	léi dǎ bú dòng	not to be shaken by thunder; (of an arrangement or plan) not to be altered under any circumstances
眉飞色舞	méi fēi sè wǔ	enraptured; exultant

【提示】

雷打不动（léi dǎ bù dòng），读“léi dǎ bú dòng”。这是“不”的变调现象。

四 跟读绕口令和经典选文，注意加点字的韵母 Read the Tongue Twister and the Adapted Classic Following the Teacher, Pay Attention to the Finals of the Characters Marked with Dots

1.

Dàmèi hé xiǎomèi yìqǐ qù gē mài. Dàmèi gē dàmài, xiǎomèi gē xiǎomài.
大妹和小妹，一起去割麦。大妹割大麦，小妹割小麦。

2.

Zǐ yuē: “ Fēi lǐ wù shì, fēi lǐ wù tīng, fēi lǐ wù yán, fēi lǐ wù dòng.”
子曰：“非礼勿视，非礼勿听，非礼勿言，非礼勿动。”

——《论语 · 颜渊》

【提示】
此系孔子回答颜渊提出仁德如何才能做得到时的具体要求。

五 听诵词，给文中注上声母和加点字的韵母 Listen and Recite the *Ci* Poem, Write the Initials for the *Ci* Poem and the Finals for the Characters Marked with Dots

醉太平 · 夺泥燕口

元 · 无名氏

夺泥燕口，削铁针头，刮金佛面细搜求，
无中觅有。鹌鹑膝里寻豌豆，鹭鸶腿上劈精肉，
蚊子腹内刳脂油，亏老先生下手！

【提示】
这首词入木三分地刻画了爱财如命者极其丑恶的行径。
刳：音 kū，挖空。

ao

一 语音视听 Audio-visual Pronunciation

1. 发音示意图 Diagrammatic Sketch of Pronunciation

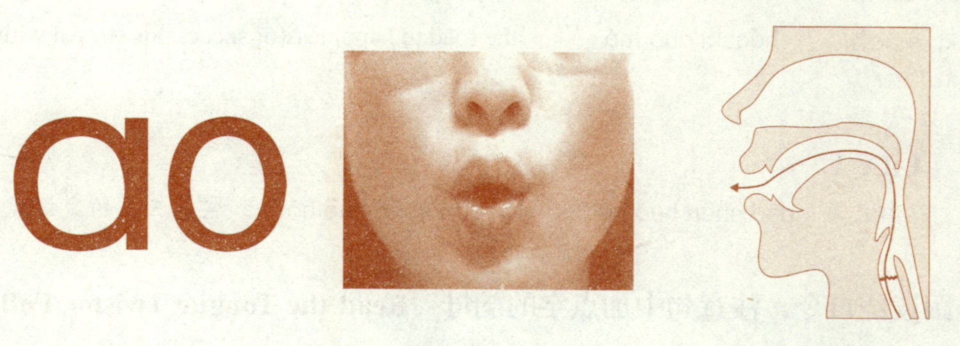

2. 发音特点 Characteristics of Pronunciation

ao [ɑu] 发音时，由 ɑ 过渡到 u。

ao [ɑu] When ao is pronounced, the sound glides from ɑ to u.

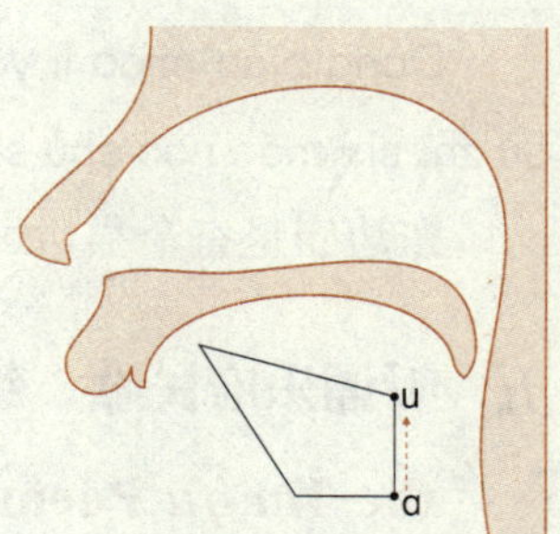

图 3-5 元音 ao 的发音舌位变化示意简图

Figure 3-5 The varied places of tongue, illustrating how to articulate vowel ao

二 听读词语 Listen and Read the Following Words

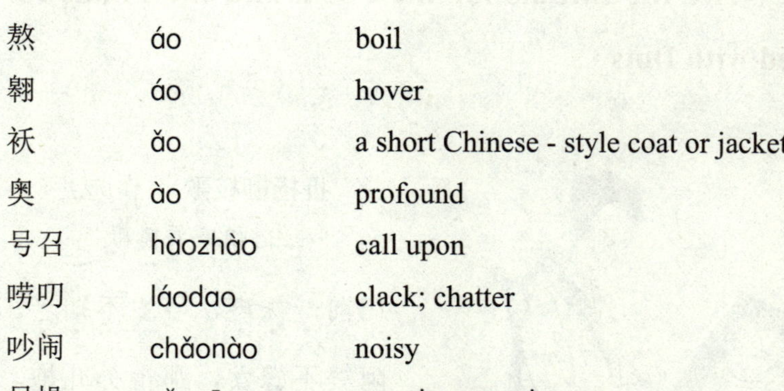

熬	áo	boil
翱	áo	hover
袄	ǎo	a short Chinese - style coat or jacket
奥	ào	profound
号召	hàozhào	call upon
唠叨	láodao	clack; chatter
吵闹	chǎonào	noisy
早操	zǎocāo	morning exercises

【提示】

唠叨（láodao）：轻声词。

三 速读短语，注意加点字的韵母 Read Phrases Quickly, Pay Attention to the Finals of the Characters Marked with Dots

宝刀不老	bǎodāo bù lǎo	the man is old, but not his sword; eldly persons still at the height of their skills
刀山火海	dāo shān huó hǎi	mountain of swords and sea of flames; most dangerous places
高高在上	gāogāo zài shàng	(of a leader) lord it over the masses; in a high rack
好事多磨	hǎoshì duō mó	the road to happiness(or success) is strewn with setbacks

【提示】

刀山火海（dāo shān huǒ hǎi），读“dāo shān huó hǎi”。这是三声的变调现象。

四 跟读绕口令，注意句中加点字的韵母 Read the Tongue Twister Following the Teacher, Pay Attention to the Finals of the Characters Marked with Dots

Dōng biān miào li yǒu gè māo, xī biān shùshāo yǒu zhī niǎo. Māo niǎo tiāntiān nào, bù zhī shì māo nào shù shàng niǎo， háishì niǎo nào miào li māo.

东边庙里有个猫，西边树梢有只鸟。猫鸟天天闹，不知是猫闹树上鸟，还是鸟闹庙里猫。

五 听诵乐府民歌，给文中注上学过的声母和加点字的韵母 Listen and Recite the *Yue-fu* Poem, Write the Initials for the Poem and the Finals for the Characters Marked with Dots

折杨柳枝歌（节选）

北朝乐府民歌

门前一株枣，岁岁不知老。

阿婆不嫁女，那得孙儿抱。

【提示】

这首歌写做女儿的希望及早出嫁，但不直说，却从母亲抱外孙的角度提出；表现上的这一波折，使诗作显得直而不露，韵味悠长。

“枣”和“早”同音双关，由“枣”引出希望早早出嫁之意。此处指枣树。

阿婆：指母亲。

孙儿：指外孙。

ou

一 语音视听 Audio-visual Pronunciation

1. 发音示意图 Diagrammatic Sketch of Pronunciation

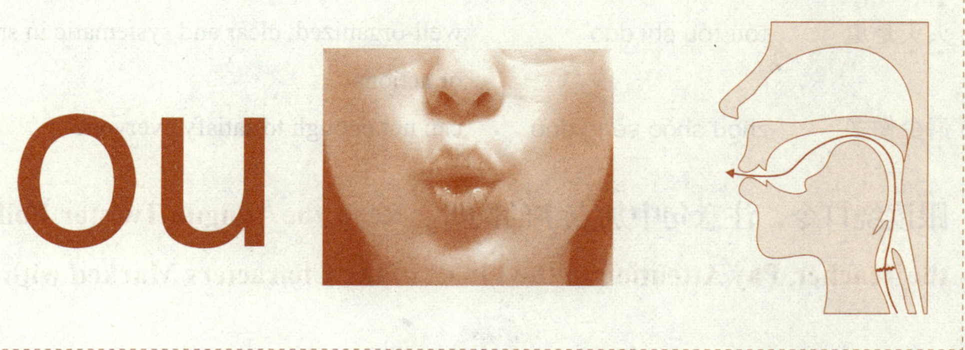

2. 发音特点 Characteristics of Pronunciation

ou [ou] 发音时，由 o 过渡到 u。

ou [ou] When ou is pronounced, the sound glides from o to u.

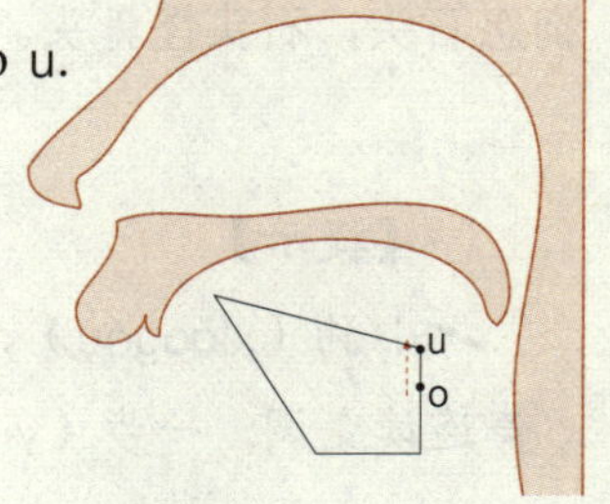

图 3-6 元音 ou 的发音舌位变化示意简图

Figure 3-6 The varied places of tongue, illustrating how to articulate vowel ou

二 听读词语 Listen and Read the Following Words

搂	lǒu	hug
喉	hóu	throat
丑	chǒu	ugly
奏	zòu	play

欧洲	Ōuzhōu	Europe
口头	kǒutóu	orally
守候	shǒuhòu	wait for
走狗	zóugǒu	lackey

【提示】

走狗（zǒugǒu），读“zóugǒu”，两个三声连读，第一个字读二声。

三 速读短语，注意加点字的韵母 Read Phrases Quickly, Pay Attention to the Finals of the Characters Marked with Dots

钩心斗角	gōu xīn dòu jiǎo	intriguing to squeeze each other out
后会有期	hòu huì yǒu qī	usu. used to comfort the other side on departing
偷鸡摸狗	tōu jī mō gǒu	(usu. theft) to steal; to be on the sly
头头是道	tóu tóu shì dào	well-organized; clear and systematic in speech or actions
粥少僧多	zhōu shǎo sēng duō	can not enough to satisfy everyone

四 跟读绕口令，注意句中加点字的韵母 Read the Tongue Twister Following the Teacher, Pay Attention to the Finals of the Characters Marked with Dots

Xiáogǒu xiǎo gǔtou, yí bù yí bù zǒu.Xiáoniǎo chàng zhītóu, xiáogǒu niǔ tóu chǒu. Gǔtou zhuàng shítou,shítou pèng gǔtou, xiáogǒu yuàn shítou, shítou guài gǔtou.

小狗小骨头，一步一步走。小鸟唱枝头，小狗扭头瞅。骨头撞石头，石头碰骨头，小狗怨石头，石头怪骨头。

【提示】

小狗（xiǎogǒu）、小鸟（xiǎoniǎo），分别读“xiáogǒu”“xiáoniǎo”，这是三声连读变调；一步（yī bù），读“yí bù”。这是“一”的变调现象。

五　听诵古诗，给全诗注上声母并给加点的字注上韵母　Listen and Recite the Ancient Poem, Write the Initials for the Poem and the Finals for the Characters Marked with Dots

黄鹤楼

唐 · 崔颢

昔人已乘黄鹤去，此地空余黄鹤楼。
黄鹤一去不复返，白云千载空悠悠。
晴川历历汉阳树，芳草萋萋鹦鹉洲。
日暮乡关何处是？烟波江上使人愁。

【提示】

晴川：指白日照耀下的汉江。

汉阳：今湖北省武汉市汉阳区，位于长江、汉水夹角地带，与武昌黄鹤楼隔江相望。

鹦鹉洲：位于汉阳东南二里长江中，后渐被江水冲没。

此诗是诗人登楼近观远眺壮丽的景色，触景生情，借神话传说表现人生有限，宇宙无穷，抒发了吊古怀乡之情。全诗信手而就，为历代推崇珍品。

黄鹤楼：位于湖北武昌蛇山，享有“天下绝景”的盛誉，与湖南岳阳楼，江西滕王阁并称为“江南三大名楼”。黄鹤楼始建于三国时期吴黄武二年（223 年），传说是为了军事目的而建的，孙权为实现“以武治国而昌”（“武昌”的名称由来于此），筑城为守，建楼以瞭望。至唐朝，逐渐成为名胜景点，历代文人墨客到此游览，曾留下不少脍炙人口的诗篇。据载，黄鹤楼原为辛氏开设的酒店，一道士为了感谢她千杯之恩，临行前在壁上画了一只鹤，告之它能下来起舞助兴。从此宾客盈门，生意兴隆。十年后，道士复来，取笛吹奏，跨上黄鹤直上云天。辛氏为纪念这位帮她致富的仙翁，便在其地起楼，取名“黄鹤楼”。

崔颢（704?—754），汴州（开封）人氏，唐玄宗开元十一年（723 年）进士。他才思敏捷，长于写诗，系盛唐诗人。

ia

一 语音视听 Audio-visual Pronunciation

1. 发音示意图 Diagrammatic Sketch of Pronunciation

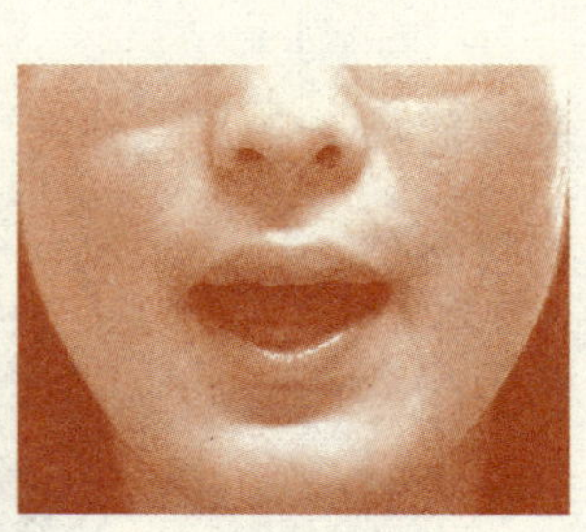

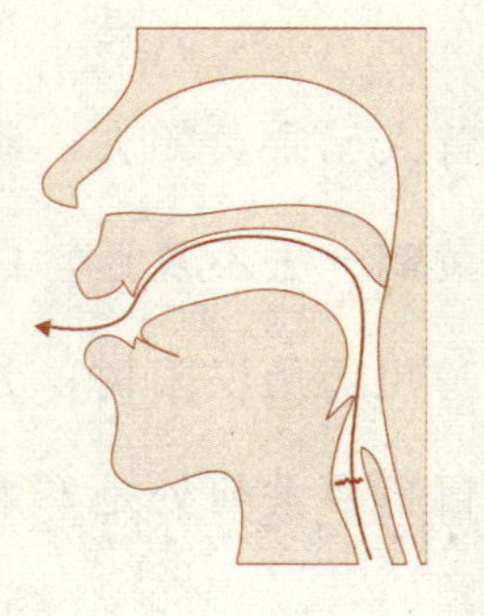

2. 发音特点 Characteristics of Pronunciation

ia [iA] 发音时，由 i 过渡到 a。

ia [iA] When ia is pronounced, the sound glides from i to a.

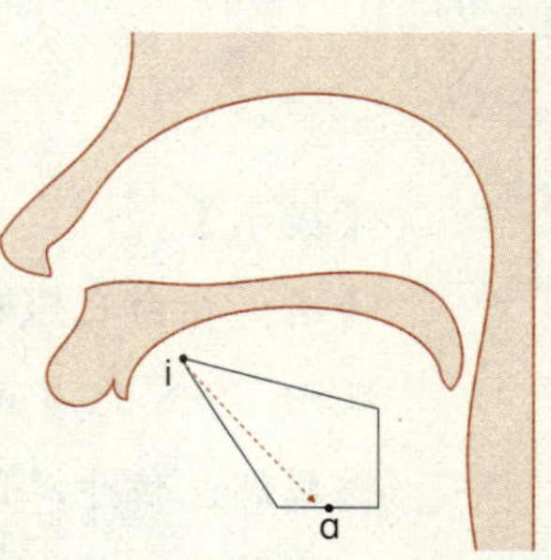

图 3-7 元音 ia 的发音舌位变化示意简图

Figure 3-7 The varied places of tongue, illustrating how to articulate vowel ia

二 听读词语 Listen and Read the Following Words

鸦	yā	crow
牙	yá	tooth
哑	yǎ	dumb
亚	yà	second
假牙	jiǎyá	artificial tooth
架下	jiàxià	under a shelf
下嫁	xiàjià	marry someone beneath herself
加价	jiā jià	price markup

【提示】

“ia” 单独成音节时，把 “i” 改为 “y” 。如 “鸦（yā）” “牙（yá）” “哑（yǎ）” “亚（yà）” 。

三 速读短语，注意加点字的韵母 Read Phrases Quickly, Pay Attention to the Finals of the Characters Marked with Dots

压岁钱	yāsuìqián	money given to children as a lunar New Year gift
雅俗共赏	yǎ sú gòng shǎng	(of a work of art or literature) appeal to all
假模假式	jiǎmojiǎshì	insincere; hypocritical
恰如其分	qià rú qí fèn	appropriate; just right
下坡路	xiàpōlù	downhill path; on the decline; going downhill

四 跟读绕口令，注意句中加点字的韵母 Read the Tongue Twister Following the Teacher, Pay Attention to the Finals of the Characters Marked with Dots

Tiānshang piāozhe yí piàn xiá, shuǐ shàng piāozhe yì qún yā. Xiá shì wǔcǎi xiá, yā shì máhuā yā.

天上飘着一片霞，水上飘着一群鸭。霞是五彩霞，鸭是麻花鸭。

【提示】

一片（yī piàn），读“yí piàn”；一群（yī qún），读“yì qún”。这是“一”的变调现象。

五 听诵古诗，给全诗注上声母并给加点的字注上韵母 Listen and Recite the Ancient Poem, Write the Initials for the Poem and the Finals for the Characters Marked with Dots

秋思

元 · 马致远

枯藤老树昏鸦，
小桥流水人家。
古道西风瘦马，
夕阳西下，
断肠人在天涯。

【提示】

该曲透露了诗人怀才不遇的悲凉情怀。全曲采取寓情于景的手法来渲染气氛，显示主题，完美地表现了漂泊天涯的旅人的愁思。

马致远（1250—1321），元代著名杂剧家，字致远，大都（今北京）人。一生以字行于世，名不详。晚号东篱，以示效陶渊明之志。一生著有杂剧16种，存世的有7种。其散曲作品也负盛名，现存辑本《东篱乐府》一卷。其杂剧内容以神化道士为主，剧本全都涉及全真教的故事，元末明初贾仲明在诗中说：“万花丛中马神仙，百世集中说致远”，“姓名香贯满梨园”。

ie

一 语音视听 Audio-visual Pronunciation

1. 发音示意图 Diagrammatic Sketch of Pronunciation

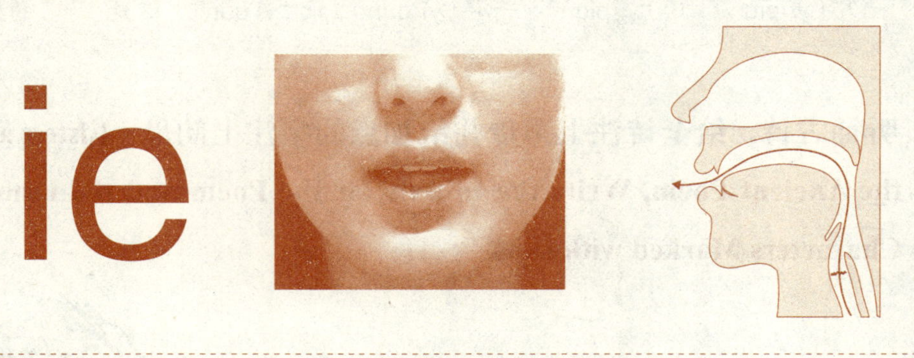

2. 发音特点 Characteristics of Pronunciation

ie [iɛ] 发音时，由 i 过渡到 ê。

ie [iɛ] When ie is pronounced, the sound glides from i to ê.

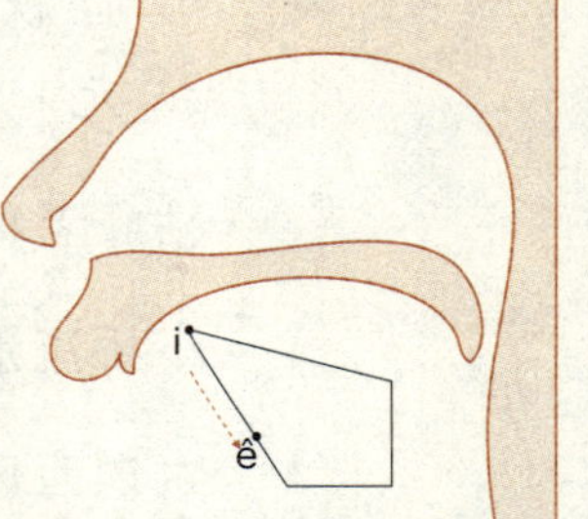

图 3-8 元音 ie 的发音舌位变化示意简图

Figure 3-8 The varied places of tongue, illustrating how to articulate vowel ie

二 听读词语 Listen and Read the Following Words

噎	yē	choke
爷	yé	grandpa

野	yě	wild
夜	yè	night
贴切	tiēqiè	proper
结业	jiéyè	finish a course of study
歇业	xiēyè	close a business
节烈	jiéliè	woman who died for protecting her chastity

【提示】

"ie"单独成音节时，把"i"变成"y"，如"噎（yē）""爷（yé）""野（yě）""夜（yè）"。

三 速读短语，注意加点字的韵母 Read Phrases Quickly, Pay Attention to the Finals of the Characters Marked with Dots

夜长梦多	yè cháng mèng duō	a long night is fraught with dreams; (fig.) a long delay means trouble
别有风味	bié yǒu fēngwèi	have a distinctive flavour or feature
跌眼镜	diē yǎnjìng	to one' s surprise; amaze; astonish
接二连三	jiē èr lián sān	one after another; in quick succession
铁石心肠	tiě shí xīncháng	be iron heated; have a heart of stone; be heartless

四 跟读绕口令和经典选文，注意加点字的韵母 Read the Tongue Twister and the Adapted Classic Following the Teacher, Pay Attention to the Finals of the Characters Marked with Dots

1.

Jiějie jiè dāo qiē qiézi, qù bà qù yèr xié qiē sī, qiēhǎo qiézi shāo qiézi, chǎo qiézi, zhēng qiézi, hái yǒu yì wǎn mèn qiézi.

姐姐借刀切茄子，去把去叶儿斜切丝，切好茄子烧茄子，炒茄子，蒸茄子，还有一碗焖茄子。

2.

Shēng, yì wǒ suǒ yù yě; yì, yì wǒ suǒ yù yě; èrzhě bù kě dé jiān, shě shēng ér qǔ yì zhě yě.

生，亦我所欲也；义，亦我所欲也；二者不可得兼，舍生而取义者也。

——《孟子·告子上》

五　听诵古诗，给全诗注上声母并给加点的字注上韵母 Listen and Recite the Poem, Write the Initials for the Poem and the Finals for the Characters Marked with Dots

春夜喜雨

唐·杜甫

好雨知时节，当春乃发生。

随风潜入夜，润物细无声。

【提示】

本诗作于宝应元年（公元762年）春，杜甫这时居住在成都草堂。从上年冬天到这年的二月间，成都一带有旱灾。当春雨来临之际，杜甫非常欣喜，他以久旱逢甘霖的喜悦心情来描写这场春夜细雨。

ua

一 语音视听 Audio-visual Pronunciation

1. 发音示意图 Diagrammatic Sketch of Pronunciation

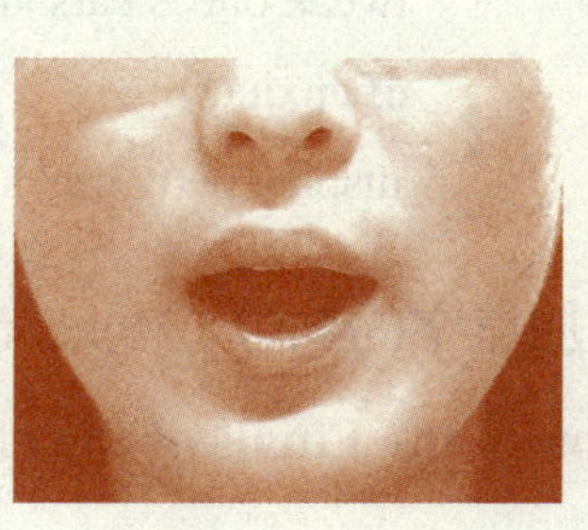

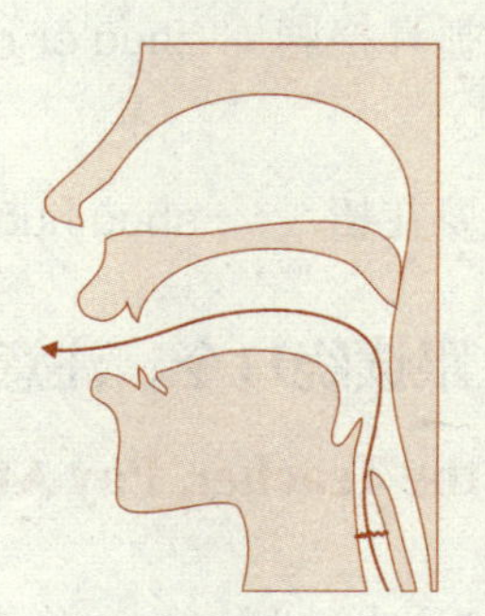

2. 发音特点 Characteristics of Pronunciation

ua [uA] 发音时，由 u 过渡到 ɑ。

ua [uA] When uɑ is pronounced, the sound glides from u to ɑ.

二 听读词语 Listen and Read the Following Words

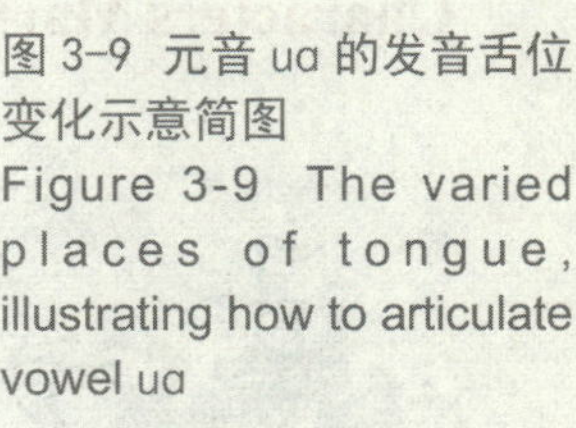

图 3-9 元音 uɑ 的发音舌位变化示意简图

Figure 3-9 The varied places of tongue, illustrating how to articulate vowel uɑ

哇	wā	wow
娃	wá	baby
瓦	wǎ	watt; tile
袜	wà	socks
挂画	guà huà	painting
抓花	zhuā huā	catch a flower
瓜花	guā huā	flower of a melon
花袜	huāwà	socks with various colors

【提示】

“uɑ”单独成音节时，把“u”变成“w”如“哇（wā）”“娃（wá）”“瓦（wǎ）”“袜（wà）”。

三 速读短语，注意加点字的韵母 Read Phrases Quickly, Pay Attention to the Finals of the Characters Marked with Dots

花好月圆	huā hǎo yuè yuán	(used as a congratulatory message for sb.' s marriage) blooming flowers and a full moon — pleasant reunion
挖空心思	wā kōng xīn sī	rack one' s brains
挖墙脚	wā qiángjiǎo	undermine wall poach
抓耳挠腮	zhuā ěr náo sāi	tweak one' s ears and scratch one' s cheeks (as a sign of anxiety)
耍花招	shuǎ huāzhāo	display petty tricks; play tricks

四 跟读绕口令，注意句中加点字的韵母 Read the Tongue Twister Following the Teacher, Pay Attention to the Finals of the Characters Marked with Dots

Xiǎohuá hé pàngwá, liǎng rén zhòng huā yòu zhòng guā. Xiǎohuá huì zhòng huā bú huì zhòng guā,pàngwá huì zhòng guā bú huì zhòng huā.

小华和胖娃，两人种花又种瓜。小华会种花不会种瓜，胖娃会种瓜不会种花。

【提示】

不会（bù huì），读“bú huì”，这是“不”的变调现象。

五 听诵古诗，给全诗注上声母并给加点的字注上韵母 Listen and Recite the Ancient Poem, Write the Initials for the Poem and the Finals for the Characters Marked with Dots

乌衣巷

唐 · 刘禹锡

朱雀桥头野草花，
乌衣巷口夕阳斜。
旧时王谢堂前燕，
飞入寻常百姓家。

【提示】

乌衣巷：曾是东晋王谢两大豪族居住的地方。全诗通过描写乌衣巷的巨大变化来感时伤怀，抒发了深沉的沧桑之感。

六 听歌学汉语，注意加点字的韵母 Learn Chinese by Listening to the Song, Pay Attention to the Finals of the Characters Marked with Dots

茉 莉 花

1= F $\frac{4}{4}$
中速 江苏民歌

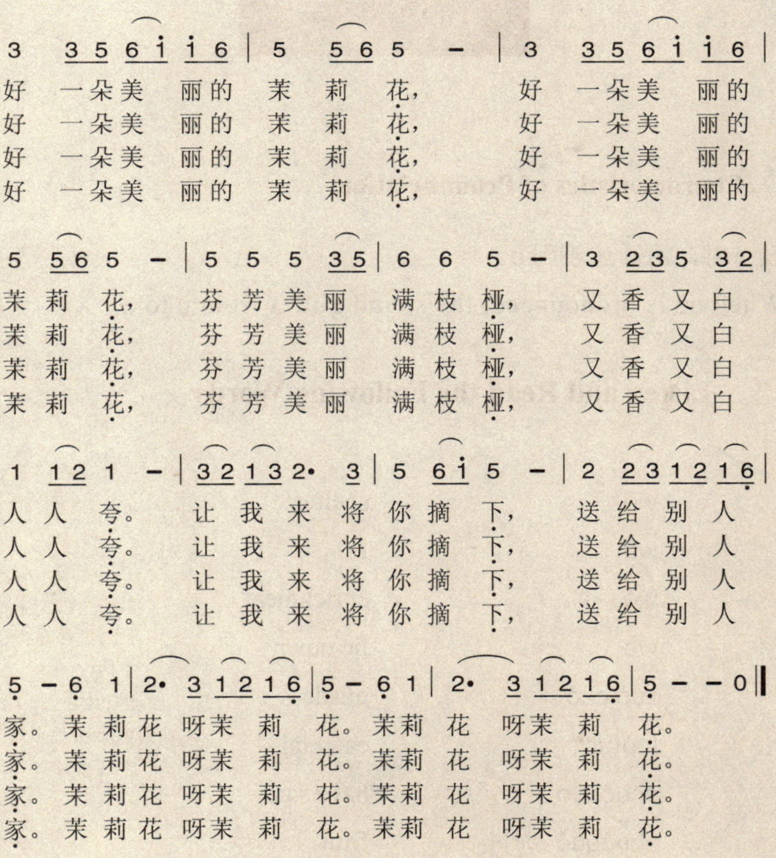

3 35 61̇ 1̇6 | 5 565 - | 3 35 61̇ 1̇6 |
好 一朵美 丽的 茉 莉 花， 好 一朵美 丽的
好 一朵美 丽的 茉 莉 花， 好 一朵美 丽的
好 一朵美 丽的 茉 莉 花， 好 一朵美 丽的
好 一朵美 丽的 茉 莉 花， 好 一朵美 丽的

5 565 - | 5 5 5 35 | 6 6 5 - | 3 235 32 |
茉 莉 花， 芬 芳 美 丽 满 枝 桠， 又 香 又 白
茉 莉 花， 芬 芳 美 丽 满 枝 桠， 又 香 又 白
茉 莉 花， 芬 芳 美 丽 满 枝 桠， 又 香 又 白
茉 莉 花， 芬 芳 美 丽 满 枝 桠， 又 香 又 白

1 12 1 - | 32 13 2· 3 | 5 61̇ 5 - | 2 23 12 16̣ |
人 人 夸。 让 我 来 将 你 摘 下， 送 给 别 人
人 人 夸。 让 我 来 将 你 摘 下， 送 给 别 人
人 人 夸。 让 我 来 将 你 摘 下， 送 给 别 人
人 人 夸。 让 我 来 将 你 摘 下， 送 给 别 人

5̣ - 6̣ 1 | 2· 3 12 16̣ | 5̣ - 6̣ 1 | 2· 3 12 16̣ | 5̣ - - 0 ‖
家。茉 莉 花 呀茉 莉 花。茉莉 花 呀茉 莉 花。
家。茉 莉 花 呀茉 莉 花。茉莉 花 呀茉 莉 花。
家。茉 莉 花 呀茉 莉 花。茉莉 花 呀茉 莉 花。
家。茉 莉 花 呀茉 莉 花。茉莉 花 呀茉 莉 花。

【提示】

每句歌词中末字“花（huā）”“桠（yā）”“夸（kuā）”“下（xiā）”的韵母中都有元音“a”，所以这些字母相同或相近，使歌唱产生和谐感。这是汉语的押韵现象，经常出现在诗歌或歌曲中。

uo

一 语音视听 Audio-visual Pronunciation

1. 发音示意图 Diagrammatic Sketch of Pronunciation

uo

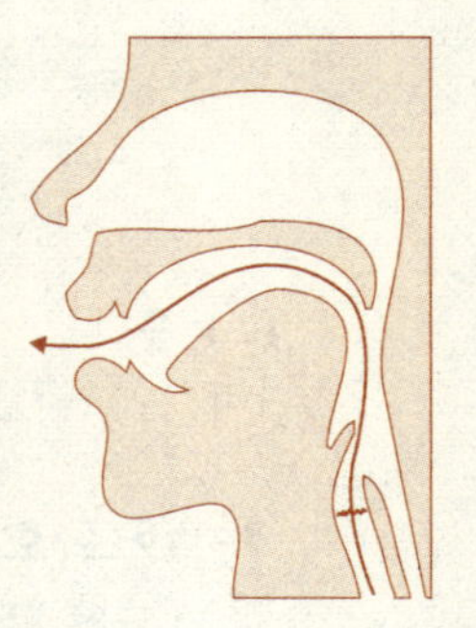

2. 发音特点 Characteristics of Pronunciation

uo [uo] 发音时，由 u 过渡到 o。

uo [uo] When uo is pronounced, the sound glides from u to o.

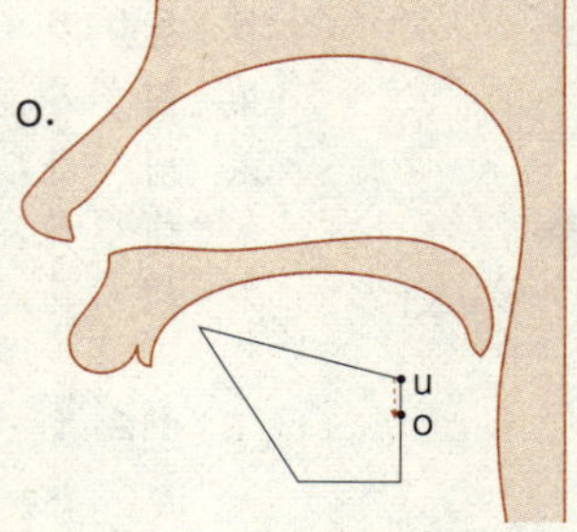

图 3-10 元音 uo 的发音舌位变化示意简图
Figure 3-10 The varied places of tongue, illustrating how to articulate vowel uo

二 听读词语 Listen and Read the Following Words

窝	wō	shelter
我	wǒ	I
沃	wò	enrichment
卧	wò	lie down
做错	zuò cuò	misdo
骆驼	luòtuo	cameral
说过	shuōguo	have said
硕果	shuòguǒ	fruit
蹉跎	cuōtuó	to idle away
哆嗦	duōsuō	shiver
过错	guòcuò	mistake
堕落	duòluò	vicious

【提示】

“uo”单独成音节时，“u”变成“w”。如“我（wǒ）”。

骆驼（luòtuo）是轻声词。说过（shuōguo）中“过”是助词，读轻声。

三 速读短语，注意加点字的韵母 Read Phrases Quickly, Pay Attention to the Finals of the Characters Marked with Dots

戳脊梁骨	chuō jǐliɑnggǔ	criticize behind sb’ s back
多多益善	duō duō yì shàn	The more, the better.
国计民生	guó jì mín shēng	national economy and the people’ s livelihood
活灵活现	huó líng huó xiàn	(of imitation or descrption of people or things) vivid; lifelike
落叶归根	luò yè guī gēn	leaves fall return to their roots; return (esp. from overseas) and settle down in one’ s native place when one get old
落汤鸡	luò tāng jī	(of a person) like a drenched chicken; like a drowned rat be soaked through

四 跟读绕口令，注意句中加点字的韵母 Read the Tongue Twister Following the Teacher, Pay Attention to the Finals of the Characters Marked with Dots

Láng dǎ chái， gǒu shāo huǒ， māor shàng kàng niē wōwo， quèr fēi lái zhēng bōbo.
狼打柴，狗烧火，猫儿上炕捏窝窝，雀儿飞来蒸饽饽。

五 听诵古诗，给全诗注上声母并给加点的字注上韵母 Listen and Recite the Ancient Poem, Write the Initials for the Poem and the Finals for the Characters Marked with Dots

子夜歌（其六）

夜长不得眠，明月何灼灼？

想闻欢唤声，虚应空中诺。

——《乐府诗集·吴声歌曲》

【提示】

灼灼：明亮。

想闻：想象中听到呼叫。

诺：表示答应的声音。

此歌写思妇想念丈夫的急切心情。

üe

一 语音视听 Audio-visual Pronunciation

1. 发音示意图 Diagrammatic Sketch of Pronunciation

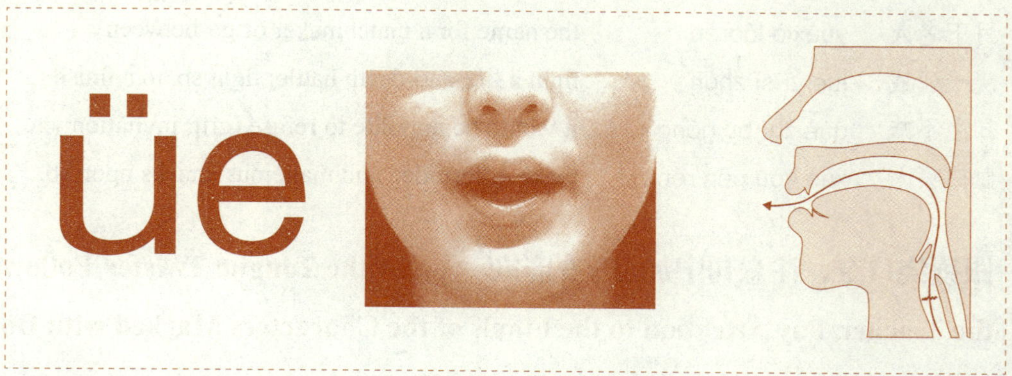

2. 发音特点 Characteristics of Pronunciation

üe [yɛ] 发音时，由 ü 过渡到 ê。

üe [yɛ] When üe is pronounced, the sound glides from ü to ê.

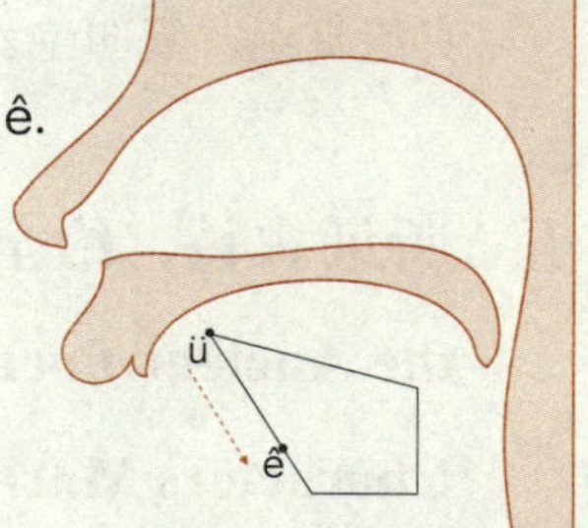

图 3-11 元音 üe 的发音舌位变化示意简图
Figure 3-11 The varied places of tongue, illustrating how to articulate vowel üe

二 听读词语 Listen and Read the Following Words

约	yuē	about
岳	yuè	high mountain
越	yuè	the more… the more
跃	yuè	jump
缺血	quēxuè	lack of blood
雀跃	quèyuè	jump for joy
决绝	juéjué	determined
约略	yuēlüè	approximate

【提示】

“üe” 单独成音节时，要在 “ü” 前加 “y”，加 “y” 后，“ü” 上两点要省写。如 “约 (yuē)”。韵母 “üe” 与声母 “j、q、x” 相拼写时，“ü” 上两点要省写。如 “缺血 (quē xuè)”。

三 速读短语，注意加点字的韵母 Read Phrases Quickly, Pay Attention to the Finals of the Characters Marked with Dots

约定俗成	yuē dìng sú chéng	(of a certain name or social habit) established or sanctioned by popular usage; accepted through common practice
月下老人	yuèxià lǎorén	the name for a matchmaker or go-between
决一死战	jué yī sǐ zhàn	fight a life-and-death battle; fight sb. to a finish
却之不恭	què zhī bù gōng	it would be impolite to refuse (gift; invitation; etc)
血口喷人	xuè kǒu pēn rén	make unformded and malicious attacks upon sb.

四 跟读绕口令，注意句中加点字的韵母 Read the Tongue Twister Following the Teacher, Pay Attention to the Finals of the Characters Marked with Dots

Zhēn jué zhēn jué, zhēn jiào jué. Hàoyuè dāngkōng xià báixuě, máquè suō tóu bù fēiyuè, què zhàn jiūcháo què xǐyuè.

真绝真绝，真叫绝。皓月当空下白雪，麻雀缩头不飞跃，鹊占鸠巢鹊喜悦。

五 听诵古诗，给全诗注上声母并给加点的字注上韵母 Listen and Recite the Ancient Poem, Write the Initials for the Poem and the Finals for the Characters Marked with Dots

忆秦娥

毛泽东

西风烈，
长空雁叫霜晨月。
霜晨月，
马蹄声碎，
喇叭声咽。
雄关漫道真如铁，
而今迈步从头越。
从头越，
苍山如海，
残阳如血。

【提示】

《忆秦娥》：词牌名。这首词作于1935年2月26日左右。全词以娄山关之战为题材。写胜利后的所见所闻所感，再现浴血奋战、英勇牺牲的激战情景。表现了作者面对失利和困难从容不迫的气度和胸怀。

六 听歌学汉语，注意加点字的韵母 Learn Chinses by Listening to the Song, Pay Attention to the Finals of the Characters Marked with Dots

满江红

宋·岳飞 词
古 曲

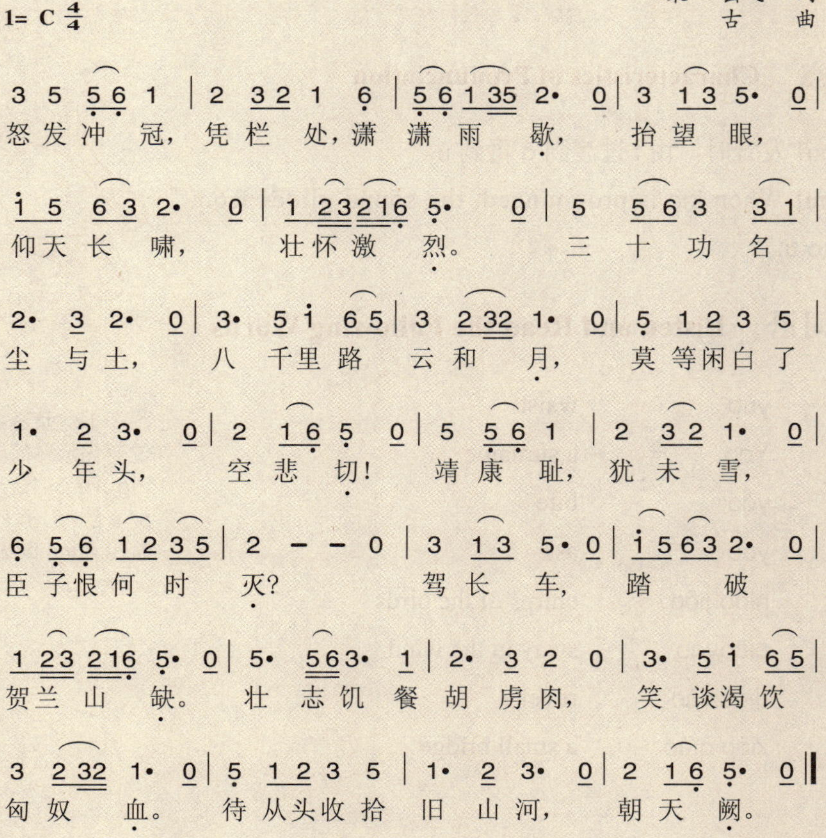

1= C 4/4

3 5 5 6 1 | 2 3 2 1 6 | 5 6 1 3 5 2· 0 | 3 1 3 5· 0 |
怒发冲冠，凭栏处，潇潇雨歇，抬望眼，

1 5 6 3 2· 0 | 1 2 3 2 1 6 5· 0 | 5 5 6 3 3 1 |
仰天长啸，壮怀激烈。三十功名

2· 3 2· 0 | 3· 5 1 6 5 | 3 2 3 2 1· 0 | 5 1 2 3 5 |
尘与土，八千里路云和月，莫等闲白了

1· 2 3· 0 | 2 1 6 5 0 | 5 5 6 1 | 2 3 2 1· 0 |
少年头，空悲切！靖康耻，犹未雪，

6 5 6 1 2 3 5 | 2 - - 0 | 3 1 3 5· 0 | 1 5 6 3 2· 0 |
臣子恨何时灭？驾长车，踏破

1 2 3 2 1 6 5· 0 | 5· 5 6 3· 1 | 2· 3 2 0 | 3· 5 1 6 5 |
贺兰山缺。壮志饥餐胡虏肉，笑谈渴饮

3 2 3 2 1· 0 | 5 1 2 3 5 | 1· 2 3· 0 | 2 1 6 5· 0 ‖
匈奴血。待从头收拾旧山河，朝天阙。

iao

一 语音视听 Audio-visual Pronunciation

1. 发音示意图 Diagrammatic Sketch of Pronunciation

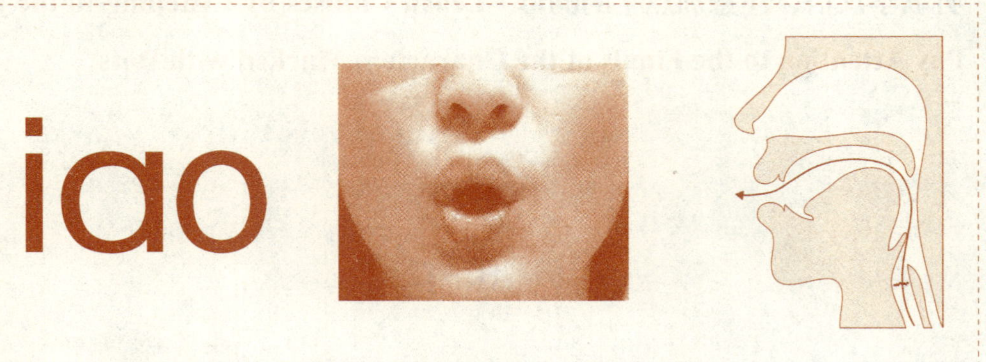

2. 发音特点 Characteristics of Pronunciation

iao [iau] 发音时，由 i 过渡到 a 再到 u。

iao [iau] When iao is pronounced, the sound glides from i to a then to u.

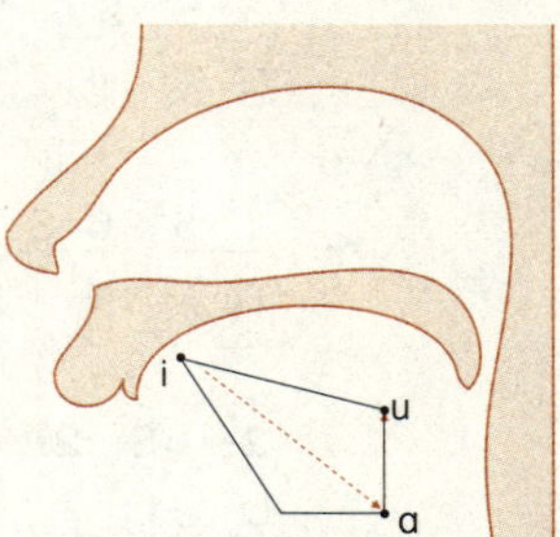

图 3-12 元音 iao 的发音舌位变化示意简图
Figure 3-12 The varied places of tongue, illustrating how to articulate vowel iao

二 听读词语 Listen and Read the Following Words

腰 yāo waist
姚 Yáo a surname
咬 yǎo bite
要 yào ask
鸟叫 niǎo jiào chirps of the birds
飘摇 piāoyáo sway in the wind
吊销 diàoxiāo revoke
小桥 xiǎo qiáo a small bridge

【提示】

“iao” 单独成音节时，“i” 变成 “y”。如腰（yāo）、姚（Yáo）、咬（yǎo）、要（yào）。

三　速读短语，注意加点字的韵母 Read Phrases Quickly, Pay Attention to the Finals of the Characters Marked with Dots

吆五喝六	yāo wǔ hè liù	arrogant
腰杆子	yāogǎnzi	backing; support
摇头摆尾	yáo tóu bái wěi	shake the head and way the tail; assume an air of complacency
咬耳朵	yáo ěrduo	whisper in sb' s ear; whisper
咬牙切齿	yǎo yá qiè chǐ	gnash one' s teeth in rage or in hatred
要面子	yào miànzi	be keen on face-saving

【提示】

摇头摆尾（yáo tóu bǎi wěi），读“yáo tóu bái wěi”；咬耳朵（yǎo ěrduo），读“yáo ěrduo”。这是三声字的连读变调现象。

四　跟读绕口令，注意句中加点字的韵母 Read the Tongue Twister Following the Teacher, Pay Attention to the Finals of the Characters Marked with Dots

Shuǐ shàng piāozhe sùliào biǎo, biǎo shàng luòzhe yì zhī niǎo. Niǎo kàn biǎo, biǎo dèng niǎo, niǎo bú rènshi biǎo, biǎo bú rènshi niǎo.

水上漂着塑料表，表上落着一只鸟。鸟看表，表瞪鸟，鸟不认识表，表不认识鸟。

【提示】

一只（yī zhī）读“yì zhī”，这是“一”的变调现象。不认识（bù rènshí）读“bú rènshi”，这是“不”的变调现象。

五　听诵古诗，给全诗注上声母并给加点的字注上韵母 Listen and Recite the Ancient Poem, Write the Initials for the Poem and the Finals for the Characters Marked with Dots

1.

春晓

唐·孟浩然

春眠不觉晓，处处闻啼鸟。
夜来风雨声，花落知多少。

【提示】

该诗意境十分优美。诗人抓住春天的早晨刚刚醒来时的一瞬间展开描写和联想，生动地表达了诗人对春天的热爱和怜惜之情。

孟浩然（689—740），唐代诗人，本名浩，字浩然，襄州襄阳（今湖北襄樊）人，世称孟襄阳。因他未曾入仕，又称之为孟山人。曾隐居于鹿门山。

2.

赤壁

唐 · 杜牧

折戟沉沙铁未销，
自将磨洗认前朝。
东风不与周郎便，
铜雀春深锁二乔。

【提示】

赤壁：魏、蜀、吴三国的古战场。

折戟：折断了的古兵器。

销：销蚀。

自将：诗人自己。

认前朝：认为是前朝战场的武器。

东风句：若无东风给予周郎机会。

铜雀：建安十五年（210年）曹操在邺城（今河北临漳县西）建造铜雀台，因楼顶铸有大铜雀而得名。

锁：关闭，藏。

二乔：吴国的两个美女。

此诗是作者感叹历史上英雄幸逢成名的机遇，而自己生不逢时，空有才能得不到施展，抒发了作者怀才不遇的思想感情。

iou

一 语音视听 Audio-visual Pronunciation

1. 发音示意图 Diagrammatic Sketch of Pronunciation

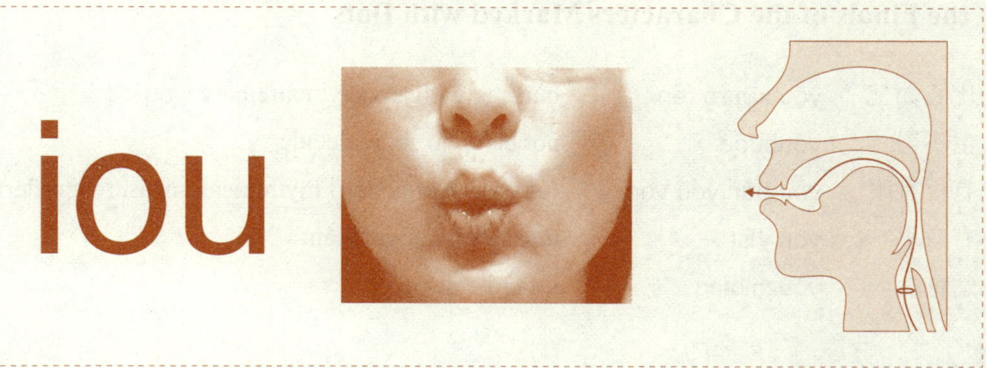

2. 发音特点 Characteristics of Pronunciation

iou [iou] 发音时，由 i 过渡到 o 再到 u。在同声母拼合时，省去 o。

iou [iou] When iou is pronounced, the sound glides from i to o then to u, but leave out o when iou combining with initials.

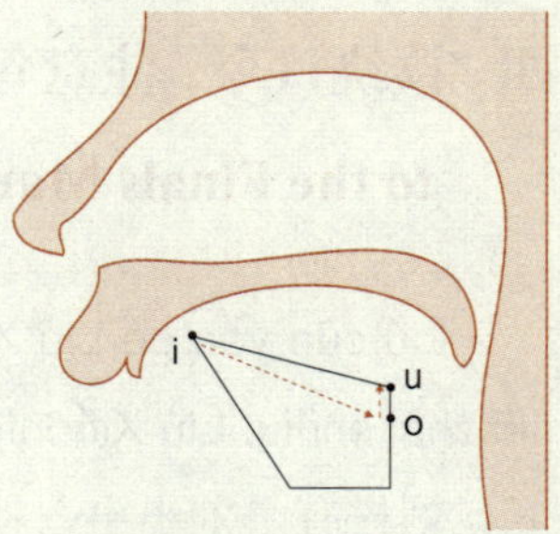

图 3-13 元音 iou 的发音舌位变化示意简图

Figure 3-13 The varied places of tongue, illustrating how to articulate vowel iou

二 听读词语 Listen and Read the Following Words

悠	yōu	remote in time or space
油	yóu	oil
有	yǒu	There be…
又	yòu	and
求救	qiújiù	ask for help
悠久	yōujiǔ	long
舅舅	jiùjiu	uncle

【提示】

“iou”单独成音节时，“i”变成“y”，如“悠（yōu）”。韵母“iou”与声母相拼时写成“iu”，调号在“u”上，如“求救（qiújiù）”。“舅舅（jiùjiu）”是轻声词。

三　速读短语，注意加点字的韵母 Read Phrases Quickly, Pay Attention to the Finals of the Characters Marked with Dots

忧心如焚	yōu xīn rú fén	burning with anxiety; extremely worried
由不得	yóubude	not be up to sb. to decide
有板有眼	yóu bǎn yóu yǎn	(of speech or action) rhythmical; measured; orderly
有意思	yǒu yìsi	meaningful; significant
幼稚病	yòuzhìbìng	infantile disorder

【提示】

有板有眼（yǒu bǎn yǒu yǎn），读“yóu bǎn yóu yǎn”，是三声字的连读变调现象。

四　读绕口令，注意句中加点字的韵母 Read the Tongue Twister, Pay Attention to the Finals Marked with Dots

Liú cūn yǒu gè Liú Xiǎoniú, liǔ cūn yǒu gè Liú Xiǎoniū. Liú Xiǎoniú qù fàngniú, Liú Xiǎo niū zhāi shíliu. Liú Xiǎoniú ràng Liú Xiǎoniū qí lǎoniú, Liú Xiǎoniū ràng Liú Xiǎoniú chī shíliu.

刘村有个刘小牛，柳村有个柳小妞。刘小牛去放牛，柳小妞摘石榴。刘小牛让柳小妞骑老牛，柳小妞让刘小牛吃石榴。

五　听诵宋词，给全词注上声母并给加点的字注上韵母 Listen and Recite the *Song Ci* Poem, Write the Initials you have learned for the *Ci* Poem and the Finals for the Characters Marked with Dots

一剪梅

宋 · 李清照

红藕香残玉簟秋，轻解罗裳，独上兰舟，云中谁寄锦书来？雁字回时，月满西楼。

花自飘零水自流。一种相思，两处闲愁。此情无计可消除，才下眉头，却上心头。

【提示】

箪：用芦苇或竹编制的席。

《一剪梅》：又名《腊梅香》，是李清照为抒写思念丈夫赵明诚之情而作的。

六　听歌学汉语，注意歌词中加点字的韵母　Learn Chinese by listening to the Song, Pay Attention to the Finals of the Characters Marked with Dots

好汉歌

电视连续剧《水浒传》片尾曲

易　茗　词
赵季平　曲
刘　欢　唱

1=♯C $\frac{4}{4}$

(2 2 1 2 2　0 | 2 2 1 2　2　0) | 5　5 7 76 5 5 |

（独）大 河 向东 流 哇，
（独）大 河 向东 流 哇，

1 16 55 336 5 5 | 55 05 1 61 2 2 |

天 上的 星星 参北 斗 哇（伴）嗨 嗨　嗨 参 北 斗 哇，
天 上的 星星 参北 斗 哇（伴）嗨 嗨　嗨 参 北 斗 哇，

2 5 2 5 321 2 2 | 5　5 7 76 5 5 |

生 死 之 交 一 碗 酒 哇，（独）说 走 咱 就 走 哇，
不 分 贵 贱 一 碗 酒 哇，（独）说 走 咱 就 走 哇，

1 16 5 5 336 5 5 | 55 55 1 6 1 2 2 |

你 有 我 有 全都 有 哇。（伴）嗨 嗨 嗨 嗨 全 都 有 哇，
你 有 我 有 全都 有 哇。（伴）嗨 嗨 嗨 嗨 全 都 有 哇，

2 5 2 5 321 2 2 ‖: 3· 3 3 3 356 1 1 |

水 里 火 里 不 回 头 哇。（独）路 见 不 平 一 声 吼 哇，
一 路 看 天 不 回 头 哇。（伴）路 见 不 平 一 声 吼 哇，

5̇· 6 5 5 654 5 5 | 5 1̇ 5̇ 1̇ 654 5 5 :‖
该 出手 时 就 出 手 哇， 风 风 火 火 闯 九 州 哇。
该 出手 时 就 出 手 哇， 风 风 火 火 闯 九 州 哇。

5̇· 3̇ 2̇ 3̇ 3̇ 1̇ 2̇ | 0 5̇ 4̇ 5̇ 6̇ 1̇ 3̇ 2̇ |
（独）嗨 呀 依儿 呀 嗨 唉 嗨 依 儿 呀，

5̇· 3̇ 2̇ 3̇ 1̇ 2̇ | 2̇ 5̇ 2̇ 5̇ 3̇ 2̇ 1̇ 2̇ |
（伴）唉 嗨 呀 依 儿 呀 唉 嗨 唉 嗨 依 儿 呀，

【提示】

此歌赞扬好汉们除暴安良、见义勇为的精神。

歌词中的“流（liú）”“斗（dǒu）”“酒（jiǔ）”“有（yǒu）”“头（tóu）”“手（shǒu）”“州（zhōu）”的韵母接近或相同，因为有复元音“ou”，所以使歌唱产生和谐感。这是汉语的押韵现象。

uai

一 语音视听 Audio-visual Pronunciation

1. 发音示意图 Diagrammatic Sketch of Pronunciation

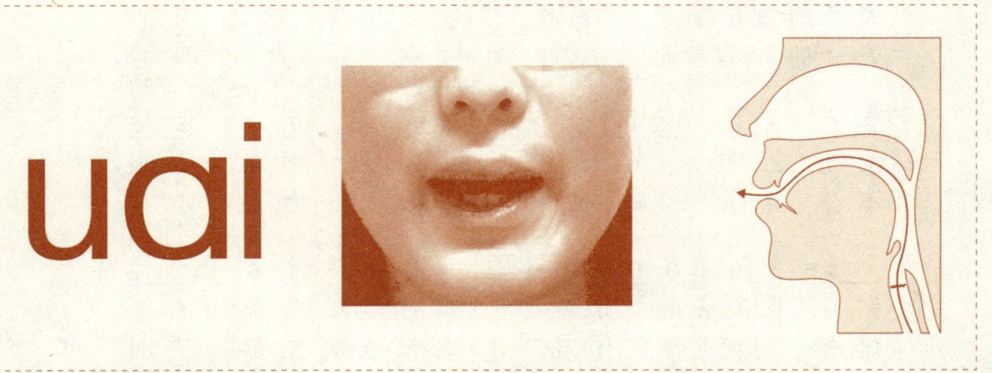

2. 发音特点 Characteristics of Pronunciation

uai [uai] 发音时，由 u 过渡到 a 再到 i。

uai [uai] When uai is pronounced, the sound glides from u to a then to i.

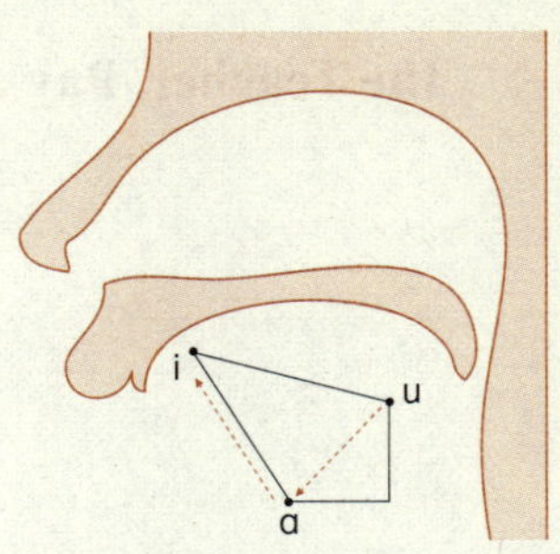

图 3-14 元音 uai 的发音舌位变化示意简图

Figure 3-14 The varied places of tongue, illustrating how to articulate vowel uai

二 听读词语 Listen and Read the Following Words

歪	wāi	bent
外	wài	outside
摔坏	shuāihuài	break
快甩	kuài shuǎi	to swing quickly
外快	wàikuài	extra income
怀揣	huáichuāi	hold; bosom

【提示】

“uai”单独成音节时，“u”变成“w”，如“歪（wāi）”。

三 速读短语，注意加点字的韵母 Read Phrases Quickly, Pay Attention to the Finals of the Characters Marked with Dots

歪七扭八	wāi qī niǔ bā	crooked; shapeless and twisted
外强中干	wài qiáng zhōng gān	outwardly strong but inwardly weak
怀才不遇	huái cái bú yù	have unrecognized talents
怪模怪样	guài mú guài yàng	queer-looking, grotesque
快人快语	kuài rén kuài yǔ	straight talk from an honest forward person

【提示】

怀才不遇（huái cái bù yù），读“huái cái bú yù”，这是“不”的变调现象。

四　跟读经典选文，注意加点字的韵母 Read the Adapted Classic Following the Teacher, Pay attention to the Finals of the Characters Marked with Dots

Láobǎn de Suànpán

Láobǎn de suànpán cái jiào guài,
Shíshī suàn chū yǎnlèi lái;
Bànnián gōngzī suàn de jīng,
Èr liǎng záliáng hái quē chái.

老板的算盘

老板的算盘才叫怪，
石狮算出眼泪来；
半年工资算得精，
二两杂粮还缺柴。

——《中国歌谣资料》

五　听诵古诗，给全诗注上声母并给加点的字注上韵母 Listen and Recite the Ancient Poem, Write the Initials for the Poem and the Finals for the Characters Marked with Dots

饮酒（节选）

晋·陶渊明

清晨闻叩门，倒裳往自开。
问子为谁欤，田父有好怀。
壶浆远相候，疑我与时乖。
且共欢此饮，吾驾不可回。

【提示】

倒裳：匆忙中穿倒了衣裳。
欤：疑问。
好怀：好情意。
疑我：怪我。
时：时俗。　乖：不合。
且：姑且。

驾：驾车。此指不再出仕。

此系节选自《饮酒》诗。全诗借与田父饮酒的交谈表达了作者不出仕的坚决态度。

陶渊明（约 365 年—427 年），字元亮，号五柳先生，谥号靖节先生，入刘宋后改名潜。东晋末期南朝宋初期诗人、文学家、辞赋家、散文家。东晋浔阳柴桑（今江西省九江市）人。曾做过几年小官，后辞官回家，从此隐居，田园生活是陶渊明诗的主要题材，相关作品有《饮酒》《归园田居》《桃花源记》《五柳先生传》《归去来兮辞》《桃花源诗》等。

uei

一 语音视听 Audio-visual Pronunciation

1. 发音示意图 Diagrammatic Sketch of Pronunciation

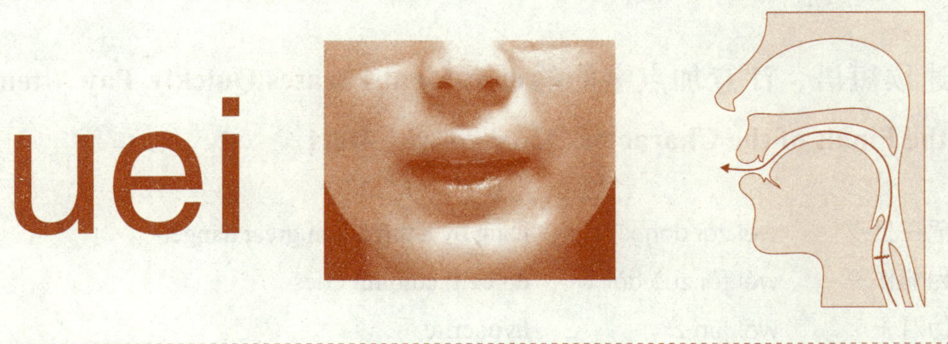

2. 发音特点 Characteristics of Pronunciation

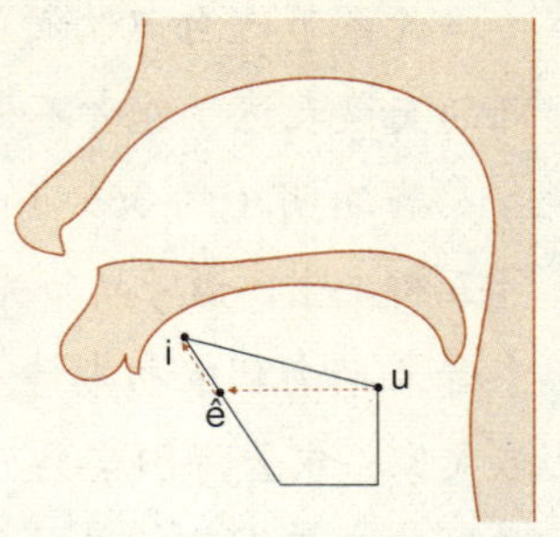

图 3-15 元音 uei 的发音舌位变化示意简图
Figure 3-15 The varied places of tongue, illustrating how to articulate vowel uei

uei [uei] 发音时，由 u 过渡到 ê 再到 i 。在同声母拼合时，省去 ê。

uei [uei] When uei is pronounced, the sound glides from u to ê then to i, but leave out ê when uei combining with initials.

二 听读词语 Listen and Read the Following Words

威	wēi	power
围	wéi	surround
伟	wěi	great
位	wèi	position
归队	guī duì	rejoin
追随	zhuīsuí	follow
退税	tuì shuì	drawback
吹灰	chuī huī	soot blowing

【提示】

"uei" 单独成音节时， "u" 变成 "w" ，如威（wēi）。

"uei" 在与辅音声母相拼时，写成 "ui" ，调号在 "i" 上，如归队（guī duì）。

三 速读短语，注意加点字的韵母 Read Phrases Quickly, Pay Attention to the Finals of the Characters Marked with Dots

危在旦夕	wēi zài dàn xī	hang by a thread; in great danger
为非作歹	wéi fēi zuò dǎi	do evil; commit cries
伪君子	wěi jūn zǐ	hypocrite
委曲求全	wěi qū qiú quán	stoop to compromise
未卜先知	wèi bǔ xiān zhī	know something without consulting an oracle; foresee

四　跟读绕口令，注意句中加点字的韵母　Read the Tongue Twister Following the Teacher, Pay Attention to the Finals of the Characters Marked with Dots

Wēiwei, wěiwei hé wèiwei, názhe shuǐbēi qù jiē shuǐ. Wēiwei ràng wěiwei, wěiwei ràng wèiwei, wèiwei ràng wēiwei, méi rén xiān jiē shuǐ. Yī èr sān, páihǎo duì, yǒu xiān yǒu hòu lái jiē shuǐ.

威威，伟伟和卫卫，拿着水杯去接水。威威让伟伟，伟伟让卫卫，卫卫让威威，没人先接水。一二三，排好队，有先有后来接水。

五　听诵古诗，给全词注上声母并给加点的字注上韵母　Listen and Recite the Poem, Write the Initials for the *Ci* Poem and the Finals for the Characters Marked with Dots

回乡偶书

唐·贺知章

少小离家老大回，乡音无改鬓毛衰。

儿童相见不相识，笑问客从何处来。

【提示】

偶书：随意写下来的。

乡音：家乡话口音。

无改：没有改变。

衰：稀疏。

此诗抒发了诗人眷恋故乡之情和“物是人非”的之感，是千百年来为人传颂的名篇。

贺知章（659—744），字季真，号四明狂客，汉族，唐越州会稽永兴（今浙江杭州市萧山区）人，贺知章诗文以绝句见长，除祭神乐章、应制诗外，其写景、抒怀之作风格独特，清新潇洒，著名的《咏柳》《回乡偶书》两首脍炙人口，千古传诵，今尚存录入《全唐诗》的共 19 首诗。

第四节 鼻韵母
Section IV Nasal Finals

普通话共有 16 个鼻韵母：an, ian, uan, üan, en, in, uen, ün 和 ang, iang, uang, eng, ing, ueng, ong, iong，又叫鼻音尾韵母。

There are sixteen nasal finals in *Putonghua*: an, ian, uan, üan, en, in, uen, ün and ang, iang, uang, eng, ing, ueng, ong, iong, also called nasal end finals.

发音时，由元音发音状态逐渐过渡到鼻辅音，除阻阶段不发音。

During the articulation of nasal finals, the pronunciation of a vowel will gradually glide to a nasal consonant. There is no articulation during the removal of blocking.

an

一 语音视听 Audio-visual Pronunciation

1. 发音示意图 Diagrammatic Sketch of Pronunciation

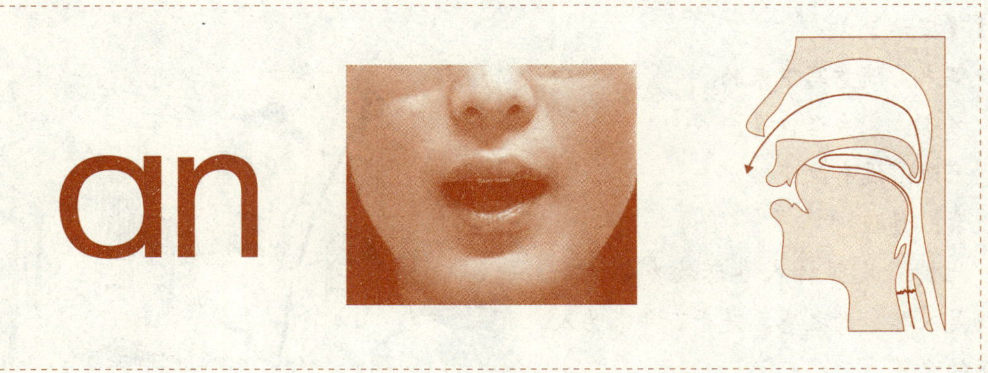

2. 发音特点 Characteristics of Pronunciation

an [an] 发音时，由 a 过渡到前鼻辅音 n。

an [an] When an is pronounced, the sound glides from a to front nasal n.

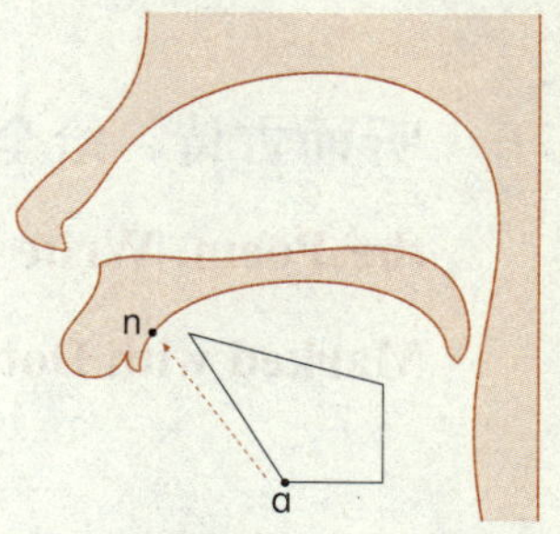

图 3-16 元音 an 的发音舌位变化示意简图

Figure 3-16 The varied places of tongue, illustrating how to articulate vowel an

二 听读词语 Listen and Read the Following Words

安	ān	install
俺	ǎn	I
暗	àn	dark
摊贩	tānfàn	street vendor
安然	ānrán	safe
漫谈	màntán	ramble
汗衫	hànshān	T-shirt

三 速读短语，注意加点字的韵母 Read Phrases Quickly, Pay Attention to the Finals of the Characters Marked with Dots

搬起石头砸自己的脚	bānqǐ shítou zá zìjǐde jiǎo	pick up a stone only to drop it on one' s own feet; suffer from one' s own actions
胆大包天	dǎn dà bāo tiān	audacious in the extreme
含辛茹苦	hán xīn rú kǔ	endure hardship and eat bitterness; suffer untold hardships and deprivations
赶鸭子上架	gǎn yāzi shàng jià	force a duck to sit on a perch; try to make sb. do sth. beyond his capabilities

四 跟读绕口令，注意加点字的韵母 Read the Tongue Twister Following the Teacher, Pay Attention to the Finals Marked of the Characters with Dots

Xuéxí jiù pà mǎn, lǎn, nán, xīn li yǒule mǎn, lǎn , nán, bù xué bù zuān yǒng bù qián, xīn li qùdiào mǎn, lǎn, nán, biān xué biān gàn, máyǐ yě néng shàng Tàishān.

学习就怕满、懒、难，心里有了满、懒、难，不学不钻永不前，心里去掉满、懒、难，边学边干，蚂蚁也能上泰山。

五　听诵古诗，给全诗注上声母并给加点的字注上韵母 Listen and Recite the Poem, Write the Initials for the Poem and the Finals for the Characters Marked with Dots

1.

无题

唐 · 李商隐

相见时难别亦难，
东风无力百花残。
春蚕到死丝方尽，
蜡炬成灰泪始干。

【提示】

《无题》：唐代以来，有的诗人不愿意标出能够表示主题的题目时，常用“无题”来表示。这是一首寄情诗，表现男女间缠绵悱恻的爱情。其中三、四两句：“春蚕到死丝方尽，蜡炬成灰泪始干。”后世多用来表达对师长奉献一生的尊敬之情。

李商隐（约 812—858），字义山，号玉溪生，晚唐著名诗人。杜牧与他齐名，两人并称“小李杜”。

2.

伐檀

坎坎伐檀兮，寘之河之干兮，河水清且涟漪。不稼不穑，胡取禾三百廛兮？不狩不猎，胡瞻尔庭有县狟兮？彼君子兮，不素餐兮！

【提示】

本诗节选自《诗经·国风·伐檀》第一节。全诗真实深刻地揭露了奴隶主对奴隶们的残酷剥削。全诗语言刚劲有力，是我国古代诗歌中的优秀诗篇。

坎坎：伐木声。

檀：树木。

寘：同“置”，放。

涟漪：清水兴起的波纹。

干：河岸。

稼：耕种。

穑：收获、收取。

胡：为什么？

廛：束、捆（三百捆）。

狩猎：打猎。

瞻：看见。

尔：你们。

庭：庭院。

县：同“悬”，悬挂。

狟：猪獾。一说幼小的貉。

君子：指剥削者（讽刺地）。

素餐：白吃饭，不劳而食。

本诗节选自《诗经·国风·伐檀》第一节。

六 听歌学汉语，注意歌词中加点字的韵母 Learn Chinese by Listening to the Song, Pay Attention to the Finals of the Characters Marked with Dots

蓝 花 花

1= F 2/4
慢　　　　陕西民歌

6 2̇ 6 6 5 | 6 2̇ 6 | 6· 2̇ | 5·6 3 3 2 |
青线线那个蓝线线　蓝个英英的
五谷里那个田苗子　唯有个高粱着

6 - | 2· 3 5 5 | 3 6 5 3 | 2 3 2 1 6 5 | 6 - ‖
采，① 生下一个蓝花花哟实　实的爱死个人。
高，一十三省的女儿哟数上那个蓝花花好。

注：① “蓝个英英的采”意即蓝得发亮。
提示： 原谱有八段词，这里只取其第一、二段。

ian

一　语音视听　Audio-visual Pronunciation

1. 发音示意图　Diagrammatic Sketch of Pronunciation

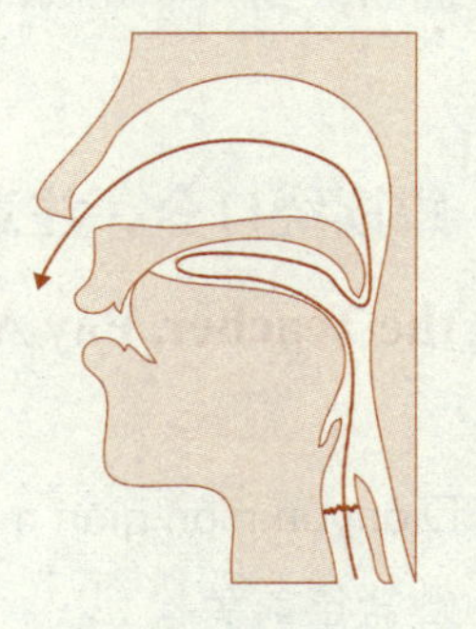

2. 发音特点　Characteristics of Pronunciation

ian [iɛn] 发音时，由 i 过渡到 ɑ 再过渡到前鼻辅音 n。

ian [iɛn] When iɑn is pronounced, the sound glides from i to ɑ then to front nasal n.

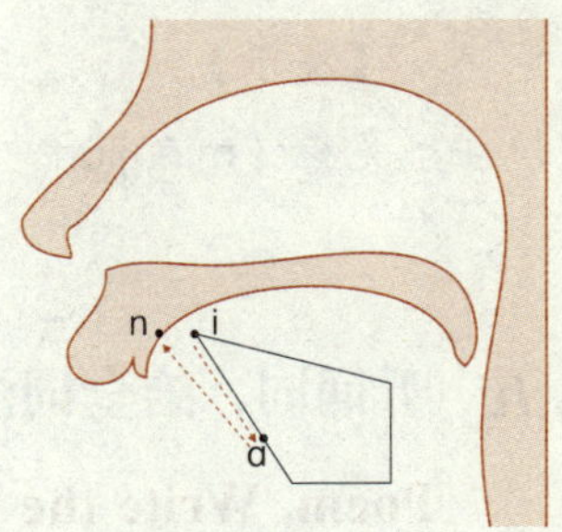

图 3-17　元音 iɑn 的发音舌位变化示意简图
Figure 3-17　The varied places of tongue, illustrating how to articulate vowel iɑn

二　听读词语　Listen and Read the Following Words

烟	yān	smoke
盐	yán	salt
眼	yǎn	eye
验	yàn	examine
颜面	yánmiàn	reputation
简便	jiǎnbiàn	simple and convenient
前线	qiánxiàn	front line
先贤	xiānxián	scholars of the past

【提示】
“ian”单独成音节“i”变成“y”。如“烟（yān）”。

三 速读短语，注意加点字的韵母 Read Phrases Quickly, Pay Attention to the Finals of the Characters Marked with Dots

变本加厉	biàn běn jiā lì	go from bad to worse;with ever-growing intensity
颠倒是非	diāndǎo shìfēi	confuse right and wrong;confuse truth and falsehood
见义勇为	jiàn yì yǒng wéi	be ready to do whatever one see right
面面俱到	miàn miàn jù dào	attend to each and every aspect of a matter

四 跟读绕口令，注意句中加点字的韵母 Read the Tongue Twister Following the Teacher, Pay Attention to the Finals of the Characters Marked with Dots

Diǎnyán nián qián miánjiǎn.
碘盐年前免检。

【提示】
免检（miǎnjiǎn），读“miánjiǎn”。这是三声的变调现象。

五 听诵词，给全词注上声母并给加点的字注上韵母 Listen and Recite the *Ci* Poem, Write the Initials for the *Ci* Poem and the Finals for the Characters Marked with Dots

水调歌头
宋 · 苏轼

明月几时有？把酒问青天。不知天上宫阙，今夕是何年。我欲乘风归去，又恐琼楼玉宇，高处不胜寒。起舞弄清影，何似在人间。

转朱阁，低倚户，照无眠，不应有恨，何事长向别时圆？人有悲欢离合，月有阴晴圆缺，此事古难全。但愿人长久，千里共婵娟。

【提示】

宫阙：神话传说中的月宫。

琼楼玉宇：指宏伟豪华的楼阁。

婵娟：神话中月宫里美丽的仙女。

本词为中秋咏月抒怀之作。作者以形象的描绘手法，将自己、社会人事、神话传说融为一体，并注入了深厚的哲学理念。富有浪漫主义色彩，是一首历来广为传诵的名作。

uan

一 语音视听　Audio-visual Pronunciation

1. 发音示意图　Diagrammatic Sketch of Pronunciation

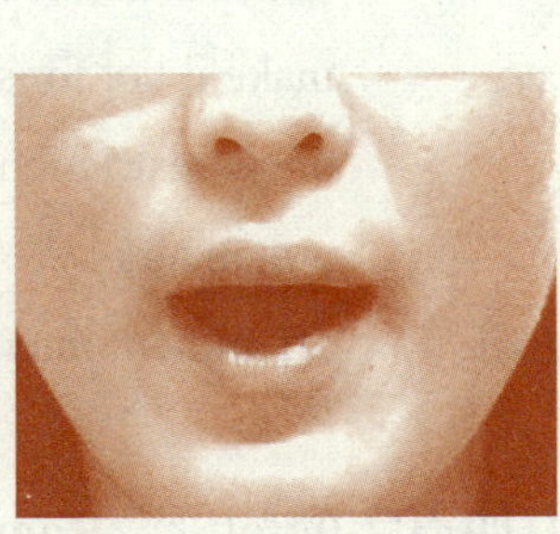

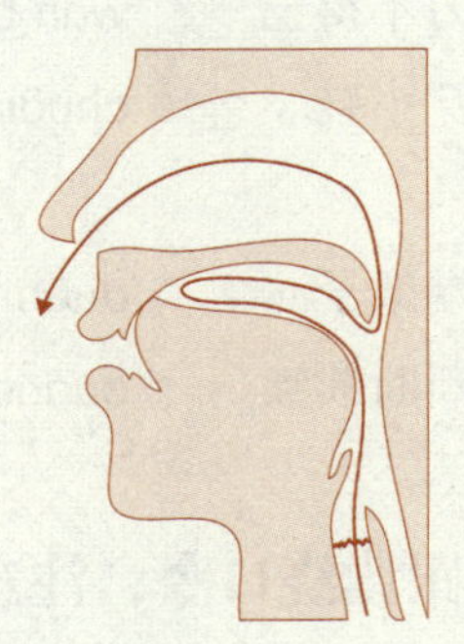

2. 发音特点 Characteristics of Pronunciation

uan [uan] 发音时，由 u 过渡到 a 再过渡到前鼻辅音 n。

uan [uan] When uan is pronounced, the sound glides from u to a then to front nasal n.

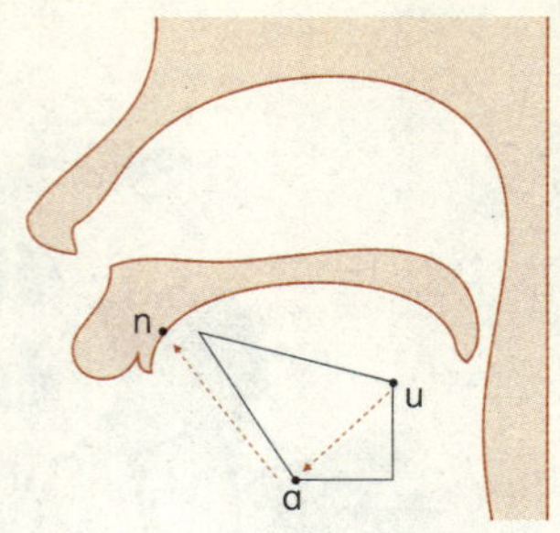

图 3-18 元音 uan 的发音舌位变化示意简图
Figure 3-18 The varied places of tongue, illustrating how to articulate vowel uan

二 听读词语 Listen and Read the Following Words

湾	wān	gulf
完	wán	finish
晚	wǎn	late
万	wàn	ten thousands
贯穿	guànchuān	run through
还款	huán kuǎn	repayment
旋转	xuánzhuǎn	spin
乱窜	luàncuàn	run around

【提示】
"uan"单独成音节时，"u"变成"w"。如"湾（wān）"。

三 速读短语，注意加点字的韵母 Read Phrases Quickly, Pay Attention to the Finals of the Characters Marked with Dots

完璧归赵	wán bì guī Zhào	return sth. intact to its owner
万不得已	wàn bù dé yǐ	out of absolute necessity; as a last resort
穿小鞋	chuān xiǎoxié	make it hot for sb.; secretly make things difficult for or set restrictions on sb. by abusing one's power
端架子	duān jiàzi	put on airs
断断续续	duànduànxùxù	off and on; intermittently

四 跟读绕口令，注意句中加点字的韵母 Read the Tongue Twister Following the Teacher, Pay Attention to the Finals of the Characters Marked with Dots

1.

Dà fānchuán xiǎo fānchuán shùqǐ wéigān chēngqǐ chuán. Fēng chuī fān, fān yǐn chuán, fānchuán shùnfēng zhuán hǎiwān.

大帆船，小帆船，竖起桅杆撑起船。风吹帆，帆引船，帆船顺风转海湾。

2.

Rén zhī chū, xìng běn shàn. Xìng xiāng jìn, xí xiāng yuǎn.
Gǒu bù jiào, xìng nǎi qiān. Jiào zhī dào, guì yǐ zhuān.
Yǎng bú jiào, fù zhī guò. Jiào bù yán, shī zhī duò.
Zǐ bù xué, fēi suǒ yí. Yòu bù xué, lǎo hé wéi?

人之初，性本善。性相近，习相远。
苟不教，性乃迁。教之道，贵以专。
养不教，父之过。教不严，师之惰。
子不学，非所宜。幼不学，老何为？

——《三字经》

五　听诵古诗，给全诗注上声母并给加点的字注上韵母 Listen and Recite the Ancient Poem, Write the Initials for the Poem and the Finals for the Characters Marked with Dots

1.

出塞

唐 · 王昌龄

秦时明月汉时关，万里长征人未还。
但使龙城飞将在，不教胡马度阴山。

【提示】

龙城：匈奴的著名城堡。因匈奴族在龙城祭祀，龙神故名龙城。其地在今蒙古人民共和国鄂尔浑河西侧的和硕柴达木湖附近。

飞将：指飞将军李广。

这是一首慨叹边战不断，国无良将的边塞诗。诗的首句最耐人寻味。

王昌龄（690—756），字少伯。盛唐著名边塞诗人，有“七绝圣手”“诗家天子”之称。

2.

关山月

唐 · 李白

明月出天山，苍茫云海间。
长风几万里，吹度玉门关。
汉下白登道，胡窥青海湾。
由来征战地，不见有人还。

【提示】

这是一首写戍兵、思妇互相思念的诗。

天山：祁连山，在今甘肃。

玉门关：在今甘肃敦煌西。

白登：山名，在今山西大同东。汉高祖征匈奴被困于此地七天，伤亡惨重。

üan

一 语音视听 Audio-visual Pronunciation

1. 发音示意图 Diagrammatic Sketch of Pronunciation

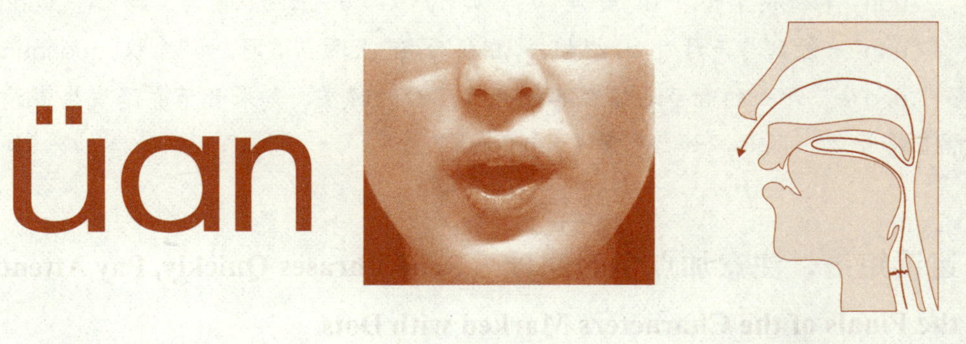

2. 发音特点 Characteristics of Pronunciation

üan [yan] 发音时，由 ü 过渡到 ɑ 再到前鼻辅音 n。

üan [yan] When üan is pronounced, the sound glides from ü to ɑ then to front nasal n.

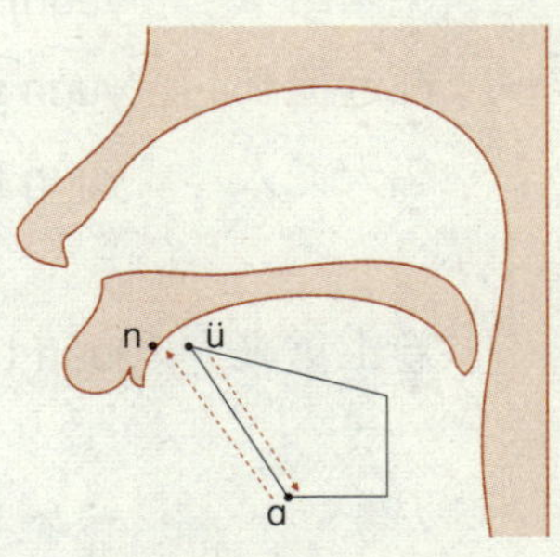

图 3-19 元音 üan 的发音舌位变化示意简图
Figure 3-19 The varied places of tongue, illustrating how to articulate vowel üan

二 听读词语 Listen and Read the Following Words

冤	yuān	grievance
元	yuán	element; unit; Yuan Dynasty; the monetary unit of China
远	yuǎn	remote
院	yuàn	yard
渊源	yuānyuán	origin
全权	quánquán	full authority
圆圈	yuánquān	round circle
花园	huāyuán	garden
权利	quánlì	right
院落	yuànluò	courtyard
元旦	yuándàn	New Year's Day

冤案	yuān’àn	unjust cast
远处	yuǎnchù	distance
源流	yuánliú	origin and development
支援	zhīyuán	support;assist

【提示】

“üan” 单独成音节，“ü” 前加 “y”，加 “y” 后 “ü” 上两点省写。如 “元（yuán）”。

“üan” 一般只与声母 “j、q、x” 相拼，相拼后 “ü” 上两点省写。如 “全权（quánquán）”。

“a, o, e” 开头的音节连读在其他音节后面的时候，如果音节界限发生混淆，就用隔音符号 “’” 隔开，如 “冤案（yuān’àn）”。

三　速读短语，注意加点字的韵母 Read Phrases Quickly, Pay Attention to the Finals of the Characters Marked with Dots

冤家路窄	yuānjiā lù zhǎi	one can’t avoid one’e enemy;It’s small world.
源远流长	yuán yuǎn liú cháng	The source is distant and stream long.
怨天尤人	yuàn tiān yóu rén	grumble against heaven and lay the blame upon other people
卷土重来	juán tǔ chóng lái	stage or launch a comeback after regaining one’ s strength

【提示】

卷土重来（juǎn tǔ chóng lái），读 “juán tǔ chóng lái”，这是两个三声连读的变调现象。

四　跟读绕口令，注意句中加点字的韵母 Read the Tongue Twister Following the Teacher, Pay Attention to the Finals of the Characters Marked with Dots

Yuánquān yuán, quān yuánquān, yuányuán juānjuan huà yuánquān. Juānjuan huà de quān lián quān, yuányuan huà de quān tào quān. Juānjuan yuányuan bǐ yuánquān, kànkan shuí de yuánquān yuán.

圆圈圆，圈圆圈，圆圆娟娟画圆圈。娟娟画的圈连圈，圆圆画的圈套圈。娟娟圆圆比圆圈，看看谁的圆圈圆。

五 听诵古诗，给全诗注上声母并给加点的字注上韵母 Listen and Recite the Poem, Write the Initials for the Poem and the Finals for the Characters Marked with Dots

村居

清 · 高鼎

草长莺飞二月天，拂堤杨柳醉春烟。

儿童散学归来早，忙趁东风放纸鸢。

【提示】

鸢：风筝。

该诗描写出一幅春天孩子们在村旁的芳草地上放风筝的图画。

高鼎：字象一、拙吾，浙江仁和（今浙江省杭州市）人，清代后期诗人。

en

一 语音视听 Audio-visual Pronunciation

1. 发音示意图 Diagrammatic Sketch of Pronunciation

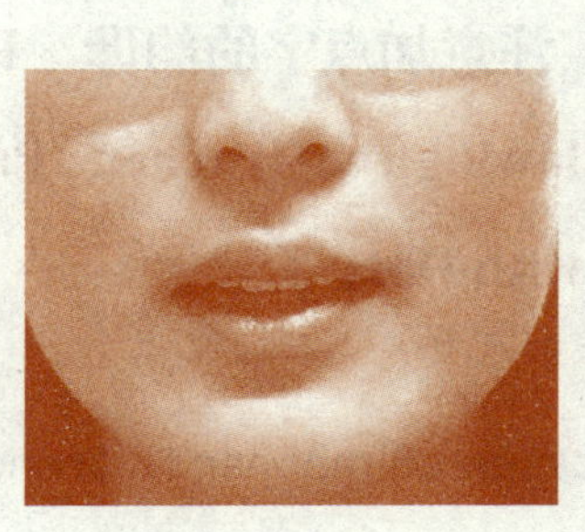

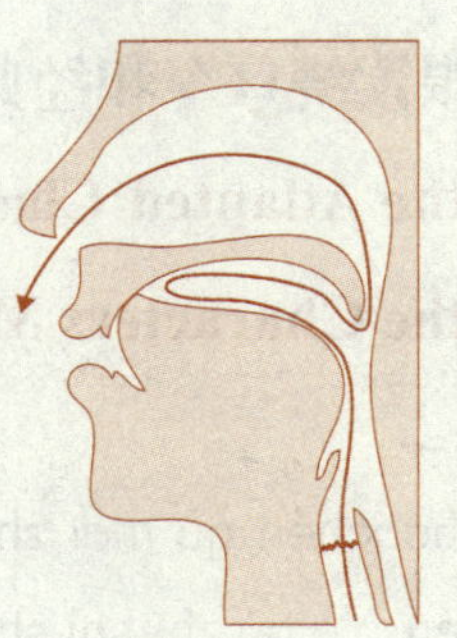

2. 发音特点 Characteristics of Pronunciation

en [ən] 发音时，由 e 过渡到前鼻辅音 n。

en [ən] When en is pronounced, the sound glides from e to front nasal n.

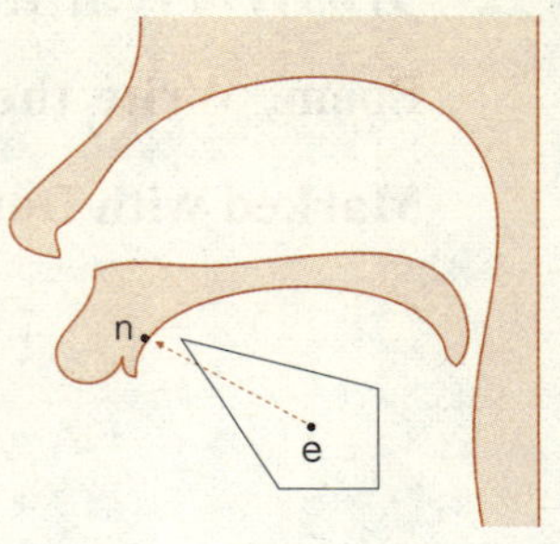

图 3-20 元音 en 的发音舌位变化示意简图

Figure 3-20 The varied places of tongue, illustrating how to articulate vowel en

二 听读词语 Listen and Read the Following Words

恩	ēn	favor
摁	èn	press
本分	běnfèn	duty
认真	rènzhēn	serious
身份	shēnfèn	identity
根本	gēnběn	basic

三 速读短语，注意加点字的韵母 Read Phrases Quickly, Pay Attention to the Finals of the Characters Marked with Dots

恩断义绝	ēn duàn yì jué	(of feelings) be estranged (mostly used to refer to divorce)
本乡本土	běn xiāng bén tǔ	native land; native country, home village
沉住气	chén zhù qì	keep calm at a critical moment
分秒必争	fēn miǎo bì zhēng	seize every minute and second; not a second to be lost
根深蒂固	gēn shēn dì gù	deep-rooted; ingrained

【提示】

本乡本土（běn xiāng běn tǔ），读“běn xiāng bén tǔ”，这是三声的变调现象。

四 跟读绕口令和经典选文，注意加点字的韵母 Read the Tongue Twister and the Adapted Classic Following the Teacher, Pay Attention to the Finals of the Characters Marked with Dots

1.

Xiǎochén qù mài zhēn, Xiáoshěn qù mài pén. Xiǎochén hǎn mài zhēn, Xiáoshěn hǎn mài pén. Yě bù zhī shì shuí mài zhēn, yě bù zhī shì shuí mài pén.

小陈去卖针，小沈去卖盆。小陈喊卖针，小沈喊卖盆。也不知是谁卖针，也不知是谁卖盆。

2.

Yú Lì Xuéwén
Bù lì xíng, dàn xué wén,
Zhǎng fúhuá, chéng hé rén.
Dàn lì xíng, bù xué wén,
Rèn jǐ jiàn, mèi zhēnlǐ.

余力学文
不力行，但学文，
长浮华，成何人。
但力行，不学文，
任己见，昧真理。

选自《弟子规》

【提示】

语意：不能身体力行孝、悌、信等本分，一味死读，纵然有知识，也只是增长浮华不实的习气，变成不切实际的人。如此读书又有何用？反之，如果只是一味地做，不肯读书学习，就容易依着自己的偏见做事，蒙蔽了真理，也是不对的。

《弟子规》：原名《训蒙文》，是启蒙养正，教育子弟敦伦尽分、防邪存诚，养成忠厚家风的最佳读物。原作者为李毓秀。全书分为五个部分，具体列述弟子在家、出外、待人、接物与学习上应该恪守的守则规范。清朝贾存仁修订改编《训蒙文》，改名为《弟子规》。

李毓秀（1662—1722），清朝康熙年间的秀才。

五　听诵古诗，给全诗注上声母并给加点的字注上韵母 Listen and Recite the Ancient Poem, Write the Initials for the Poem and the Finals for the Characters Marked with Dots

夜宿山寺
唐 · 李白

危楼高百尺，手可摘星辰。
不敢高声语，恐惊天上人。

【提示】

这是李白的一首记游写景的短诗。诗人用夸张的艺术手法，描绘了山寺的高耸，给人以丰富的联想。山上的这座高楼好像有一百尺高，站在楼上就可以用手摘下月亮和星星，我不敢在这儿大声说话，恐怕惊动了天上的仙人。全诗语言朴素自然，生动形象。

in

一　语音视听　Audio-visual Pronunciation

1. 发音示意图　Diagrammatic Sketch of Pronunciation

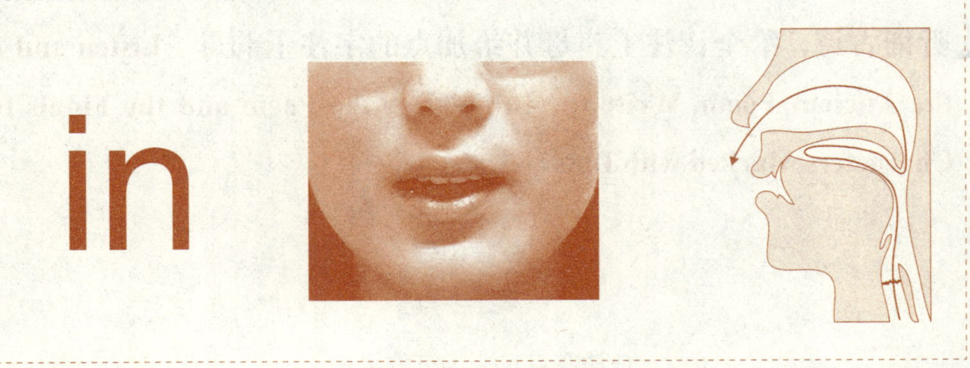

2. 发音特点 Characteristics of Pronunciation

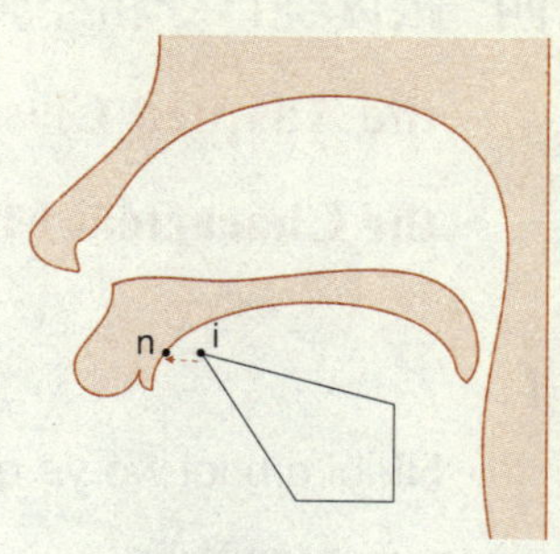

图 3-21 元音 in 的发音舌位变化示意简图
Figure 3-21 The varied places of tongue, illustrating how to articulate vowel in

in [in] 发音时，由 i 过渡到前鼻辅音 n。

in [in] When in is pronounced, the sound glides from i to front nasal n.

二 听读词语 Listen and Read the Following Words

因	yīn	reason
银	yín	silver
引	yǐn	quote
印	yìn	print
金印	jīnyìn	golden seal
贫民	pínmín	the poor
辛勤	xīnqín	hardworking
邻近	línjìn	near

【提示】

“in”单独成音节时，“in”前加“y”，如“因（yīn）”。

三 速读短语，注意加点字的韵母 Read Phrases Quickly, Pay Attention to the Finals of the Characters Marked with Dots

因人成事	yīn rén chéng shì	depend on others for success in one' s work
寅吃卯粮	yín chī mǎo liáng	eat the food the next of year; live beyond one' s income
引火烧身	yín huǒ shāo shēn	draw fire against/on oneself; “to draw fire” to oneself — to bring trouble to oneself
饮水思源	yín shuǐ sī yuán	When drinking water, think of its source. / While living in happiness, keep mind the source of it.

【提示】

引火烧身（yǐn huǒ shāo shēn），读“yín huǒ shāo shēn”；饮水思源（yǐn shuǐ sī yuán），读“yín shuǐ sī yuán”；这都是三声字连读时的变调现象。

四　跟读绕口令和经典选文，注意加点字的韵母 Read the Tongue Twister and the Adapted Classic Following the Teacher, Pay Attention to the Finals of the Characters Marked with Dots

1.

Nǐ lái qín lái wó yě qín,shēngchǎn tóngxīn tǔ biàn jīn. Dàjiā dōu shì qīn xiōngdì, xīn xīn xiāng yìn tuánjié jǐn.

你来勤来我也勤，生产同心土变金。大家都是亲兄弟，心心相印团结紧。

2.

Guān jīn yí jiàn gǔ, wú gǔ bù chéng jīn.

观今宜鉴古，无古不成今。

——《增广贤文》

【提示】

观察当今社会，应以古代为镜子加以借鉴。

3.

Yòu ér xué, zhuàng ér xíng, shàng zhì jūn, xià zé mín.

幼儿学，壮而行，上致君，下泽民。

——《三字经》

【提示】

幼年志在求学，长大之后步入社会就要学以致用，将自己的学问反馈给社会。上报国家，下为苍生造福。

五　听诵古诗，给全诗注上声母并给加点的字注上韵母 Listen and Recite the Ancient Poem, Write the Initials for the Poem and the Finals for the Characters Marked with Dots

送杜少府之任蜀州

唐·王勃

城阙辅三秦，风烟望五津。
与君离别意，同是宦游人。
海内存知己，天涯若比邻。
无为在歧路，儿女共沾巾。

【提示】

该诗是送别诗的名作，诗意在慰勉朋友勿在离别之时悲伤。诗中“海内存知己，天涯若比邻”成为朋友之间表达情谊的名句。

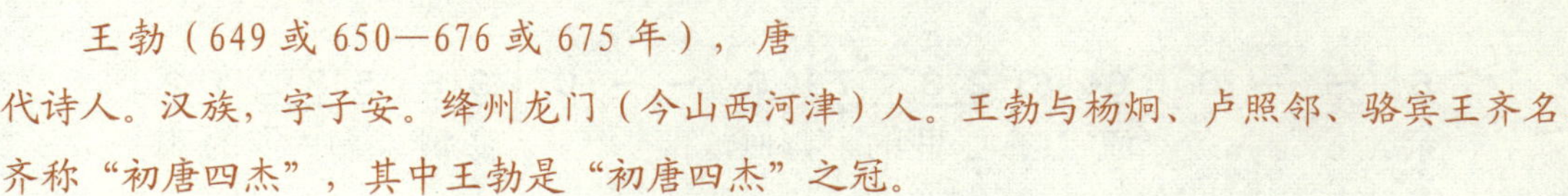

王勃（649或650—676或675年），唐代诗人。汉族，字子安。绛州龙门（今山西河津）人。王勃与杨炯、卢照邻、骆宾王齐名，齐称“初唐四杰”，其中王勃是“初唐四杰”之冠。

六 听歌学汉语，注意歌词中加点字的韵母 Learn Chinese by Listening to the Song, Pay Attention to the Finals of the Characters Marked with Dots

我的中国心

1=^{b}B $\frac{4}{4}$

黄霑 词
王福龄 曲

(3 – 6 – | i 76 3 i | 6 – – – | 6 – – –) |

3 – 3 – | 2 32 i 7 | 6 – – – | 6 – – – |

6· 32 31 7 | 6 – – 0 | 36 53 2 12 | 3 – – 35 |
河 山只在我梦 萦， 祖国 已多年未亲 近， 可是

6· 76 53 2 | 11 23 – | 2· 376 5 | 6 – – 0 |
不 管怎样也改 变不 了， 我 的中 国 心。

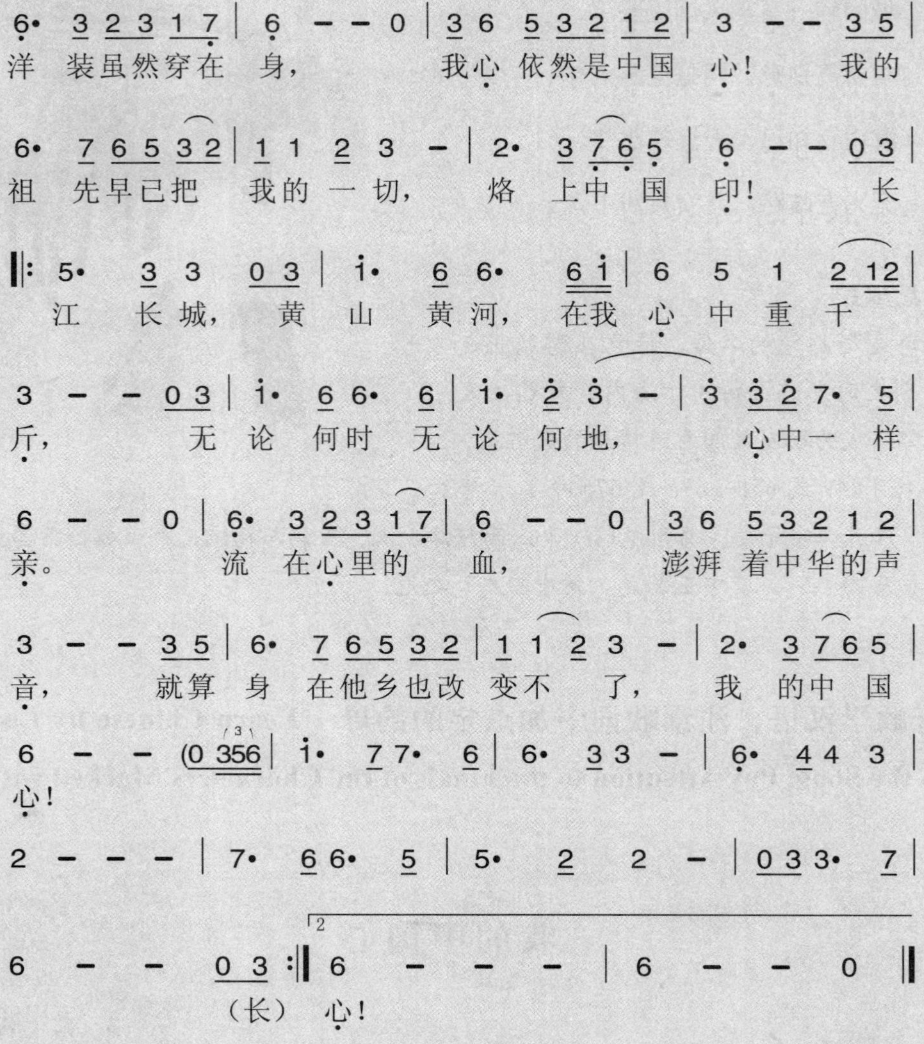

6· 3 2 3 1 7 | 6 – – 0 | 3 6 5 3 2 1 2 | 3 – – 3 5 |
洋 装虽然穿在 身， 我心 依然是中国 心！ 我的

6· 7 6 5 3 2 | 1 1 2 3 – | 2· 3 7 6 5 | 6 – – 0 3 |
祖 先早已把 我的 一 切， 烙 上中 国 印！ 长

‖: 5· 3 3 0 3 | i· 6 6· 6 i | 6 5 1 2 1 2 |
江 长城， 黄 山 黄 河， 在我 心 中 重 千

3 – – 0 3 | i· 6 6· 6 | i· 2 3 – | 3 3 2 7· 5 |
斤， 无 论 何时 无 论 何 地， 心中一 样

6 – – 0 | 6· 3 2 3 1 7 | 6 – – 0 | 3 6 5 3 2 1 2 |
亲。 流 在心里的 血， 澎湃 着中华的声

3 – – 3 5 | 6· 7 6 5 3 2 | 1 1 2 3 – | 2· 3 7 6 5 |
音， 就算 身 在他乡也改 变不 了， 我 的中 国

6 – – (0 356 | i· 7 7· 6 | 6· 3 3 – | 6· 4 4 3 |
心！

2 – – – | 7· 6 6· 5 | 5· 2 2 – | 0 3 3· 7 |

6 – – 0 3 :‖ [2] 6 – – – | 6 – – 0 ‖
（长） 心！

uen

一 语音视听 Audio-visual Pronunciation

1. 发音示意图 Diagrammatic Sketch of Pronunciation

2. 发音特点 Characteristics of Pronunciation

uen [uən]（un）发音时，由 u 过渡到 e 再到前鼻辅音 n。在同声母拼合时，省去 e，可自成音节，写作 wen。

uen [uən] When uen (un) is pronounced, the sound glides from u to e then to front nasal n, but leave out "e" when combining with other initials. It can stand alone as a syllable, written as wen.

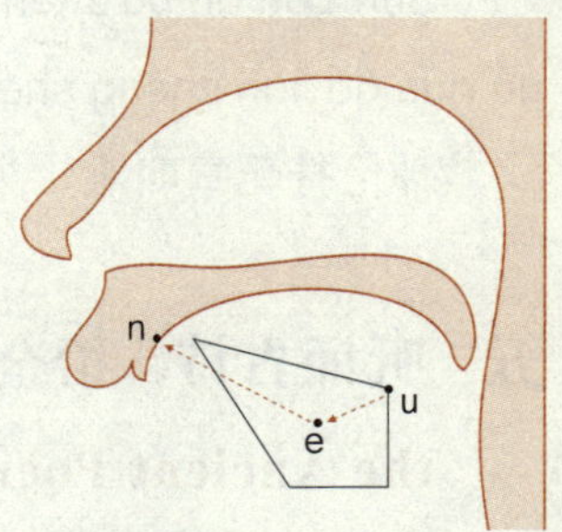

图 3-22 元音 uen 的发音舌位变化示意简图
Figure 3-22 The varied places of tongue, illustrating how to articulate vowel uen

二 听读词语 Listen and Read the Following Words

温	wēn	warm
文	wén	art
稳	wěn	stable
问	wèn	ask
温顺	wēnshùn	obedient
昆仑	Kūnlún	Kunlun Mountain
春笋	chūnsǔn	bamboo shoots in spring

【提示】

“uen”单独成音节，“u”变成“w”，如“温（wēn）”。“uen”在与辅音声母相拼时，写成“un”，调号在“u”上。如“昆仑（kūnlún）”。

三 速读短语，注意加点字的韵母 Read Phrases Quickly, Pay Attention to the Finals of the Characters Marked with Dots

温故知新	wēn gù zhī xīn	gain some knowledge by reviewing old
文从字顺	wén cóng zì shùn	readable and fluent
稳操胜券	wěn cāo shèngquàn	be certain (or confident) of success
问长问短	wèn cháng wèn duǎn	when showing one' s concern for sb.; make detailed enquires

四 跟读绕口令，注意句中加点字的韵母 Read the Tongue Twister Following the Teacher, Pay Attention to the Finals of the Characters Marked with Dots

Sūn Lún dá bǎ zhēn jiào zhǔn, bàn dūn shèjìn bǎ zhōngxīn. Běn shì bànlù xuéyì rén, mō pá gún dǎ lián chéng shén.

孙伦打靶真叫难，半蹲射进靶中心。本是半路学艺人，摸爬滚打连成神。

五 听诵古诗，给全诗注上声母并给加点的字注上韵母 Listen and Recite the Ancient Poem, Write the Initials for the Poem and the Finals for the Characters Marked with Dots

清明

唐·杜牧

清明时节雨纷纷，路上行人欲断魂。
借问酒家何处去，牧童遥指杏花村。

【提示】

该诗描绘了一幅《雨中问路图》，借清明的景物抒发思乡的内心。

清明：二十四节气之一。在每年的4月4日或4月5、6日。清明是表征物候的节气，含有天气晴朗、草木繁茂的意思。清明这天，民间有踏青、寒食、扫墓等习俗。

杏花村：位于安徽省池州市城西，古时曾有“十里烟村一色红，村酒村花两共幽”的佳境记载，是全国唯一以村建志书的村。古时的杏花村，村内茅屋酒帘，亭台楼榭，十里杏花、灿若红霞，是历代仕宦文人赏花沽酒之地。

ün

一 语音视听 Audio-visual Pronunciation

1. 发音示意图 Diagrammatic Sketch of Pronunciation

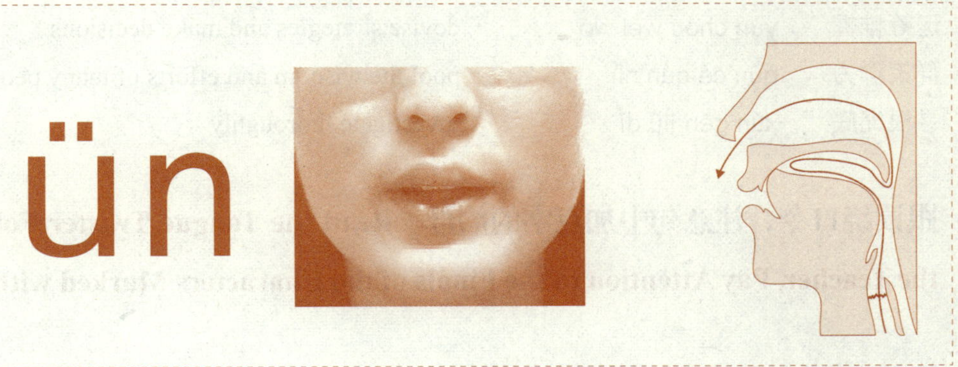

2. 发音特点 Characteristics of Pronunciation

ün [yn] 发音时，由ü过渡到前鼻辅音n。

ün [yn] When ün is pronounced, the sound glides from ü to front nasal n.

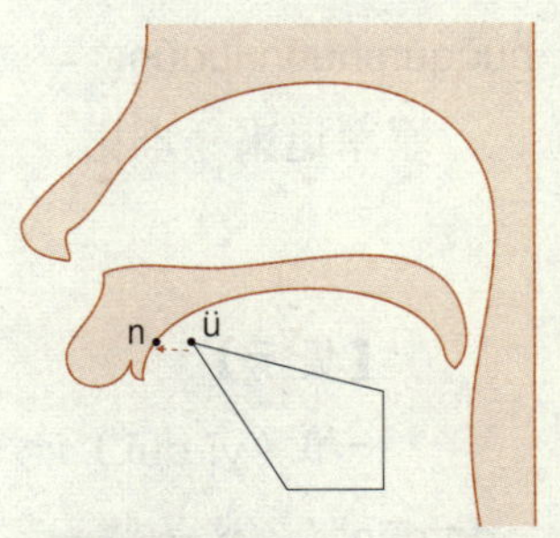

图3-23 元音ün的发音舌位变化示意简图

Figure 3-23 The varied places of tongue, illustrating how to articulate vowel ün

二 听读词语 Listen and Read the Following Words

晕	yūn	faint
云	yún	cloud

允	yǔn	allow
运	yùn	transport
军训	jūnxùn	military training
均匀	jūnyún	well-distributed
逡巡	qūnxún	to hang back

【提示】

"ün"单独成音节时，"ü"前加"y"，加"y"后"ü"上两点省写。如"晕（yūn）"。"ün"一般与辅音声母"j、q、x"相拼后"ü"上两点省写。如"军训（jūnxùn）"。

三 速读短语，注意加点字的韵母 Read Phrases Quickly, Pay Attention to the Finals of the Characters Marked with Dots

晕头转向	yūn tóu zhuàn xiàng	dizzy; giddy; muddle-headed
芸芸众生	yún yún zhòng shēng	all living things
运筹帷幄	yùn chóu wéi wò	devise strategies and make decisions
群策群力	qún cè qún nlì	pool the wisdom and efforts of many people
寻根究底	xún gēn jiū dǐ	investigate thoroughly

四 跟读绕口令，注意句中加点字的韵母 Read the Tongue Twister Following the Teacher, Pay Attention to the Finals of the Characters Marked with Dots

Jūnjun yùnlai yì duī qún, yísè jūnyòng lǜsè qún. Jūnxùn nǚshēng yí dà qún, huàn xià huāqún huàn lǜqún.

军军运来一堆裙，一色军用绿色群。军训女生一大群，换下花裙换绿裙。

【提示】

一堆（yī duī）读"yì duī"；一色（yīsè）读"yísè"；一大群（yī dà qún）读"yí dà qún"，这是"一"的变调现象。

五 听诵古诗，给全诗注上声母并给加点的字注上韵母 Listen and Recite the Ancient Poem, Write the Initials for the Poem and the Finals for the Characters Marked with Dots

宿新市徐公店

宋 · 杨万里

篱落疏疏一径深，
树头新绿未成阴。
儿童急走追黄蝶，
飞入菜花无处寻。

【提示】

这首诗运用白描手法，平易自然，形象鲜明。杨万里为官清廉，曾遭奸相嫉恨，被罢官后长期村居，对农村生活十分熟悉，描写自然真切感人，别有风趣。

篱落：篱笆。

ang

一 语音视听 Audio-visual Pronunciation

1. 发音示意图 Diagrammatic Sketch of Pronunciation

2. 发音特点 Characteristics of Pronunciation

ang [ɑŋ] 发音时，由 ɑ 过渡到后鼻辅音 ng。

ang [ɑŋ] When ɑng is pronounced, the sound glides from ɑ to back nasal ng.

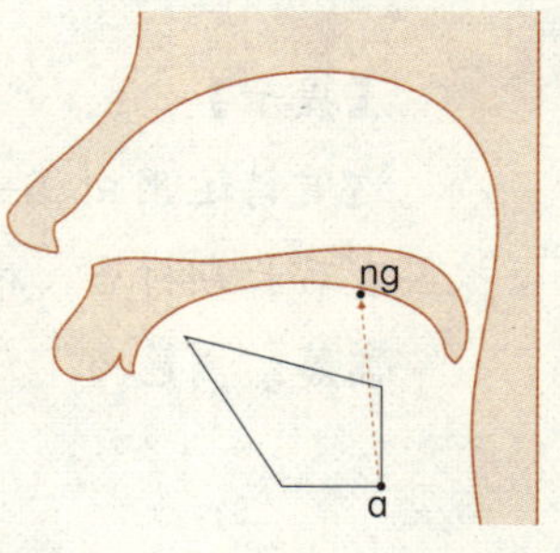

图 3-24 元音 ɑng 的发音舌位变化示意简图
Figure 3-24 The varied places of tongue, illustrating how to articulate vowel ɑng

二 听读词语 Listen and Read the Following Words

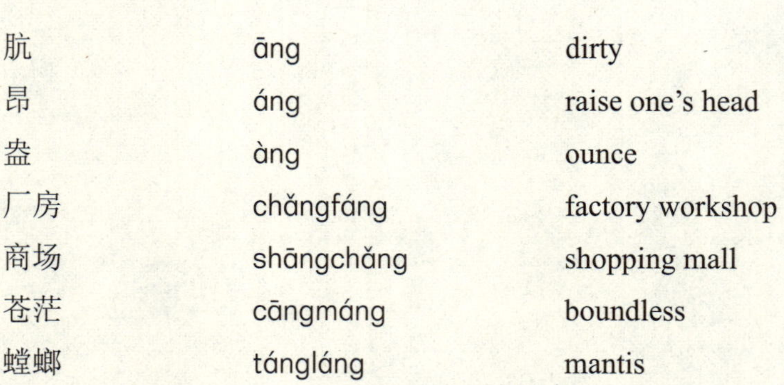

肮	āng	dirty
昂	áng	raise one's head
盎	àng	ounce
厂房	chǎngfáng	factory workshop
商场	shāngchǎng	shopping mall
苍茫	cāngmáng	boundless
螳螂	tángláng	mantis

三 速读短语，注意加点字的韵母 Read Phrases Quickly, Pay Attention to the Finals of the Characters Marked with Dots

长话短说	cháng huà duǎn shuō	make a short of long; make a long story short
当务之急	dāng wù zhī jí	most pressing matter of the moment
刚柔相济	gāng róu xiāng jì	couple hardness with softness (in dealing with people)
忙里偷闲	máng lǐ tōu xián	snatch a little of leisure from a busy life

四 跟读绕口令，注意句中加点字的韵母 Read the Tongue Twister Following the Teacher, Pay Attention to the Finals of the Characters Marked with Dots

1.

Chángchéng cháng,chéngqiáng cháng,cháng cháng Chángchéng cháng chéngqiáng,chéngqiáng cháng cháng chéng cháng cháng.

长城长，城墙长，长长长城长城墙，城墙长长城长长。

2.

Cǎi Bīngláng（jiéxuǎn）

Yīn Yìqiū

Gāogāo de shù shang jiē bīngláng,
Shuí xiān pá shàng shuí xiān cháng,
Shuí xiān pá shàng wǒ tì shuí xiān zhuāng,
Shàonián láng a cǎi bīngláng,
Xiǎo mèimei tílán táitóu wàng,
Dī tóu xiǎng yòu xiǎng a,
Tā yòu měi tā yòu zhuàng,
Shuí rén bǐ tā qiáng,
Gǎnmáng lái jiào shēng wǒ de láng a!
Qīngshān gāo a liúshuǐ cháng,
Nà tàiyáng yǐ cán,
Nà guīniǎo zài chàng,
Jiào wóliǎ gǎnkuài huí jiāxiāng!

采槟榔（节选）
殷忆秋

高高的树上结槟榔，
谁先爬上谁先尝，
谁先爬上我替谁先装。
少年郎啊采槟榔，
小妹妹提篮抬头望，
低头想又想啊，
他又美他又壮，
谁人比他强，
赶忙来叫声我的郎啊！
青山高啊流水长，
那太阳已残，
那归鸟在唱，
教我俩赶快回家乡！

【提示】

槟榔：一种常绿乔木，一般生长在季雨林中，喜温、喜湿。具有独特的御瘴功能，是历代医家治病的药果，又有“洗瘴丹”的别名。

五　听诵古诗，给全诗注上声母并给加点的字注上韵母 Listen and Recite the Poem, Write the Initials for the Poem and the Finals for the Characters Marked with Dots

秋浦歌
唐·李白

白发三千丈，缘愁似个长。
不知明镜里，何处得秋霜。

【提示】

秋浦：在今安徽池州市贵池区西南。唐时是著名产铜、银的地方。

缘：因为。

秋霜：秋天的白霜，这里用来形容白发。

个：这般。

缘：因为。

这首诗采用浪漫夸张的手法，抒发了诗人怀才不遇的苦闷之情。

iang

一 语音视听 Audio-visual Pronunciation

1. 发音示意图 Diagrammatic Sketch of Pronunciation

iang

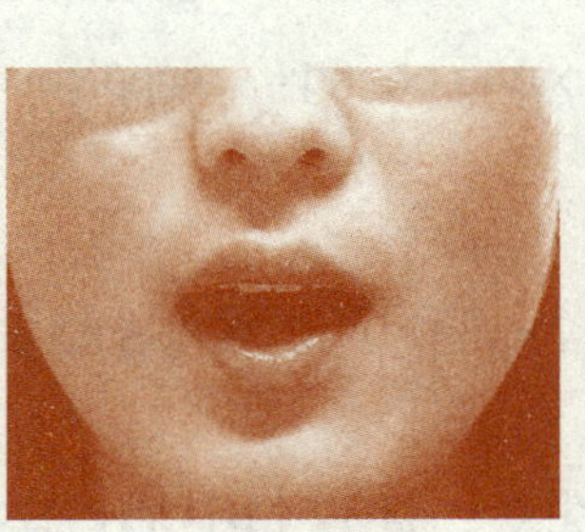

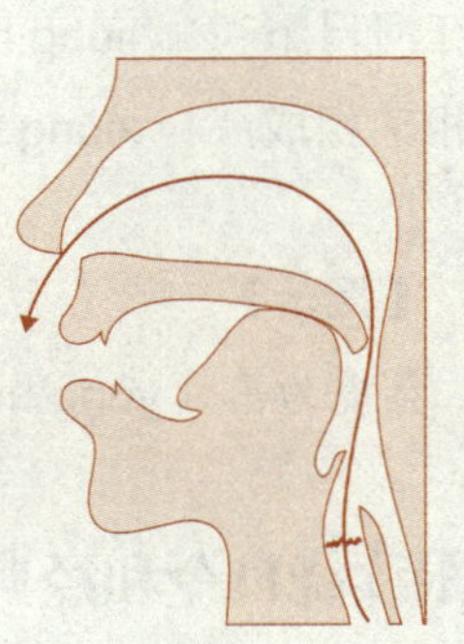

2. 发音特点 Characteristics of Pronunciation

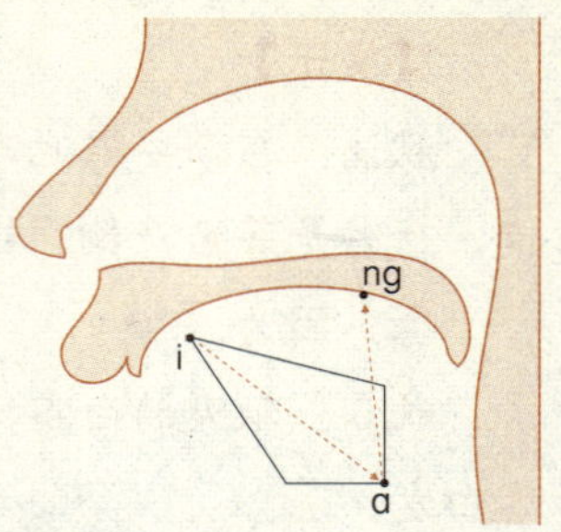

图 3-25 元音 iang 的发音舌位变化示意简图
Figure 3-25 The varied places of tongue, illustrating how to articulate vowel iang

iang [iaŋ] 发音时，由 i 过渡到 ɑ 再到后鼻辅音 ng。

iang [iaŋ] When iang is pronounced, the sound glides from i to ɑ then to back nasal ng.

二 听读词语 Listen and Read the Following Words

秧	yāng	seeding
羊	yáng	sheep
养	yǎng	raise
样	yàng	example
洋枪	yángqiāng	foreign rifles
强将	qiángjiàng	a good general
两辆	liǎng liàng	two (cars)
江洋	jiāng yáng	rivers and seas

【提示】
"iang"单独成音节。"i"变成"y"。如"秧（yāng）"。

三 速读短语，注意加点字的韵母 Read Phrases Quickly, Pay Attention to the Finals of the Characters Marked with Dots

扬长避短	yáng cháng bì duǎn	show one' s strong points and hide one' s weaknesses
仰人鼻息	yǎng rén bí xī	be dependent on the whims of others
养虎遗患	yáng hǔ yí huàn	appeasement brings disaster
江河日下	jiāng hé rì xià	go from bad to worse
相辅相成	xiāng fǔ xiāng chéng	supplement and complement each other

【提示】
养虎为患（yǎng hǔ yí huàn），读"yáng hǔ yí huàn"。

四 跟读绕口令和经典选文，注意句中加点字的韵母 Read the Tongue Twister and the Adapted Classic Following the Teacher, Pay Attention to the Finals of the Characters Marked with Dots

Jiǎng jiā yáng, jiǎ jiā qiáng, jiǎng jiā yáng zhuàngdǎo le jiǎ jiā qiáng, jiǎ jiā qiáng yāsǐ le jiǎng jiā yáng, jiǎ jiā yào jiǎng jiā péi qiáng, jiǎng jiā yào jiǎ jiā péi yáng.

蒋家羊，贾家墙，蒋家羊撞倒了贾家墙，贾家墙压死了蒋家羊，贾家要蒋家赔墙，蒋家要贾家赔羊。

五　听诵古诗，给全诗注上声母并给加点的字注上韵母 Listen and Recite the Ancient Poem, Write the Initials of the Characters and the Finals for the Characters Marked with Dots

闻官军收河南河北

唐·杜甫

剑外忽传收蓟北，初闻涕泪满衣裳。
却看妻子愁何在，漫卷诗书喜欲狂。
白日放歌须纵酒，青春作伴好还乡。
即从巴峡穿巫峡，便下襄阳向洛阳。

【提示】

此诗极自然地写出了所有遭受战乱离乡人的共同感受，抒发了听到胜利时难以抑制的喜悦之情，是首流传千古的抒情名篇。

uang

一 语音视听 Audio-visual Pronunciation

1. 发音示意图 Diagrammatic Sketch of Pronunciation

2. 发音特点 Characteristics of Pronunciation

uang [uaŋ] 发音时，由 u 过渡到 a 再过渡到后鼻辅音 ng。

uang [uaŋ] When uang is pronounced, the sound glides from u to a then to back nasal ng.

图 3-26 元音 uang 的发音舌位变化示意简图
Figure 3-26 The varied places of tongue, illustrating how to articulate vowel uang

二 听读词语 Listen and Read the Following Words

汪	wāng	vast
王	wáng	a surname
网	wǎng	net
忘	wàng	forget
狂妄	kuángwàng	arrogant
矿床	kuàngchuáng	mineral deposit
装潢	zhuānghuáng	decorate
双簧	shuānghuáng	oboe

【提示】
“uang” 单独成音节时，“u” 变成 “w”，如汪（wāng）。

三 速读短语，注意加点字的韵母 Read Phrases Quickly, Pay Attention to the Finals of the Characters Marked with Dots

汪洋大海	wāngyáng dà hǎi	(of sea) immense
亡羊补牢	wáng yáng bǔ láo	take remedial measure after loss is done to prevent further losses; better late than never
网开一面	wǎng kāi yí miàn	give the wrongdoer a way out; put sb. on the way of escaping
忘乎所以	wàng hū suǒ yǐ	be carried away; be swollen-headed

【提示】

一面（yī miàn），读“yí miàn”。这是“一”的变调现象。

四 跟读绕口令，注意句中加点字的韵母 Read the Tongue Twister Following the Teacher, Pay Attention to the Finals of the Characters Marked with Dots

Wángzhuāng mài kuāng,Kuāngzhuāng mài wǎng, Wángzhuāng mài kuāng bú mài wǎng,Kuāngzhuāng mài wǎng bú mài kuāng.

王庄卖筐，匡庄卖网，王庄卖筐不卖网，匡庄卖网不卖筐。

【提示】

“王庄（Wángzhuāng）”“匡庄（Kuāngzhuāng）”中的“王”和“匡”是姓，在汉语拼音拼写时第一个字母需要大写。

不卖（bù mài），读“bú mài”，这是“不”的变调现象。

五 听诵古诗，给全诗注上声母并给加点的字注上韵母 Listen and Recite the Poem, Write the Initials for the Poem and the Finals for the Characters Marked with Dots

木兰诗（节选）

开我东阁门，坐我西间床。脱我战时袍，著我旧时裳。当窗理云鬓，对镜帖花黄。出门看伙伴，伙伴皆惊惶。同行十二年，不知木兰是女郎。

【提示】

《木兰诗》是一首歌咏女英雄木兰代父从军出征的叙事诗。本文节选的是她参战取得胜利后，回到家中时的喜悦情景。全诗千百年来始终流传不绝。

eng

一　语音视听　Audio-visual Pronunciation

1. 发音示意图　Diagrammatic Sketch of Pronunciation

eng

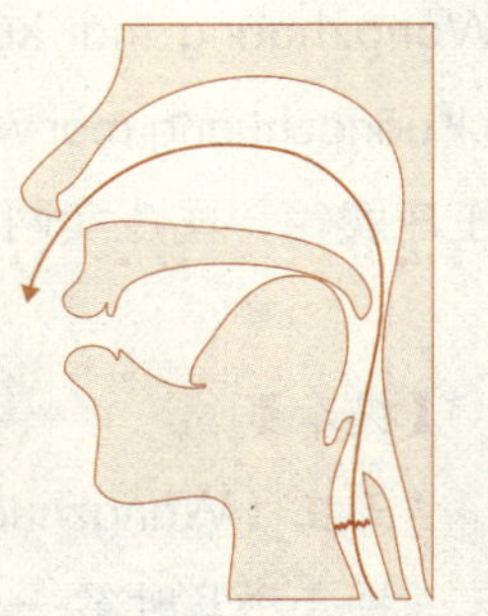

2. 发音特点　Characteristics of Pronunciation

eng [əŋ]　发音时，由 e 过渡到后鼻辅音 ng。

eng [əŋ]　When eng is pronounced, the sound glides from e to back nasal ng.

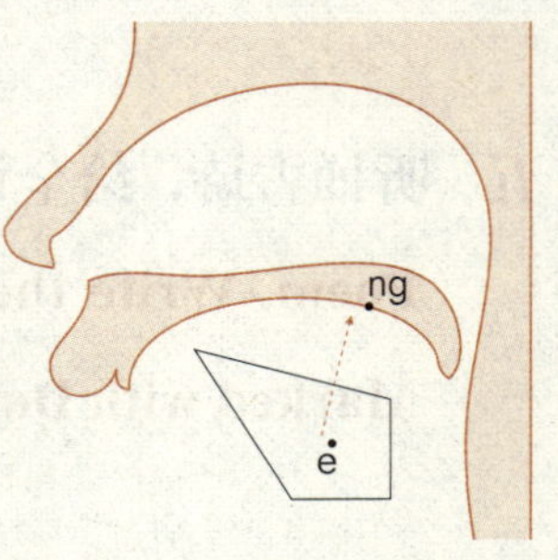

图 3-27 元音 eng 的发音舌位变化示意简图

Figure 3-27 The varied places of tongue, illustrating how to articulate vowel eng

二 听读词语 Listen and Read the Following Words

崩	bēng	collapse
腾	téng	jump
耿	gěng	bright or upright
政	zhèng	political
更冷	gèng lěng	colder
征程	zhēngchéng	journey
风筝	fēngzheng	kite
增生	zēngshēng	proliferate

三 速读短语，注意加点字的韵母 Read Phrases Quickly, Pay Attention to the Finals of the Characters Marked with Dots

层出不穷	céng chū bù qióng	emerge in an endless stream; appear one after another
等而下之	děng ér xià zhī	from that grade down; lower down
梦幻泡影	mèng huàn pào yǐng	(fig.) empty and easily shattered fantasy
碰一鼻子灰	pèng yì bízi huī	be snubbed;be slighted

【提示】

碰一鼻子灰（pèng yībízi huī），读“pèng yì bízi huī”。这是“一”的变调现象。

四 跟读经典选文，注意加点字的韵母 Read the Adapted Classic Following the Teacher, Pay attention to the Finals of the Characters Marked with Dots

Jì kāngzǐ wèn zhèng yú Kǒngzǐ. Kǒngzǐ duì yuē: “Zhèngzhě, zhèng yě. Zǐ shuài yǐ zhèng, shú gǎn bú zhèng.”

季康子问政于孔子。孔子对曰：“政者，正也。子帅以正，孰敢不正？”

——《论语 · 颜渊篇》

【提示】

政：公正。 子：指季康子，你。 帅：带头，指领导者。 孰：谁，哪一个。

五　听诵古诗，给全诗注上声母并给加点的字注上韵母 Listen and Recite the Ancient Poem, Write the Initials for the Poem and the Finals for the Characters Marked with Dots

1.

离离原上草

唐 · 白居易

离离原上草，一岁一枯荣。
野火烧不尽，春风吹又生。

【提示】

这首诗是通过对古原上野草的描绘，抒发送别友人时的依依惜别之情。

白居易（772—846），唐代诗人，字乐天，号香山居士，祖籍太原，晚年官至太子少傅，谥号“文”，世称白傅、白文公。他在文学上积极倡导新乐府运动，主张“文章合为时而著，歌诗合为事而作”。

2.

赠从弟（其二）

魏 · 刘桢

亭亭山上松，瑟瑟谷中风。
风声一何盛，松枝一何劲。
冰霜正惨凄，终岁常端正。
岂不罹凝寒，松柏有本性。

【提示】

全诗以物喻人，以挺立高山之上，敢于抗迎风寒、冰霜的松树比堂弟，鼓励他坚守刚强不屈的品格，不要屈服于外力。

刘桢（186—217），字公干，东平（今山东东平县）人，东汉著名文学家，“建安七子”之一。他的五言诗写得有气势，语言质朴，不重雕饰，平畅中显示出刚劲清新的风格。

ing

一 语音视听 Audio-visual Pronunciation

1. 发音示意图 Diagrammatic Sketch of Pronunciation

ing

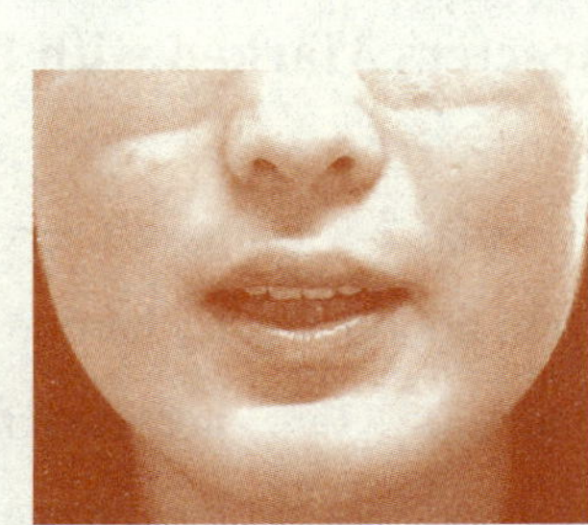

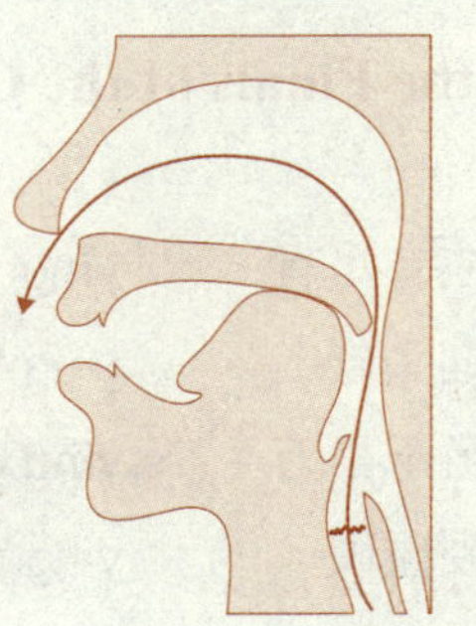

2. 发音特点 Characteristics of Pronunciation

ing [iŋ] 发音时，由 i 过渡到后鼻辅音 ng。

ing [iŋ] When ing is pronounced, the sound glides from i to back nasal ng.

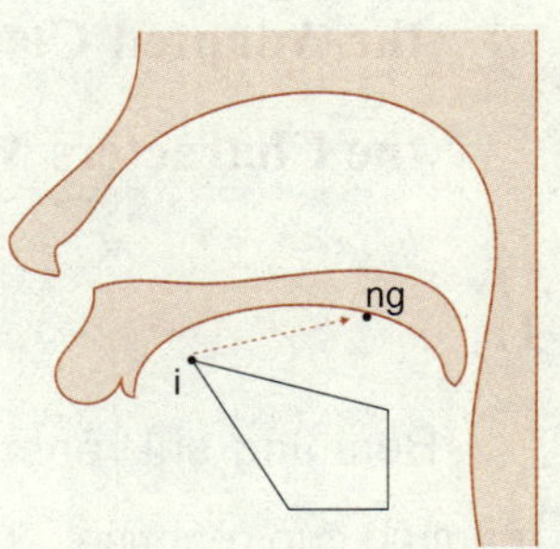

图 3-28 元音 ing 的发音舌位变化示意简图
Figure 3-28 The varied places of tongue, illustrating how to articulate vowel ing

二 听读词语 Listen and Read the Following Words

英	yīng	English
迎	yíng	welcome
影	yǐng	shadow
硬	yìng	hard
评定	píngdìng	evaluate
倾听	qīngtīng	listen
命令	mìnglìng	order
叮咛	dīngníng	exhort

【提示】

"ing"单独成音节时，在"i"前加"y"。如英（yīng）。

三 速读短语，注意加点字的韵母 Read Phrases Quickly, Pay Attention to the Finals of the Characters Marked with Dots

应有尽有	yīng yǒu jìn yǒu	have everything that one could wish for
迎头赶上	yíng tóu gǎn shàng	try hard to catch up (with those ahead)
盈千累万	yíng qiān lěi wàn	in a great number
硬碰硬	yìng pèng yìng	meet force with force

四 跟读绕口令和经典选文，注意加点字的韵母 Read the Tongue Twister and the Adapted Classic Following the Teacher, Pay Attention to the Finals of the Characters Marked with Dots

1.

Rènmìng shì rènmìng,rénmíng shì rénmíng,rènmìng rénmíng bù néng cuò,cuò le rénmíng cuò rènmìng.

任命是任命，人名是人名，任命人名不能错，错了人名错任命。

2.

Lù bù chǎn bù píng, shì bú wéi bù chéng, rén bú quàn bú shàn, zhōng bù qiāo bù míng.
路不铲不平，事不为不成，人不劝不善，钟不敲不鸣。

——《增广贤文》

【提示】

钟：古代打击乐器。盛行于青铜时代，不仅是乐器，还是象征地位和权力的礼器。王公贵族在朝聘、祭祀等各种仪典、宴飨与日常燕乐中，广泛使用着钟乐。

不劝（búquàn），读“búquàn”；不善（bù shàn），读“bú shàn”。这是“不”的变调现象。

五　听诵古诗，给全诗注上声母并给加点的字注上韵母 Listen and Recite the Poem, Write the Initials for the Poem and the Finals for the Characters Marked with Dots

正气歌（节选）

宋·文天祥

天地有正气，杂然赋流形。
下则为河岳，上则为日星。
于人曰浩然，沛乎塞苍冥。
皇路当清夷，含和吐明庭。
时穷节乃见，一一垂丹青。

【提示】

天地正气：意为形成万事万物的根源，体现在人身上则为浩然之气，也即气质、气节。
杂然：万事万物各有不同的形态。
赋：给予。
沛乎：充沛洋溢在无穷无尽的天地间。
苍冥：天空。
皇路：指朝政。国家的政治等局面。
清夷：国家清平安顺。

含和：有正气的人当朝执政，使国泰民安，和谐发展。

时穷：国家遇到困危时。

节乃见：公正廉洁刚毅的气节才能体现出来。

丹青：绘画。指对治理国家有杰出贡献的人物画像陈列表彰。

这首诗是南宋末宰相文天祥在元大都监狱中所作。全诗充分表现了诗人坚贞不屈的爱国情操。

文天祥，宋吉水人，字宋瑞，号文山。曾官为左丞相、信国公，时元兵入侵，举兵抗元，为元将所败，被俘解拘元都燕京三年，狱中作《正气歌》以明志，终不屈被杀。元世祖称其为“真男子”。

六　听歌学汉语，注意歌词中加点字的韵母　Learn Chinese by Listening to the Song, Pay Attention to the Finals of the Characters Marked with Dots

秋水伊人

1936年影片《古塔奇案》插曲

1= F $\frac{4}{4}$

贺绿汀　词曲

5 5 3　2　– | 2 3 1 2 3 7 6 5 | 5 5 5　5　– |
望穿秋　水，　不见伊人的倩　影，　更残漏　尽，
望断云　山，　不见妈妈的慈　颜，　漏尽更　残，

5 6 7 6 5 5 3　2　– | 3 2 3 2 7 6　5　0 3 2 3 | 5 5 6 5 3　1　– |
孤雁两三　声。　往日的温　情，　只换得　眼前的凄　清，
难对锦衾　寒。　往日的欢　乐，　只映出　眼前的孤　单，

5·　6　1 2　3 | 2 3 2 6 7 6　5　– | 6· 6 5 3 5 6· 7 6 |
梦　魂　无所　寄，　空有泪满　襟。　几　时归来　呀，
梦　魂　无所　依，　空有泪栏　杆。　几　时归来　呀，

5 6 5 3 5 － | 5 5 5 5 3 3 2 5 5 7 6 | 5· 6 7 7 7 7 6 |
伊 人 哟， 几时你会穿过那边的丛 林？ 那亭亭的塔
妈 妈 哟， 几时你会穿过故乡的家 园？ 这篱边的雏

2 － 6 7 6 3 5 4 3 | 2 － 3 3 3 2 5 5 | 3 2 7 6 － |
影， 点点的鸦 阵， 依旧是当年的 情 景。
菊， 空阶的落 叶， 依旧是当年的 庭 院。

6 6 6 6 5 3 5 6 5 6 7 | 6· 3 5· 5 6 5 3 2 | 1· 2 3 5 3 2 － |
只有你的女儿 哟， 已长得活 泼 天 真，
只有你的女儿 哟， 已堕入绝 望 的深 渊，

0 5 5 5 6 7 6 5 6 5 3 2· 3 | 5 5 3 2 3 3 2· 7 6 | 5 － － 0 ‖
只有你留下的女儿 哟，来 安慰我这 破 碎的 心。
只有你被弃的女儿 哟，在 忍受无尽的摧 残。

ueng

一 语音视听 Audio-visual Pronunciation

1. 发音示意图 Diagrammatic Sketch of Pronunciation

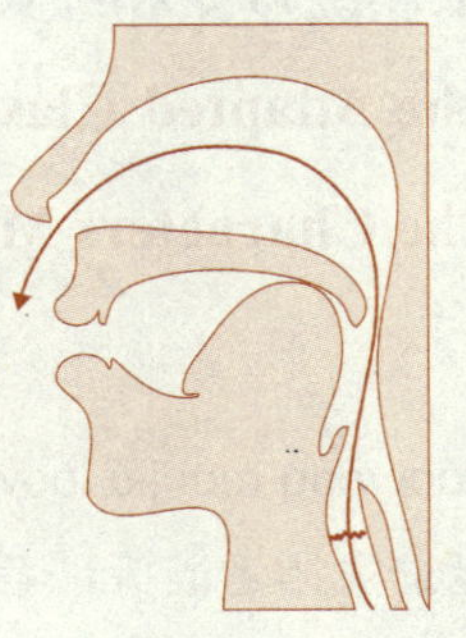

2. 发音特点 Characteristics of Pronunciation

ueng [uəŋ] 发音时，由 u 过渡到 e 再到后鼻辅音 ng。不拼声母能自成音节。

ueng [uəŋ] When ueng is pronounced, the sound glides from u to e then to back nasal ng. It can stand in consolation.

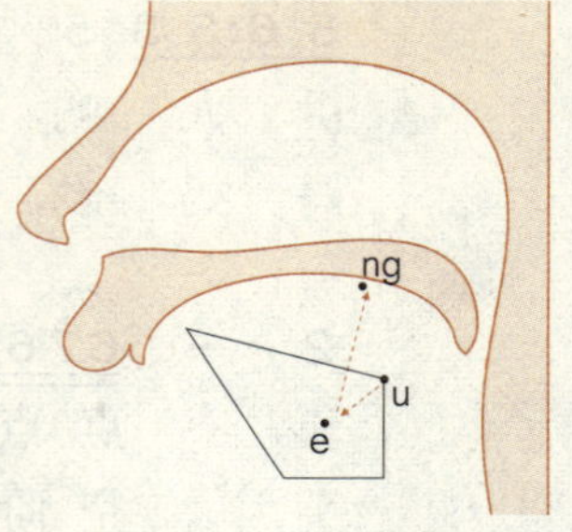

图 3-29 元音 ueng 的发音舌位变化示意简图
Figure 3-29 The varied places of tongue, illustrating how to articulate vowel ueng

二 听读词语 Listen and Read the Following Words

翁	wēng	old man
瓮	wèng	pot
老翁	lǎowēng	old man; greybeard
渔翁	yúwēng	old fisherman

【提示】
"ueng" 单独成音节时，"u" 变成 "w"。如翁（wēng）。

三 速读短语，注意加点字的韵母 Read Phrases Quickly, Pay Attention to the Finals of the Characters Marked with Dots

瓮中之鳖	wèng zhōng zhī biē	a turtle in the jar-bottle up; inescapable situation
请君入瓮	qǐng jūn rù wèng	treat sb. with the way he has devised against others

四 跟读绕口令和经典选文，注意加点字的韵母 Read the Tongue Twister and the Adapted Classic Following the Teacher, Pay Attention to the Finals of the Characters Marked with Dots

1.

Lǎowēng mài jiǔ lǎowēng mǎi, lǎowēng máijiǔ lǎowēng mài.
老翁卖酒老翁买，老翁买酒老翁卖。

2.

Rénshēng yíshì, cǎomù yìchūn. Hēifà bùzhī qín xué zǎo, zhuányǎn biàn shì báitóuwēng.
人生一世，草木一春。黑发不知勤学早，转眼便是白头翁。

【提示】

一世（yīshì），读“yíshì”；一春（yīchūn），读“yìchūn”。这是“一”的变调现象。

五　听诵古诗，给全诗注上声母并给加点的字注上韵母 Listen and Recite the Poem, Write the Initials for the Poem and the Finals for the Characters Marked with Dots

示儿

宋·陆游

死去元知万事空，但悲不见九州同。
王师北定中原日，家祭无忘告乃翁。

【提示】

这是陆游的绝笔。他在弥留之际，还念念不忘被女真贵族霸占着的中原领土和人民，热切地盼望着祖国的重新统一，因此他特地写这首诗作为遗嘱，谆谆告诫自己的儿子。从这里我们可以领会到诗人的爱国激情是何等的执著、深沉、热烈、真挚！

九州：《禹贡》中分中国为冀州、兖州、青州、徐州、扬州、荆州、豫州、梁州、雍州。一般情况下，“九州”泛指中国。

王师：朝廷的部队。

中原：历史上指包括河南省中北部，山西省南部，陕西省及山东省各一部分在内的黄河中下游地区，这里是中华文明的发源地，是华夏民族的摇篮。

祭：对死者表示追念的仪式。

翁：老人，这里指作者，作父亲解。

ong

一 语音视听 Audio-visual Pronunciation

1. 发音示意图 Diagrammatic Sketch of Pronunciation

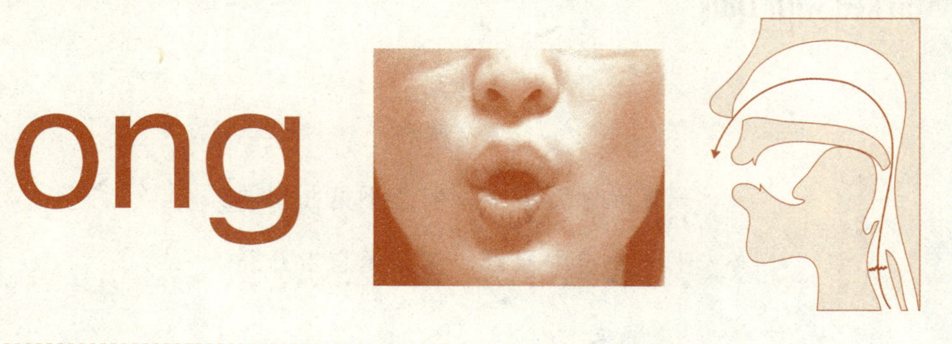

2. 发音特点 Characteristics of Pronunciation

ong [uŋ] 发音时，由 u 过渡到后鼻辅音 ng。不能自成音节，只能拼部分声母。

ong [uŋ] When ong is pronounced, the sound glides from u to the back nasal ng. It cannot stand in consolation, but can only spell with some of the initials.

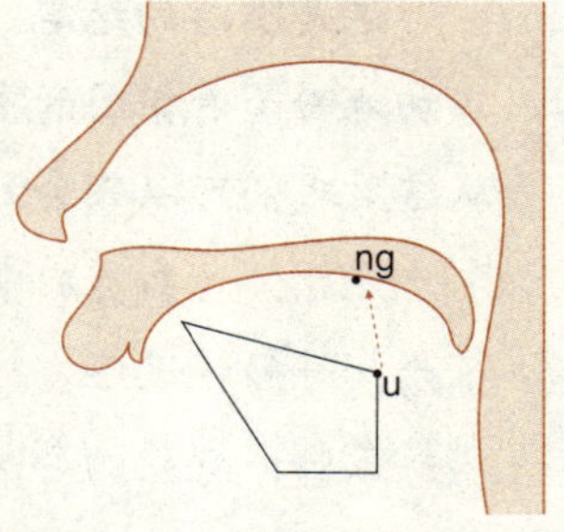

图 3-30 元音 ong 的发音舌位变化示意简图

Figure 3-30 The varied places of tongue, illustrating how to articulate vowel ong

二 听读词语 Listen and Read the Following Words

东	dōng	east
懂	dǒng	understand
动	dòng	act
冬宫	dōnggōng	winter palace
空桶	kōngtǒng	empty barrel
总统	zóngtǒng	president
从容	cóngróng	leisurely

【提示】

总统（zǒngtǒng），读“zóngtǒng”。两个三声字连读，第一个字读二声。

三　速读短语，注意加点字的韵母　Read Phrases Quickly, Pay Attention to the Finals of the Characters Marked with Dots

东倒西歪	dōng dǎo xī wāi	jumbled; in a mess
鸿门宴	Hóngményàn	a meeting contrived as a clearly trap
空口无凭	kōng kǒu wú píng	mere verbal statement without conclusive evidence
公报私仇	gōng bào sī chóu	abuse public power to retaliate against a personnel enemy

四　跟读绕口令，注意句中加点字的韵母　Read the Tongue Twister Following the Teacher, Pay Attention to the Finals of the Characters Marked with Dots

Chōngchong zāile shíkē sōng, sōngsong zāile shíkē cōng. Chōngchong shuō zāi sōng bù rú zāi cōng, sōngsong shuō zāi cōng bù rú zāi sōng.

冲冲栽了十棵松，松松栽了十棵葱。冲冲说栽松不如栽葱，松松说栽葱不如栽松。

五　听诵古诗，给全诗注上声母并给加点的字注上韵母　Listen and Recite the Poem, Write the Initials for the Poem and the Finals for the Characters Marked with Dots

题西林壁

宋 · 苏轼

横看成岭侧成峰，远近高低各不同。
不识庐山真面目，只缘身在此山中。

【提示】

西林：指庐山西林寺。

这首诗是作者苏轼游览庐山后的总结，它描写了庐山变化多姿的面貌，并借景说理，从中揭示一种生活哲理来启发读者的思考和领悟。这首绝句的长处不在于形象或感情，而在于富有理趣。

六 听歌学汉语，注意加点字的韵母 Learn Chinese by Listening to the Song, Pay Attention to the Finals of the Characters Marked with Dots.

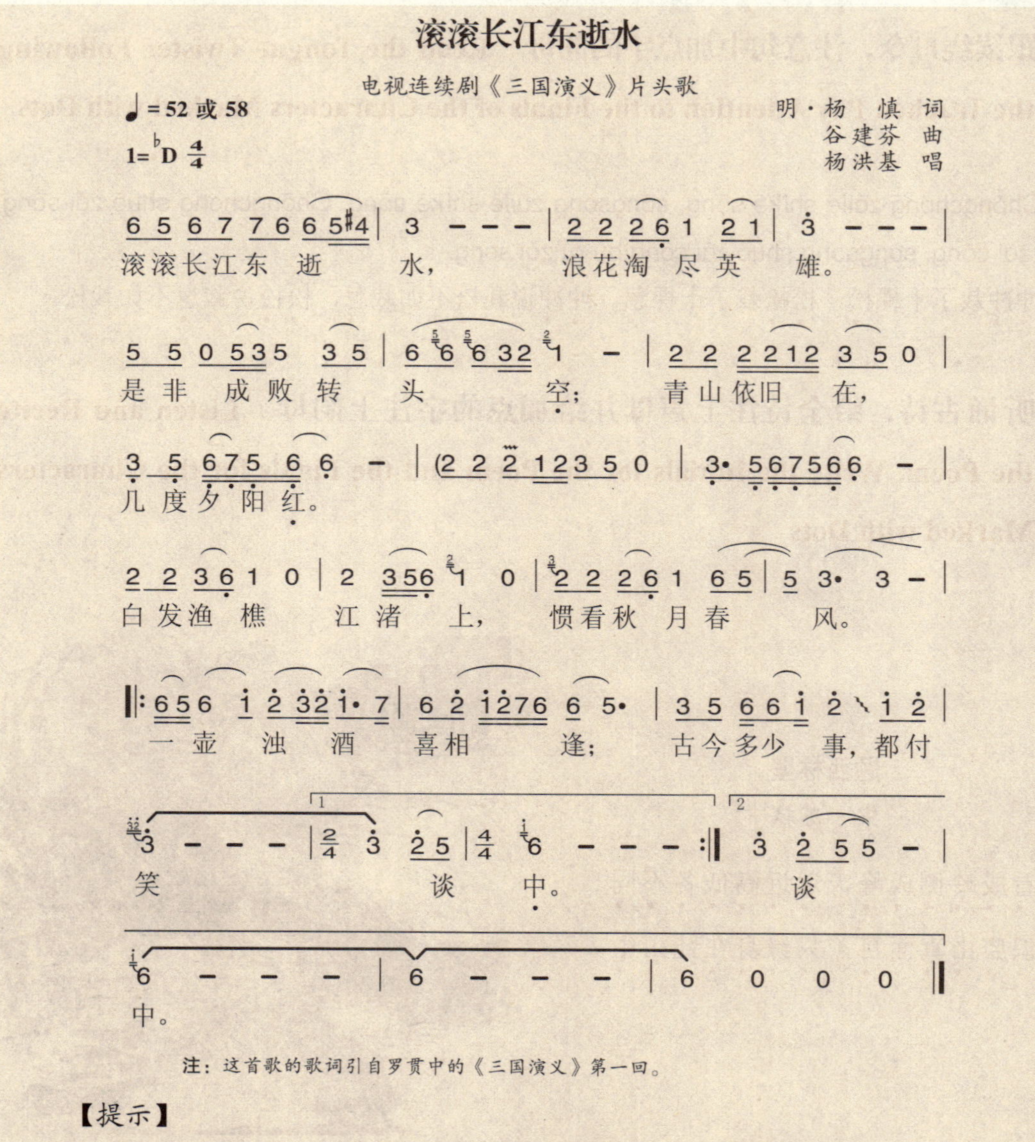

【提示】

歌词中“空（kōng）”“红（hóng）”“中（zhōng）”的韵母相同，押 ong 韵。

iong

一 语音视听 Audio-visual Pronunciation

1. 发音示意图 Diagrammatic Sketch of Pronunciation

2. 发音特点 Characteristics of Pronunciation

iong [yŋ] 发音时，由 ü 过渡到后鼻辅音 ng（io 在《汉语拼音方案》中标为两个字母，实际是偏后的 ü [y]）。

iong [yŋ] When iong is pronounced, the sound glides from ü to ng. (In *The scheme for the Chinese Phonetic Alphabet*, there are two letters in io, but actually, it is ü [y]).

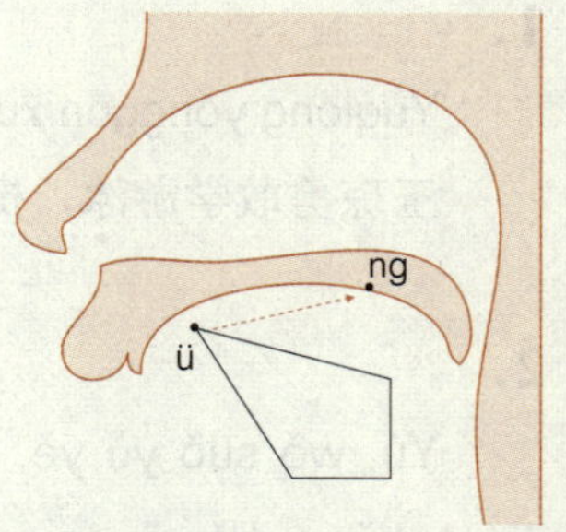

图 3-31 元音 iong 的发音舌位变化示意简图
Figure 3-31 The varied places of tongue, illustrating how to articulate vowel iong

二 听读词语 Listen and Read the Following Words

拥	yōng	embrace
永	yǒng	forever
用	yòng	use
雄熊	xióngxióng	male bear
汹涌	xiōngyǒng	swell
炯炯	jióngjiǒng	shining
茕茕	qióngqióng	lonely

【提示】

“iong”单独成音节时，“i”变成“y”。如“拥（yōng）”。

炯炯（jiǒngjiǒng），读“jióngjiǒng”。这是三声的变调现象。

三 速读短语，注意加点字的韵母 Read Phrases Quickly, Pay Attention to the Finals of the Characters Marked with Dots

拥政爱民	yōng zhèng ài mín	(of the army) support the government and cherish the people
永垂不朽	yǒng chuí bù xiǔ	(memory of sb' s name, deeds, spirit, etc) live forever
迥然不同	jiǒngrán bùtóng	far apart; vastly different
胸中有数	xiōng zhōng yǒu shù	know the situation and problem with certainty
雄才大略	xióng cái dà lüè	(a man of) great talent and bold vision

四 跟读绕口令和经典选文，注意加点字的韵母 Read the Tongue Twister and the Adapted Classic Following the Teacher, Pay Attention to the Finals of the Characters Marked with Dots

1.

Yùqióng yónggǎn xué yóuyǒng, tǐngxiōng yángyǒng shì yīngxióng.

玉琼勇敢学游泳，挺胸仰泳是英雄。

2.

Yú, wǒ suǒ yù yě, xióngzhǎng yì wǒ suǒ yù yě; èrzhě bù kě dé jiān, shě yú ér qǔ xióngzhǎng zhě yě.

鱼，我所欲也，熊掌亦我所欲也；二者不可得兼，舍鱼而取熊掌者也。

——《孟子 · 告子上》

3.

Rén lǎo xīn bù lǎo, rén qióng zhì bù qióng. Rén wú bǎirì hǎo, huā wú bǎirì hóng.

人老心不老，人穷志不穷。人无百日好，花无百日红。

——《朱子家训》

五 听诵词，给词中加点字注上声母和韵母 Listen and Recite the *Ci* Poem, Write the Initials and the Finals for the Characters Marked with Dots

临江仙

明 · 杨慎

滚滚长江东逝水，浪花淘尽英雄。是非成败转头空。青山依旧在，几度夕阳红。白发渔樵江渚上，惯看秋月春风。一壶浊酒喜相逢。古今多少事，都付笑谈中。

选自《二十一史》弹词

【提示】

《临江仙》：词牌名。

这是一首咏史词。借叙述历史兴亡抒发人生感慨。

杨慎（1488—1559），字用修，别号升庵，原籍庐陵，元末迁居四川新都。因被流放到滇南，故自称“博南山人”“金马碧鸡老兵”。明代著名的学者、文学家。

长江：中国第一大河，古时简称江，六朝以后才有大江和长江之称。

复习二 分辨前鼻韵母和后鼻韵母

Revision 2
Distinguish the Front Nasal Finals and Back Nasal Finals

an，ian，uan，üan，en，in，uen，ün 八个鼻韵母都是由元音和前鼻辅音构成的，又叫前鼻尾韵。

These eight nasal finals an, ian, uan, üan, en, in, uen, ün are made up of vowels and front nasals, so they are also called front nasal end finals.

ang, iang, uang, eng, ing, ueng, ong, iong 八个韵母，都是由元音和后鼻辅音构成的，又叫后鼻尾韵。

ang, iang, uang, eng, ing, ueng, ong, iong, these eight finals are all composed by vowels and back nasal consonants, also called nasal ending.

部分方言中把普通话前鼻韵母 en, in, uen, ün 读作后鼻音韵母 eng, ing, ueng, iong，练学时要区分两组韵母发音部位和方法的不同。

In some dialects, the front nasal final syllable in *Putonghua*, such as en, in, uen, ün, are pronounced as back nasal finals eng, ing, ueng, ong. So when practising, one should distinguish between the two groups of final syllables in the place-of-articulation and manner-of-articulation.

n 与 ng 发音部位不同，n 是舌尖中、浊、鼻音，又叫前鼻音。ng 是舌根、浊鼻音，又叫后鼻音。

The places of articulation of n and ng are different. The former is an alveolar and voiced nasal, also called front nasal; while the latter is a velar and voiced nasal, called back nasal.

如图所示：

As the following diagrammatic sketch:

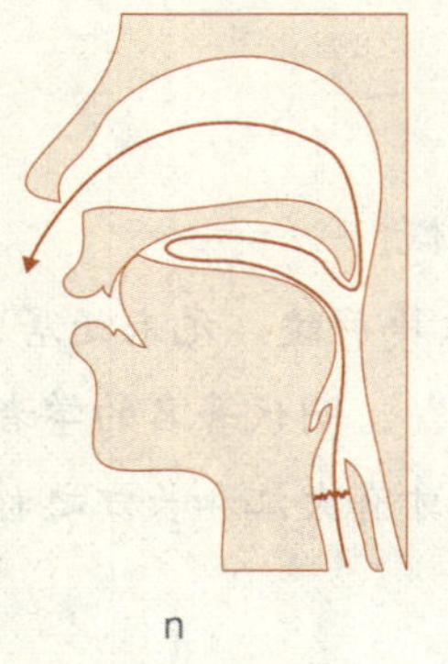
n

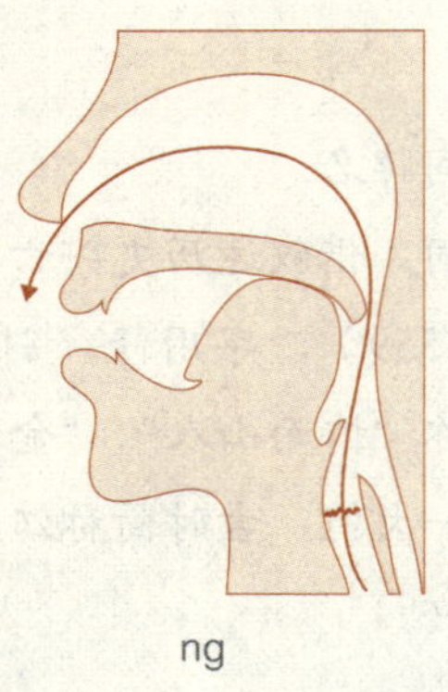
ng

如：

深沉（shēnchén）————→生成（shēngchéng）
金银（jīnyín）————→经营（jīngyíng）
频频（pínpín）————→平平（píngpíng）
分针（fēnzhēn）————→风筝（fēngzheng）
沉沦（chénlún）————→成龙（chénglóng）
春分（chūnfēn）————→冲锋（chōngfēng）

为了便于广大读者朋友在语音学习过程中更好地了解汉语声母、韵母的发音部位，现将其在口腔内外的相互关系综合于下图中以做参考。

In order to help our readers better learn and understand the places of articulations of the initials and finals, we illustrate their interrelations both in and out the oral cavity in the following table.

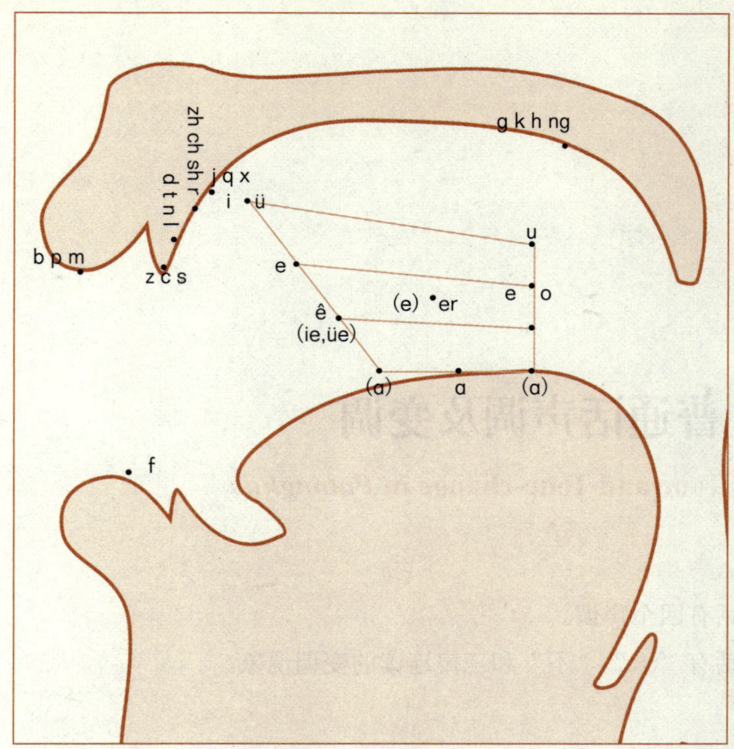

图 3-32 拼音发音部位相互关系示意总图
Figure 3-32 Relationship between each sound in places of pronunciation

第四章　普通话声调及变调

Chapter IV　Tone and Tone-change in *Putonghua*

★ 普通话有四个声调。

★ 普通话有“一”“不”和三声连读的变调现象。

普通话声调标记示例表

The Table of Tone Marks

调类 Tone Category	阴平 High-level tone	阳平 Raising tone	上升 Falling-rising tone	去声 Falling tone
调值 Tone Pitch	高平调 ˥ 55 High-level tone	高升调 ˧˥ 35 Raising tone	降升调 ˨˩˦ 214 Falling-rising tone	全降调 ˥˩ 51 Falling tone
调号 Tone	ˉ	ˊ	ˇ	ˋ
例字 Examples	chūn tiān 春天　huā kāi 花开	rén mín 人民　tuán jié 团结	yǒng yuǎn 永远　yǒu hǎo 友好	shèng lì 胜利　jiàn shè 建设

汉语是声调语言，声调是汉语每个音节中绝对不可缺少的成分，它同声母、韵母一样，有区别意义的作用。如：qiān（千），qián（钱）, qiǎn（浅）, qiàn（欠）四个音节，它们的声母、韵母都相同，但意义不同，这是由声调的不同而形成的。发音中声调的不同，主要是由音高的不同决定的。

Chinese is a language of tone. Tones, which are indispensable parts of every syllable in Chinese, similar to initial syllables and final syllables, have an effect of characterizing meanings. For example, qiān(千, thousand), qián(钱, money), qiǎn(浅, shallow), qiàn(欠, owe), the initial and final syllables are completely the same, but they differ in meanings because of the different tones. The differences of tones lie in the differences of pitches.

第一节　普通话声调的分类

Section I　Classification of Tones in *Putonghua*

普通话的声调可分作四类，是根据普通话全部字音的实际读法将调值相同的字归纳在一起分类定出的，并采用“五度标记法”（见表 4-1）表示声调、调值、调号的变化。

According to the actual pronunciation of all the words in *Putonghua*, the tones are classified into four different kinds. The variations of tones, pitches and tone marks are illustrated by “Five-degree Marks” (see Table 4-1).

表 4-1 五度标记法

Table 4-1 Five-degree Marks

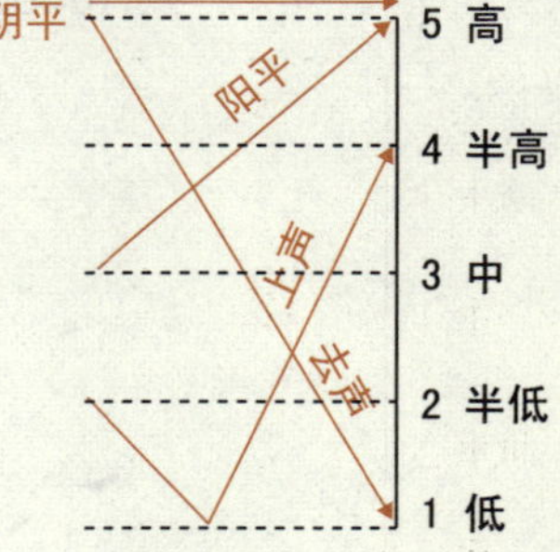

五度标记法 Five-degree Marks

现将五度标记法分述如下：

The following are Five-degree Marks described respectively:

1. 阴平调［第一声］声音高而平，由 5 度到 5 度，无升降变化，又叫高平调或 55 调（见表 4-2）。如：

High-level tone (the 1st), from degree 5 to degree 5, no variation (see also Table 4-2). For example:

ā ī ū ǖ　高（gāo）　空（kōng）
　　　　飞（fēi）　机（jī）

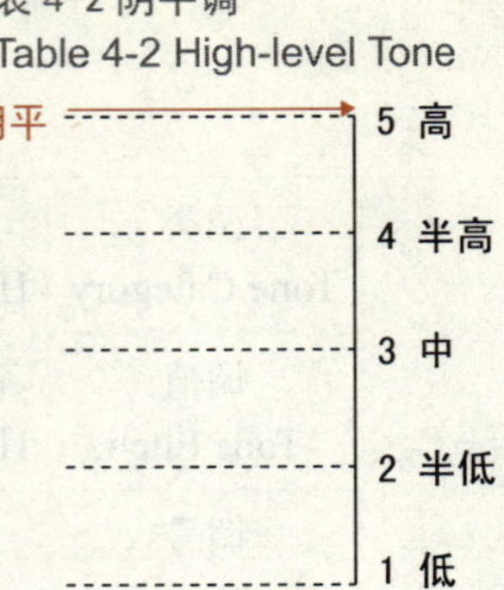

表 4-2 阴平调
Table 4-2 High-level Tone

2. 阳平调［第二声］声音由中 3 度升到 5 度，又叫中升调或 35 调（见表 4-3）。如：

Raising tone(the 2nd tone), from degree 3 to degree 5(see also Table 4-2). For example:

á í ú ǘ　平（píng）　层（céng）　宁（níng）
　　　　人（rén）　行（xíng）　红（hóng）

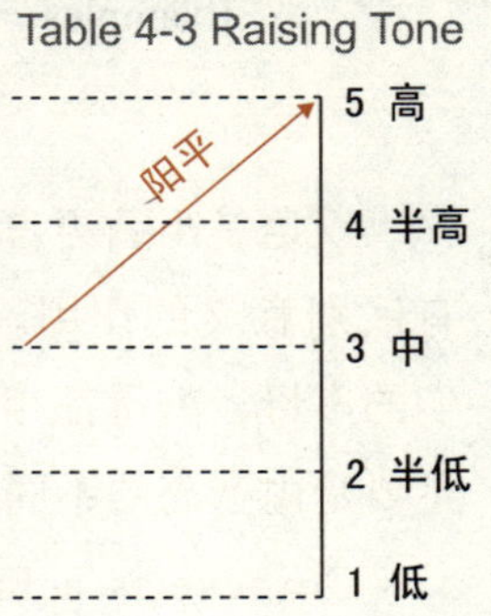

表 4-3 阳平调
Table 4-3 Raising Tone

3. 上声调［第三声］声音由半低 2 度降到 1 度，再由 1 度升到半高 4 度，又叫降升调、曲折调或 214 调（见表 4-4）。如：

Falling-rising tone(the 3rd tone), from degree 2 to degree 1, and then from degree 1 to degree 4 (see also Table 4-4) . For example:

ǎ ǐ ǔ ǚ　米（mǐ）　吃（chǐ）　子（zǐ）
　　　　李（lǐ）　起（qǐ）　苦（kǔ）

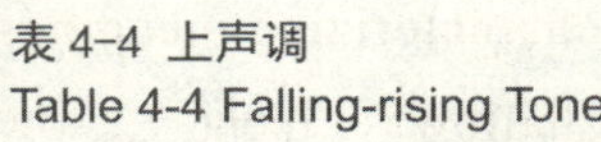
表 4-4 上声调
Table 4-4 Falling-rising Tone

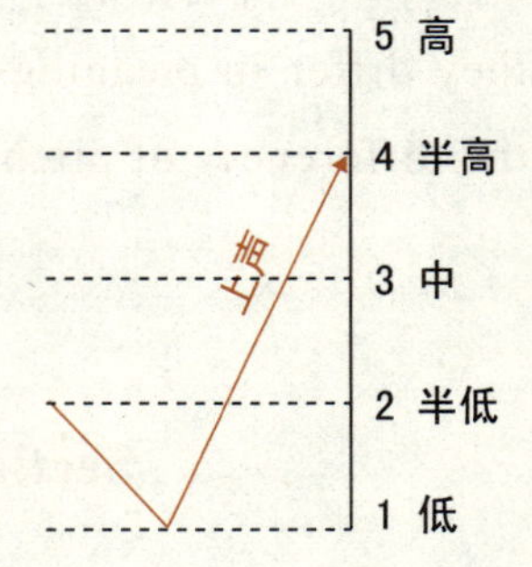

4. 去声调［第四声］声音由高 5 度降低到 1 度，又叫全降调、高降调或 51 调（见表 4-5）。如：

Falling tone (the 4th tone), from degree 5 to degree 1(see also Table 4-5). For example:

à ì ù ǜ　抱（bào）　造（zào）　照（zhào）
　　　　到（dào）　叫（jiào）　号（hào）

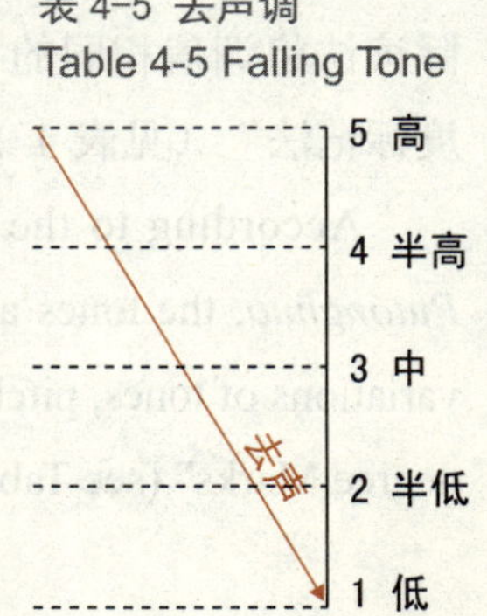

表 4-5 去声调
Table 4-5 Falling Tone

第二节 调号

Section II Tone-marks

普通话的四种基本声调可归纳为“一平、二升、三曲、四降”。表示声调的符号叫调号，是“五度标记法”图式上去掉竖线后的四种不同变化的线型，即 55ˉ、35ˊ、214ˇ、51ˋ。

Four basic tones in Chinese are separately called “level, rising, curving and falling”. The marks used are called tone marks(55ˉ, 35ˊ,214ˇ, 51ˋ).

《拼音方案》规定：调号标在主要元音上。

The Scheme for the Chinese Phonetic Alphabet prescribes that the tone marks are positioned on the head of the vowels.

如：

For example:

妈 mā　　麻 má　　马 mǎ　　骂 mà

期 qī　　其 qí　　起 qǐ　　气 qì

呼 hū　　胡 hú　　虎 hǔ　　护 hù

多 duō　　夺 duó　　躲 duǒ　　垛 duò

标调号的规律是：

Rules for the tone-marks are:

ɑ 母出现莫放过，如：

Mark each ɑ, for example:

bā 巴　　gāo 高　　xiá 匣　　yuán 元

没有 ɑ 母找 e, o，如：

Mark e or o when ɑ is absent, for example:

léi 雷　　qiè 切　　tōng 通　　duō 多

有了 iu, ui 标在后，如：

Mark the latter syllable of iu and ui, for example:

jiù 救　　xiù 绣　　duī 堆　　chuī 吹

i 上调号把点抹，如：

Omit the dot over the letter “i” when a rising mark is placed over it, for example:

yī 衣　　jīn 金　　yīng 英　　qīng 青

轻声不标调，如：

No marks on neutral voices, for example:

yīfu 衣服　　jīnzi 金子　　shítou 石头　　zhàngfu 丈夫。

练习
Exercises

1. 请读下列按四声顺序排列的同声同韵字。

Read the following characters with the same sound and syllables arranged in the four-tone order.

巴	拔	把	罢	疵	磁	此	次
bā	bá	bǎ	bà	cī	cí	cǐ	cì
低	敌	底	地	知	直	纸	志
dī	dí	dǐ	dì	zhī	zhí	zhǐ	zhì
妻	齐	起	气	分	坟	粉	奋
qī	qí	qǐ	qì	fēn	fén	fěn	fèn
诗	时	使	是	灰	回	悔	汇
shī	shí	shǐ	shì	huī	huí	huǐ	huì

2. 请读由同声调的字组成的短语。

Read the phrases made by the characters with the same tones.

春天花开　　江山多娇
chūntiān huā kāi　　jiāngshān duō jiāo

人民团结　　豪情昂扬
rénmín tuán jié　　háoqíng ángyáng

永远友好　　美好理想
yóngyuǎn yóuhǎo　　méihǎo líxiǎng
（yǒngyuǎn yǒuhǎo）　　（měihǎo lǐxiǎng）

日夜变化　　创造世界
rìyè biànhuà　　chuàngzào shìjiè

3. 请读由不同声调的字组成的短语。

Read the phrases made by the characters with different tones.

忠	言	逆	耳	卓	有	成	效
zhōngyán		nì	ěr	zhuó	yǒu	chéngxiào	
身	体	力	行	集	思	广	益
shēn	tǐ	lì	xíng	jí	sī	guǎng	yì
得	心	应	手	语	重	心	长
dé	xīn	yìng	shǒu	yǔ	zhòng	xīn	cháng

第三节 变调
Section III Tone-change

普通话中，有些音节在连读时，前一音节的声调受后一音节声调的影响，使声调发生变化，这就是“变调”。变调只出现在口语中，书面上的调号不变。（本书为方便读者，将变调后的调号标记出来）

In *Putonghua*, when read in succession, the variation of tones happens because of the influence of the former syllable on the following syllable. This is called “tone-change”, it appears the spoken Chinese, tones don’t change in the written Chinese. (To be convenient for the readers, the changed tones are marked in the book.)

常见的有以下几种：

The following types are commonly used:

1. 上声的变调 Tone-change in the rising tone

凡上声字是一个音节或在其他音节之后时，读 214 调不变，只在两个上声音节相连发音时，前一音节变读为 35 调（像阳平）。在非上声音节前变读为 21 调“半上”。如：

When the rising tone happens on an only syllable or after other syllables, it remains as the tone 214. Only when two rising tones are in succession will the former tone change into the tone 35, the high-level tone (or similar to the high-level tone). When the rising tone happens before a non-rising tone, it changes into the tone 21(half rising tone). For example:

(1) 在上声前　Before a Rising Tone

选举（xuánjǔ）　　冷水（léngshuǐ）

美好（méihǎo）　　野草（yécǎo）

(2) 在非上声前　Before a Non-rising Tone

首都（shǒudū）　　海洋（hǎiyáng）

解放（jiěfàng）　　尾巴（wěiba）

凡是两个或两个以上的上声字连读时，可按照上述规律变调。如：

Whenever two or more rising tones are in succession, tone-change follow the rules mentioned above. For example:

展览馆（zhánlánguǎn）　　管理组（guánlízǔ）

水果好（shuíguó hǎo）　　土产品（tǔ chánpǐn）

永远友好（yóngyuǎn yóuhǎo）

转眼两载（zhuányǎn liángzǎi）

养 马 场 养 有 五 百 匹 好 母 马。

Yángmá chǎng yǎng yǒu wúbǎi pǐ hǎo múmǎ.

(3) 上声字与原为上声改读为轻声的字相连时，有两种变调，有的变"阳平"，有的变"半上"。

When the rising tone is connected with a neutral rising tone, there are two kinds of tone-change. Some are changed into rising tone, some into half-rising.

如：For example:

早起（záoqi）　等等（déngdeng）　讲讲（jiángjiang）　（阳平）

姐姐（jiějie）　奶奶（nǎinai）　毯子（tǎnzi）　（半上）

2. 去声的变调　Tone-change in the falling tone

两个去声相连，前一个音节的调值变"半去"，　如：

When two falling tones are in succession, the first tone is changed into half-falling. For example:

木炭（mùtàn）　　办事（bànshì）

电话（diànhuà）　　报废（bàofèi）

正确（zhèngquè）　　大会（dàhuì）

3. "一（yī）""不（bù）"的变调　The tone-change of yī(一) and bù(不)

（1）"一""不"在单念或出现在词句末尾以及"一"在序数中声调不变，"一"读阴平，"不"仍读去声。如：一（yī）、十一（shíyī）、第一（dìyī）、统一（tǒngyī）、划一（huàyī）、不（bù）。

When yī(一)or bù(不) is pronounced in isolation or at the end of a phrase or sentence, yī(一) is in high-level tone and bù(不) still in falling tone. For example: 一（yī）、十一 (shíyī)、第一 (dìyī)、统一 (tǒngyī)、划一 (huàyī)、不（bù）。

（2）“一”“不”在去声前，一律读阳平。如：一样 (yíyàng)、一向 (yíxiàng)、一架 (yíjià)、一阵 (yízhèn)、不怕 (búpà)、不够 (búgòu)、不去 (búqù)、不对 (búduì)。

When followed by a falling tone, yī(一) or bù(不) is pronounced in the rising-tone. For example: 一样 (yíyàng)、一向 (yíxiàng)、一架 (yíjià)、一阵 (yízhèn)、不怕 (búpà)、不够 (búgòu)、不去 (búqù)、不对 (búduì).

（3）“一”“不”在阴平、阳平、上声前“一”变为去声，“不”仍读去声。如：一般 (yìbān)、一天 (yìtiān)、一年 (yìnián)、一条 (yìtiáo)、一早 (yìzǎo)、一晚 (yìwǎn)、不说 (bùshuō)、不开 (bùkāi)、不同 (bùtóng)、不来 (bùlái)、不想 (bùxiǎng)、不走 (bùzǒu)。

When followed by a high-level tone, rising tone or falling-rising tone, yī(一) is pronounced in the falling tone, bù(不) still in the falling-tone. For example: 一般 (yìbān)、一天 (yìtiān)、一年 (yìnián)、一条 (yìtiáo)、一早 (yìzǎo)、一晚 (yìwǎn)、不说 (bùshuō)、不开 (bùkāi)、不同 (bùtóng)、不来 (bùlái)、不想 (bùxiǎng)、不走 (bùzǒu).

（4）“一”“不”出现在两个相同的动词中间时，读轻声。如：想一想（xiǎng yi xiǎng）、看一看 (kàn yi kàn)、走一走 (zǒu yi zǒu)、试一试 (shì yi shì)、说不说 (shuō bu shuō)、肯不肯 (kěn bu kěn)、行不行 (xíng bu xíng)、去不去 (qù bu qù)。

When between two verbs, yī(一) or bù(不) is pronounced in the neutral tone. For example: 想一想（xiǎng yi xiǎng）、看一看 (kàn yi kàn)、走一走 (zǒu yi zǒu)、试一试 (shì yi shì)、说不说 (shuō bu shuō)、肯不肯 (kěn bu kěn)、行不行 (xíng bu xíng)、去不去 (qù bu qù).

4. “七（qī）”“八 (bā)”的变调 The tone-change of “七（qi）” and “八 (ba)”

“七”“八”在去声前读阳平，其他声调前仍读阴平。如：七岁 (qísuì)、七件 (qíjiàn)、七次 (qícì)、七辆 (qíliàng)；八岁 (básuì)、八件 (bájiàn)、八次 (bácì)、八辆 (báliàng)（变阳平）；七天 (qītiān)、七人 (qīrén)、七亩 (qīmǔ)、七碗 (qīwǎn)，八株 (bāzhū)、八瓶 (bāpíng)、八本 (bāběn)、八块 (bākuài)（仍读阴平）。

When followed by a falling tone, qī(七)and bā(八) are pronounced in the rising tone; while followed by other tones, they remain as the high-level tone. For example: 七岁 (qísuì)、七件 (qíjiàn)、七次 (qícì)、七辆 (qíliàng)；八岁 (básuì)、八件 (bájiàn)、八次 (bácì)、八辆 (báliàng)（变阳平）；七天 (qītiān)、七人 (qīrén)、七亩 (qīmǔ)、七碗 (qīwǎn)，八株 (bāzhū)、八瓶 (bāpíng)、八本 (bāběn)、八块 (bākuài).

第五章　音节

Chapter V　Syllables

★ 音节的结构。

★ 音节的拼合。

★ 拼音的方法。

★ 普通话声、韵拼合规律。

第一节 音节的结构

Section I Structure of the Syllables

普通话的音节一般由声母、韵母、声调三部分构成。如：

The syllables in *Putonghua* are composed of initials, finals and tones. For example:

biāo（标） huán（还） niǎo（鸟） lüè（略）

一个音节可以没有辅音，但必须有主要元音和声调。如：

Consonants are not necessary, but main vowels and tone are necessary. For example:

ā（阿） ō（喔） é（鹅） wú（吴）

第二节 音节的拼合

Section II Connections between Syllables

普通话声、韵拼合成音节时应注意：

Pay attention when initials and finals are combined into syllables.

1. 声母、韵母拼合时，两者之间不要停顿。如：gǔ（谷）拼读时，g 与 u 之间有了停顿，就会拼为 g(e)-ǔ（歌舞）。

No pause is required when the initial and final are spelled. Take the syllable gu for example. When g and u are combined, if there is a pause, the sound would be g(e)-ǔ, a different meaning.

2. 要读准韵头。有些音节有韵头(声母后的第一个元音，即介音)，如果读不出或读不准，就会出现丢失或改变韵头的现象。如：luàn(乱)拼读时，丢失了 u，就会成为 làn（滥）；quán(全)拼读时，把 ü 读成 i，就会成为 qián(前)。

Read the head of finals correctly. Some syllables have a head of finals (the first vowel after the initial). If not correctly read, the head of the final would be lost or changed. For example, if u is lost in the pronunciation of luàn(乱, chaos), it would be làn（滥, too much）; if ü is misread as i in the pronunciation of quán（全，whole）, it would be qián（前，before）.

第三节 普通话声、韵拼合方法

Section III Ways of Spelling of Initials and Finals

声、韵拼合时不要把声母拉长，采用“声母短促，韵母长，两音合一紧相连”的快拼法较好。如：

When the initials are spelled with the finals, do not prolong the initials. The initial short, the final long, these two are spelled with pause. For example:

b-ɑ— bā（巴） d-ɑ—dà（大）

d-ou—dōu（都） g-en—gēn（根）

j-i—jī（机） sh-u—shū（叔）

g-uɑng—guāng（光） m-ing—míng（明）

第四节 普通话声、韵拼合规律

Section IV Rules of Spelling of Initials and Finals

普通话声、韵拼合主要有以下一些规律：

Main rules of the spelling of the initials and finals in *Putonghua*:

1. 双唇音 b, p, m, 舌尖中音 d, t 能与开口、齐齿、合口呼韵母 ɑ, o, e, i, u 相拼，不能与撮口呼韵母 ü 相拼。

The bilabial b, p, m and the alveolar d, t could spell with some finals such as ɑ, o, e, i, u, but not with ü.

2. 舌尖前音 z, c, s, 舌尖后音 zh, ch, sh, r 和舌根音 g, k, h 能与开口呼 ɑ, o, e 和合口呼 u 韵母相拼。永远不与齐齿呼 i 和撮口呼 ü 韵母相拼。

The supra-dental z, c, s, retroflex zh, ch, sh, r and velar g, k, h could spell with open vowel ɑ, o, e and closed vowel u, but never with even vowel i and pursed vowel ü.

3. 舌面音 j、q、x 只能与齐齿呼 i 和撮口呼 ü 韵母相拼。永远不与开口呼 ɑ, o, e 和合口呼 u 相拼。

Dorsal j, q, x could only spell with even vowel i and pursed vowel ü, never with open vowel ɑ, o, e or closed vowel u.

4. 舌尖中音 n, l 能与所有的韵母相拼。自成音节的“零声母”音节在四呼中均有。

Alveolar n, l could spell with all the finals. Non-initial could spell with all the finals.

普通话声韵拼合规律可用下图表示。

Spelling rules of *Putonghua* are exemplified in the following table.

普通话声韵配合简表

The Table of Spelling of Initials and Finals in *Putonghua*

例字 Examples / 韵母 Finals / 声母 Initials		开口呼 Open vowel	齐齿呼 Even vowel	合口呼 Closed vowel	撮口呼 Pursed vowel
双唇音 Bilabial	b, p, m	+	+	只和 u 相拼 only spelled with u	
唇齿音 Labiodental	f	+		只和 u 相拼 only spelled with u	
舌尖中音 Alveolar	d, t	+	+	+	
	n, l				+
舌面音 Dorsal	j, q, x		+		+
舌根音 Velar	g, k, h	+		+	
舌尖后音 Retroflex	zh, ch, sh, r	+		+	
舌尖前音 Supra-dental	z, c, s	+		+	
零声母 Non-initial		+	+	+	+

注：+表示声韵能相拼，空白表示不能相拼。

Note: + stands for the possibility of spelling, blank stands for the impossibility of spelling.

第六章　语音阅读和汉字的书写

Chapter VI　Reading of Pronunciation Practice and Writing of Chinese Characters

★ 古典诗文阅读。

★ 现代文阅读。

★ 汉字的书写。

第一节 古典诗文阅读
Section I Reading Poems and the Adapted Classics

Kóngzǐ Yǔlù (Bāzé Jiéxuǎn)
孔子语录（八则节选）

《论语》，儒家经典，主要记载孔子及其弟子的言行，由孔子弟子及再传弟子记录编纂。

孔子（公元前551—前479），名丘，字仲尼，春秋时鲁国陬邑（今山东曲阜）人，中国古代伟大的思想家，教育家，儒家学派的创始人。

节选 一

Zǐyuē: Xué ér shí xí zhī, bú yì yuè hū? Yǒu péng zì yuǎnfāng lái, bú yì lè hū? Rén bù zhī ér bú yùn， bú yì jūnzǐ hū?

—《Lúnyǔ • Xué'ér Piān》

子曰："学而时习之，不亦说乎？有朋自远方来，不亦乐乎？人不知而不愠，不亦君子乎？

——《论语 • 学而篇》

【注】

时：经常。Shí: jīngcháng.

习：复习、练习、实习。Xí: fùxí, liànxí, shíxí.

说：高兴、愉快。Yuè: gāoxìng, yúkuài.

朋：志同道合的人。 Péng: zhì tóng dào hé de rén.

知：了解。Zhī: liáojiě.

愠：不愉快，怨恨。Yùn: bù yúkuài, yuànhèn.

君子：指有学问、有道德的人。Jūnzǐ: zhǐ yǒu xuéwèn, yǒu dàodé de rén.

【译】

Kóngzǐ shuō: "Xuéxí le,ránhòu yào jīngcháng fùxí tā, bù yě hěn yúkuài ma? Yǒu péngyou cóng hényuǎn de dìfang lái, bù yě hěn kuàilè ma? Rénjia bù lǐjiě zìjǐ, zìjǐ què bù shēngqì, zhèyàng de rén, bù yě jiùshì yǒu dàodé, yǒu xiūyǎng de rén ma?"

孔子说："学习了，然后要经常复习它，不也很愉快吗？有朋友从很远的地方来，不也很快乐吗？人家不理解自己，自己却不生气，这样的人，不也就是有道德、有修养的人吗？"

节选 二

Zǐ yuē: "Jūnzǐ shí wú qiū bǎo, jū wú qiú ān, mǐn yú shì ér shèn yú yán, jiù yǒu dào ér zhèng yān, kě wèi hào xué yě yǐ."

—《Lúnyǔ•Xué'ér Piān》

子曰："君子食无求饱，居无求安，敏于事而慎于言，就有道而正焉，可谓好学也已。"

——《论语・学而篇》

【注】

饱：过多、满足。Bǎo: guòduō,mǎnzú.

安：安逸。Ān: ānyì.

敏：快捷。Mǐn: kuàijié.

慎：慎重。Shèn: shènzhòng.

就：去，到。Jiù: qù, dào.

有道：有道德学问的人。Yǒu dào: yǒu dàodé xuéwèn de rén.

正：端正、改正。Zhèng: duānzhèng, gǎizhèng.

好：喜爱。 Hào: xǐ'ài.

【译】

Kóngzǐ shuō: "Jūnzǐ yǐnshí bù yāoqiú guòfèn fēngfù, jūzhù bù yāoqiú guòyú shūshì, zuòshì yào qínkuài ér shuōhuà yào jǐnshèn, bìng néng zhǔdòng dào yǒu dàodé, yǒu xuéwèn de rén nàli qù qǐngjiào, yǐ duānzhèng zìjǐ de sīxiǎng hé yánxíng, zhèyàng jiù kéyǐ chēng zhī wéi hàoxué le."

孔子说"君子饮食不要求过分丰富，居住不要求过于舒适，做事要勤快而说话要谨慎，并能主动到有道德、有学问的人那里去请教，以端正自己的思想和言行，这样就可以称之为好学了。"

节选 三

Zǐ yuē: "Yóu! Huì rǔ zhī zhī hū? Zhī zhī wéi zhī zhī, bù zhī wéi bù zhī, shì zhī yě."

—《Lúnyǔ · Wéi Zhèng Piān》

子曰："由！诲女知之乎？知之为知之，不知为不知，是知也。"

——《论语·为政篇》

【注】

由：孔子的贤弟子，姓仲名由，字子路。Yóu:Kóngzǐ de xián dìzǐ, xìng Zhòng míng Yóu, zì Zǐlù.

诲：教诲、讲授。Huì:jiàohuì, jiǎngshòu.

女（通"汝"）：你。 Rǔ (tōng rǔ) :nǐ.

是：此、这。Shì:cǐ, zhè.

知：聪明、智慧、态度端正。Zhī: cōngming, zhìhuì, tàidu duānzhèng.

【译】

Kóngzǐ wèn: "Yóu! Jiāogěi nǐ de shìlǐ nòng míngbai le ma? Zhīdào jiù shì zhīdào, bù zhīdào jiù shì bù zhīdào, zhè shì míngzhì de tàidu a !"

孔子问：" 由！教给你的事理弄明白了吗？知道就是知道，不知道就是不知道，这是明智的态度啊！"

节选 四

Zǐ yuē: "Bú huàn rén zhī bù jǐ zhī, huàn bù zhī rén yě."

—《Lúnyǔ•Xué'ér Piān》

子曰："不患人之不己知，患不知人也。"

——《论语·学而篇》

【注】

患：忧虑、怕。Huàn: yōulǜ, pà.

不己知：不了解自己。Bù jǐ zhī: bù liáojiě zìjǐ.

【译】

Kóngzǐ shuō: “Bú yào pà biérén bù liáojiě zìjǐ, zhòngyào de shì pà zìjǐ bù liáojiě bié rén.”

孔子说：“不要怕别人不了解自己，重要的是怕自己不了解别人。”

节选 五

Zǐ yuē: “Sān rén xíng, bì yǒu wǒ shī yān; zé qí shàn zhě ér cóng zhī, qí bú shàn zhě ér gǎi zhī.”

—《Lúnyǔ• Shù'ér Piān》

子曰：“三人行，必有我师焉；择其善者而从之，其不善者而改之。”

——《论语·述而篇》

【译】

Kóngzǐ shuō: “Rúguǒ yǒu sān rén zài yìqǐ gōngzuò, qízhōng bìdìng yǒu kéyǐ zuò wǒ de lǎoshī de rén, cóngzhōng xuánqǔ yōuliáng de bùfēn ér gēnzhe xuéxí,kàndào bù liáng de dìfang, jiù kéyǐ duìzhào zhe gǎijìn zìjǐ.”

孔子说：“如果有三人在一起工作，其中必定有可以做我的老师的人，从中选取优良的部分而跟着学习，看到不良的地方，就可以对照着改进自己。”

节选 六

Zǐ yuē: “Qí shēn zhèng, bú lìng ér xíng; qí shēn bú zhèng, suī lìng bù xíng.”

—《Lúnyǔ•Zǐlù Piān》

子曰：“其身正，不令而行；其身不正，虽令不行。”

——《论语·子路篇》

【译】

Kóngzǐ shuō: “Zuòwéi lǐngdǎozhě de rén, rúguǒ tā de yánxíng, júzhǐ dōu shì duānzhèng de, bú xià mìnglìng, shìqing yě huì xíng de tōng; rúguǒ tā zìshēn de xíngwéi bùduān, jíshǐ sān lìng wǔ shēn, bǎixìng yě búhuì tīngcóng de.”

孔子说：“作为领导者的人，如果他的言行、举止都是端正的，不下命令，事情也会行得通；如果他自身的行为不端，即使三令五申，百姓也不会听从的。”

节选 七

Zǐyuē: "Xué ér bù sī zé wǎng, sī ér bù xué zé dài."

—《Lúnyǔ•Wéi Zhèng Piān》

子曰："学而不思则罔， 思而不学则殆。"

——《论语·为政篇》

【注】

罔：无，无所得。Wǎng: wú, wú suǒdé.

殆：疑惑。Dài: yíhuò

【译】

Kóngzǐ shuō: " Zhǐshì dúshū, ér zìjǐ bù kāidòng nǎojīn dúlì sīkǎo, jiù bú huì zhēnzhèng de shòuyì; zhǐshì kōngxiǎng, ér bú rènzhēn xuéxí, jiùhuì yíhuò bù jiě."

孔子说："只是读书，而自己不开动脑筋独立思考，就不会真正的受益；只是空想，而不认真学习，就会疑惑不解。"

节选 八

"Diǎn， ěr hé rú?"

Gǔ sè xī, kēng ěr, hé sè ér zuò, duì yuē: "Yì hū sān zǐ zhě zhī zhuàn."

Zǐ yuē: " Hé shāng hū? Yì gè yán qí zhì yě!"

Yuē: "Mùchūnzhě, chūn fú jì chéng,guànzhě wǔ-liùrén, tóngzǐ liù-qī, yù hū yí, fēng hū wǔ yú, yǒng ér guī."

Fūzǐ kuìrán tàn yuē: "Wú yǔ diǎn yě."

—《Lúnyǔ•Xiān Jìn Piān》

"点，尔何如？"

鼓瑟稀，铿尔，合瑟而作，对曰："异乎三子者之撰。"

子曰："何伤乎？亦各言其志也！"

曰："暮春者，春服既成，冠者五六人，童子六七，浴乎沂，风乎舞雩，咏而归。"

夫子喟然叹曰："吾与点也。"

——《论语·先进篇》

【译】

Wèn: “Zēngdiǎn, nǐ zěnmeyàng?”

Tā tánsè zhèng jìn wěishēng, kēng de yì shēng bǎ sè fàngxià, zhànle qǐlái dá dào :“Wǒ de zhìxiàng hé tāmen sān wèi suójiǎng de bù tóng.” Kǒngzǐ dào: “Nà yǒu shénme fáng 'ài ne? Zhèngshì yào gè rén shuōchū zìjǐ de zhìxiàng a!”

Zēngxī biàn dào: “Mùchūn sānyuè, chūntiān yīfu dōu chuāndìng le, péitóng wǔ-liù wèi chéngnián rén, liù-qī gè xiǎohái zài Yíshuǐ pángbiān xíxǐ zǎo, zài wǔyútái shàng chuīchuī fēng, yílù chànggē, yílù zǒuhuílai.” Kóngzǐ chángtàn yì shēng dào: “Wǒ tóngyì Zēngdiǎn de zhǔzhāng ya!”

问：“曾点！你怎么样？”

他弹瑟正近尾声，铿的一声把瑟放下，站了起来答道：“我的志向和他们三位所讲的不同。”孔子道：“那有什么妨碍呢？正是要各人说出自己的志向呵！”

曾皙便道：“暮春三月，春天衣服都穿定了，陪同五六位成年人，六七个小孩，在沂水旁边洗洗澡，在舞雩台上吹吹风，一路唱歌，一路走回来。”孔子长叹一声道：“我同意曾点的主张呀！”

【提示】

这是孔子教导弟子时所说的内容中的部分语录。

儒家倡导“好学”。孔子所说的学习，包括读书、治学、做人。他把好学精神放在首要的地位，认为“君子食无求饱，居无求安”，最重要的是好学上进，做一个既有学问又有道德的人。他非常看重道德修养和以身作则的力量，“其身正，不令而行；其身不正，虽令不行。”这对于领导者来说，意义非常重要。他对道德修养提出了很高的要求：“人不知而不愠”，“不患人之不己知，患不知人也”，是强调谦虚、谨慎，永不患得患失，永不自我满足，方能不断有所进取；“无求生以害仁，有杀身以成仁”，要求具有为崇高的道义和理想而勇于自我牺牲的精神，这可以说是儒家道德、节操的最高境界。

关于学习态度和学习方法，他重视：一是要“知之为知之，不知为不知”，实事求是，老老实实；二是要懂得“三人行，必有我师焉”的道理，善于发现别人的智能优点，取长补短；三是要主动求教，“就有道而正焉”，乐于切磋，为有高尚道德、有学问的朋友来访而高兴；四是既要善于读书，又要善于思考，学思结合，学活学透。

Mèngzǐ Yǔlù（Wǔzé Jiéxuǎn）
孟子语录（五则节选）

孟子

《孟子》，儒家经典，主要记载孟子的言行，由孟子和他的弟子万章等编撰。

孟子（约公元前 372—前 289），名轲，字子舆，战国中期邹国（今山东邹县）人。他继承并发展了孔子的学说，成为孔子之后儒家学派的主要代表人物。

节选 一

Lǎo wú lǎo, yǐ jí rén zhī lǎo;yòu wú yòu, yǐ jí rén zhī yòu; tiānxià yùn yú zhǎng.

—《Mèngzǐ•Liáng Huìwáng Shàng》

老吾老，以及人之老；幼吾幼，以及人之幼；天下运于掌。

——《孟子·梁惠王上》

【译】

Gōnggōng jìngjìng de shìfèng zìjǐ de zhǎngbèi, yě zūnjìng biérén de zhǎngbèi; cíài jìnxīn de yǎngyù zìjǐ de zínǚ, yě àihù biérén de zínǚ; rúguǒ zhèyàng le, shèhuì jiù héxié píngshùn de fāzhǎn le.

恭恭敬敬地侍奉自己的长辈，也尊敬别人的长辈；慈爱尽心地养育自己的子女，也爱护别人的子女；如果这样了，社会就和谐平顺地发展了。

节选 二

Mín wéi guì, shèjì cì zhī, jūn wéi qīng.

—《Mèngzǐ•Jìnxīn Xià》

民为贵，社稷次之，君为轻。

——《孟子·尽心下》

【注】

Shèjì: Shè wéi zhúguǎn tǔdì de shén, jì wéi zhúguǎn gǔzi de shén. Hòulái yǐ shèjì zhǐdài guójiā. Yǒu “Jiāngshān Shèjì” zhī shuō.

社稷：社为主管土地的神，稷为主管谷子的神。后来以社稷指代国家。有“江山社稷”之说。

【译】

Bàixìng shì zuì zhòngyào de, dàibiǎo guójiā de túgǔ zhī shén wéi cì, jūnzhǔ shì zuì qīng de.

百姓是最重要的，代表国家的土谷之神为次，君主是最轻的。

节选 三

Dé dào zhě duō zhù, shī dào zhě guǎ zhù. Guǎ zhù zhī zhì, qīnqi pàn(pàn) zhī. Dé dào zhī zhì, tiānxià shùn zhī.

—《Mèngzǐ•Gōngsūn Chǒu Xià》

得道者多助，失道者寡助。寡助之至，亲戚畔（叛）之。得道之至，天下顺之。

——《孟子・公孙丑下》

【译】

Héhū mínxīn mínyì, jiù huì dédào rénmín de yōnghù, shīqù mínxīn mínyì, jiù huì bèi rénmín suǒ pāoqì.Shī jìn mínxīn, jiù zhòng pàn qīn lí, jìn dé mínxīn, rénmín jiù yōnghù. Wèicǐ, guójiā jiù huì cháng zhì jiǔ ān le.

合乎民心民意，就会得到人民的拥护，失去民心民意，就会被人民所抛弃。失尽民心，就众叛亲离，尽得民心，人民就拥护。为此，国家就会长治久安了。

节选 四

Wèi mín shàng ér bù yǔ mín tóng lè zhě, yì fēi yě. Lè mín zhī lè zhě, mín yì lè qí lè; yōu mín zhī yōu zhě, mín yì yōu qí yōu.Lè yǐ tiānxià, yōu yǐ tiānxià, rán ér bú wàng zhě, wèi zhī yǒu yě.

—《Mèngzǐ•Liáng Huìwáng Xià》

为民上而不与民同乐者，亦非也。乐民之乐者，民亦乐其乐；忧民之忧者，民亦忧其忧。乐以天下，忧以天下，然而不王者，未之有也。

——《孟子·梁惠王下》

【注】

非，不对，不当。Fēi, bú duì, búdàng.

【译】

Zuòwéi láobǎixìng de fùmǔguān, néng gēn láobǎixìng huànnàn yǔ gòng, tóng gān gòng kǔ, shíkè xiǎngdào láobǎixìng, xiǎngdào guójiā, rúguǒ zhèyàng hái bù néng chēng wáng tiānxià,cónglái méiyǒu zhèyàng de shì.

作为老百姓的父母官，能跟老百姓患难与共，同甘共苦，时刻想到老百姓，想到国家，如果这样还不能称王天下，从来没有这样的事。

节选 五

Tiān jiāng jiàng dàrèn yú sī rén yě, bì xiān kǔ qí xīn zhì, láo qí jīn gǔ, è qí tǐ fū, kōng fá qí shēn, xíng fú luàn qí suǒ wéi, suóyǐ dòng xīn rěn xìng, zēng yì qí suǒ bù néng.

—《Mèngzǐ•Gào Zǐ Xià》

天将降大任于斯人也，必先苦其心志，劳其筋骨，饿其体肤，空乏其身， 行拂乱其所为，所以动心忍性，曾益其所不能。

——《孟子·告子下》

【注】

拂：原指执法大臣、贤士，可泛指官吏。Fú: yuánzhǐ zhífǎ dàchén, xiánshì, kě fànzhǐ guānlì.

曾（通“增”）：增加。Zēng: (tōng zēng) zēngjiā.

【译】

(Shíshì) jiāng xūyào yí wèi néng chéngdān zhòngdà rènwù de rén, jiù yào lìliàn tā de jīngshén yìzhì, jīngshòu shēnxīn bù néng rěnshòu de jiānnán kùnkǔ, shǐ tā de yánxíng bú yào bèilí zhèngdào, shīqù yǐ dìng de fāngxiàng, yào rèn láo rèn yuàn, zēngjiā yǒuyì yú tā de yíwǎng méiyǒu jùbèi de cáinéng.

（时势）将需要一位能承担重大任务的人，就要励练他的精神意志，经受身心不能忍受的艰难困苦，使他的言行不要背离正道，失去已定的方向，要任劳任怨，增加有益于他的已往没有具备的才能。

【提示】

孔子的核心思想是“仁”，政治上主张“仁政”“仁者爱人”“克己复礼”，教育上主张“有教无类”“因材施教”；孟子主张施行仁政、行王道，斥责暴虐，反对战争，宣扬性善论，重视后天教化。孔子的不为富贵违仁、从善如流、身正令行、杀身成仁等思想；孟子的为民父母，推善及人，与民同忧乐，得道者多助、失道者寡助，生于忧患而死于安乐，民贵君轻等思想，都是社会经验和渊博学识的结合，充满真知灼见，是“孔孟之道”的精华，几千年来一直得到国内外读者广泛传诵，有许多已成为家喻户晓的格言和志士仁人的座右铭。

孔子强调“仁爱”，孟子重视“仁政”，从修身到治国，仁义之心一脉相承，这说明儒家学说一贯把人格修养看做是经世治国的精神基础和先决条件。孔孟这一思想，不仅在历史上对中国后世的政治、思想、文化、教育乃至人格修养上，都产生过长期而深刻的影响，而且在今后也仍具有重要的教育意义。

Lǐ Jì • Lǐyùn Dàtóng Piān
礼记·礼运大同篇

Dàdào zhī xíng yě, tiānxià wéi gōng. Xuǎn xián yǔ néng, jiǎng xìn xiū mù. Gù rén bù dú qīn qí qīn, bù dú zǐ qí zǐ, shǐ lǎo yǒu suǒzhōng,zhuàng yǒu suǒyòng, yòu yǒu suǒ cháng,guān guǎ gū dú fèi jí zhě jiē yǒu suóyǎng. Nán yǒu fèn, nǚ yǒu guī. Huò wù qí qì yú dì yě, búbì cáng yú jǐ. Lì wù qí bù chū yú shēn yě, búbì wéi jǐ. Shì gù móu bì ér bù xīng, dào qiè luàn zéi ér bú zuò, gù wài hù ér bú bì, shì wèi dàtóng.

—《Lǐ Jì•Juan Qī》

大道之行也，天下为公。选贤与能，讲信修睦。故人不独亲其亲，不独子其子，使老有所终，壮有所用，幼有所长，鳏寡孤独废疾者皆有所养。男有分，女有归。货恶其弃于地也，不必藏于己。力恶其不出于身也，不必为己。是故谋闭而不兴，盗窃乱贼而不作，故外户而不闭，是谓大同。

——《礼记·卷七》

【注】

大道：理也。大道理。Dàdào: lǐ yě. Dà dàoli.

【译】

Shèngrén de dàdào nénggòu shíxíng de niándài, tiānxià shì tiānxià rén suǒ gòngyǒu de. Dàjiā xuánjǔ yǒu xiánnéng de rén lái gòngtóng zhìlǐ, rénrén jiǎngqiú chéngxìn, bícǐ hémù xiāngchǔ. Bù dú àihù zìjǐ de qīnrén, bùdú àihù zìjǐ de zínǚ, gèng néng tuīguǎng àixīn dào qítā rén shēnshang, shǐ dé shèhuì shang niánzhǎng de lǎorén dōu néng ānxiǎng tiānnián, qīngzhuàngzhě dōu néng gòngxiàn yì jǐ zhī lì, qīngshàonián yǔ yòu'ér yě dōu néng shòudào liánghǎo de jiàoyǎng, nàxiē gūkǔ wúyī jí cánjí de rén, yě dōu néng shòudào hénhǎo de guānzhào. Nánde néng kèshǒu zìjǐ běnfèn yìngjìn de zhízé, nǚde yě gè yǒu zìjǐ de guīsù. Gè zhǒng huòwù zīyuán, zuì kěwù de shì bèi làngfèi, qìzhì, gèng bù néng sīcáng zhàn wéi jǐ yǒu. Yǒu nénglì gèng yīnggāi wèi dàzhòng zuòchū fèngxiàn, bù néng zhǐwèi zìjǐ móulì. Ruò néng rúcǐ, zhěnggè shèhuì jiù bú huì yǒu gōu xīn dòu jiǎo, sǔn rén lì jǐ de shì, yě bú huì yǒu qiǎngjié, tōudào, shārén yuèhuò de shì fāshēng. Jíshǐ ménhù bù guānbì, yě búyòng dān jīng shòu pà, shēnghuó zìzài ānlè. Zhèyàng, shèhuì héxié, zhēn kě wèi shì dàtóng shìjiè le.

圣人的大道能够实行的年代，天下是天下人所共有的。大家选举有贤能的人来共同治理，人人讲求诚信，彼此和睦相处。不独爱护自己的亲人，不独爱护自己的子女，更能推广爱心到其他人身上，使得社会上年长的老人都能安享天年，青壮者都能贡献一己之力，青少年与幼儿也都能受到良好的教养，那些孤苦无依及残疾的人，也都能受到很好的关照。男的能恪守自己本分应尽的职责，女的也各有自己的归宿。各种货物资源，最可恶的是被浪费、弃置，更不能私藏占为己有。有能力更应该为大众作出奉献，不能只为自己谋利。若能如此，整个社会就不会有钩心斗角、损人利己的事，也不会有抢劫、偷盗、杀人越货的事发生。即使门户不关闭，也不用担惊受怕，生活自在安乐。这样，社会和谐，真可谓是大同世界了。

【提示】

《礼记》是战国至秦汉年间儒家学者解释说明经书《仪礼》的文章选集，是一部儒家思想的资料汇编。《礼记》作者不止一人，写作时间也有先有后，其中多数篇章可能是孔子的72名关门弟子及其学生们的作品，还兼收先秦其他典籍。其内容主要是记载和论述先秦礼制、礼仪，解释仪礼，记录孔子和弟子等的问答，记述修身做人的准则。实际上，这部9万字左右的著作内容广博，门类杂多，涉及政治、法律、道德、哲学、历史、祭祀、文艺、日常生活、历法、地理等方面，可以说是包罗万象，集中体现了先秦儒家政治、哲学和伦理思想，是研究先秦社会的重要资料。全书用散文写成，一些篇章具有很高的文学价值。有的用短小生动的故事阐明某一道理，有的气势磅礴、结构谨严，有的言简意赅、意味隽永，有的擅长心理描写和刻画，书中还收有大量富有哲理的格言、警句，精辟而深刻。

《礼记》与《仪礼》《周礼》合称“三礼”，对中国文化产生过深远影响。

Jiè Zǐ Shū
诫子书

Zhūgě Liàng
诸葛亮

Fū jūnzǐ zhī xíng, jìng yǐ xiū shēn, jián yí yǎng dé, fēi dànbó wú yǐ míng zhì, fēi níngjìng wú yǐ zhì yuǎn. Fū xué xū jìng yě, cái xū xué yě, fēi xué wú yǐ guǎng cái, fēi zhì wú yǐ chéng xué. Yín màn zé bù néng lì jīng, xiǎn zào zé bù néng zhì xìng, nián yǔ shí chí, yì yǔ rì qù, suí chéng kū luò, duō bù jiē shì, bēi shǒu qióng lú, jiāng fù hé jí!

—《Zhūgě Liàng Jí》

夫君子之行，静以修身，俭以养德，非淡泊无以明志，非宁静无以致远。夫学须静也，才须学也，非学无以广才，非志无以成学。淫漫则不能励精，险躁则不能治性，年与时驰，意与日去，遂成枯落，多不接世，悲守穷庐，将复何及！

——《诸葛亮集》

【译】

Yǒu dàodé xiūyǎng de rén, shì zhèyàng jìnxíng xiūyǎng duànliàn de. Tāmen yǐ jìngsī fánxǐng lái shǐ zìjǐ jìn shàn jìn měi, yǐ jiánpǔ jiéyuē lái péiyǎng zìjǐ gāoshàng de pǐndé. Bù qīng xīn guǎyù jiù bù néng shǐ zìjǐ de zhìxiàng míngquè jiāndìng, bù āndìng qīngjìng jiù bù néng wèile shíxiàn yuǎndà lǐxiǎng ér chángqī kèkǔ xuéxí. Yào xué dé zhēnzhī bìxū shǐ shēnxīn zài níngjìng zhōng yánjiū tàntǎo,rén de cáinéng shì cóng búduàn de xuéxí zhōng jīlěi qǐlái de; rúguǒ bú xià kǔgōng xuéxí jiù bù néng zēngzhǎng yǔ fāyáng zìjǐ de cáigàn; rúguǒ méiyǒu jiāndìng bù yí de yìzhì jiù bù néng shǐ xuéyè chénggōng. Zòng yù fàngdàng, xiāojí dàimàn jiù bù néng miǎnlì xīnzhì shǐ jīngshén zhènzuò; màoxiǎn cǎoshuài, jízào bù'ān jiù bù néng táoyě xìngqíng shǐ jiécāo gāoshàng. Rúguǒ niánhuá yǔ suìyuè xūdù, zhìyuàn suí shírì xiāomó, zuìzhōng jiùhuì xiàng kūzhī luòyè bān yìtiāntiān shuāilǎo xiàqu, zhèyàng de rén bù huì wéi shèhuì suǒyòng ér yǒuyì yú shèhuì, zhíyǒu bēishāng de kùnshǒu zài zìjǐ de qióngjiā pòshě li, dào nàshí zài huǐhèn yě láibují le.

有道德修养的人，是这样进行修养锻炼的，他们以静思反省来使自己尽善尽美，以俭朴节约来培养自己高尚的品德。不清心寡欲就不能使自己的志向明确坚定，不安定清静就不能为了实现远大理想而长期刻苦学习。要学得真知必须使身心在宁静中研究探讨，人的才能是从不断地学习中积累起来的；如果不下苦功学习就不能增长与发扬自己的才干；如果没有坚定不移的意志就不能使学业成功。纵欲放荡、消极怠慢就不能勉励心志使精神振作；冒险草率、急躁不安就不能陶冶性情使节操高尚。如果年华与岁月虚度，志愿随时日消磨，最终就会像枯枝落叶般一天天衰老下去。这样的人不会为社会所用而有益于社会，只有悲伤地困守在自己的穷家破舍里，到那时再悔恨也来不及了。

【提示】

《诫子书》是三国时期著名的政治家诸葛亮54岁临终前写给8岁儿子诸葛瞻的一封家书，成为后世历代学子修身立志的名篇。它可以看做是诸葛亮对其一生的总结。诸葛亮也是一位品格高洁、才学渊博的父亲，对儿子的殷殷教诲与无限期望尽在言中。通过这些智慧理性、简练谨严的文字，将普天下为人父者的爱子之情表达得如此深切。

Jiàn Tàizōng Shí Sī Shū

谏太宗十思疏

Táng · Wèi Zhēng

唐 · 魏征

Chén wén qiú mù zhī zhángzhě, bì gù qí gēnběn; yù liú zhī yuán zhě, bì jùn qí quányuán; sī guó zhī ānzhě, bì jī qí dé yì. Yuán bù shēn ér wàng liú zhī yuǎn, gēn bú gù ér qiú mù zhī zhǎng, dé bú hòu ér sī guó zhī ān, chén suī xià yú, zhī qí bù kě, ér kuàng yú míng zhé hū? Rén jūn dāng shénqì zhī zhòng, jū yù zhōng zhī dà, bú niàn jū ān sī wēi, jiè shē yí jiǎn, sī yì fá gēn yǐ qiú mù mào, sāi yuán ér yù liú cháng yě.

Fán bǎi yuán shǒu, chéng tiān jǐng mìng, shàn shízhě shí fán, kè zhōng zhě gài guǎ. Qǐ qǔ zhī yì, shǒu zhī nán hū?Gài zài yīn yōu, bì jiéchéng yǐ dài xià; jì dé zhì, zé zòng qíng yǐ ào wù. Jiéchéng, zé Wú, Yuè wéi yìtǐ; ào wù, zé gǔròu wéi xíng lù. Suī dǒng zhī yǐ yánxíng, zhèn zhī yǐ wēinù, zhōng gǒu miǎn ér bù huái rén, mào gōng ér bù xīn fú. Yuàn búzài dà, kě wèi wéi rén, zài zhōu fù zhōu, suǒ yí shēn shèn.

Chéng néng jiàn kě yù, zé sī zhīzú yǐ zì jiè; jiāng yǒu zuò, zé sī zhī zhǐ yǐ ān rén; niàn gāo wēi, zé sī qiān chōng ér zì mù; jù mǎn yì, zé sī jiāng hǎi xià bǎi chuān; lè pán yóu, zé sī sān qū yǐ wéi dù; yōu xiè dài, zé sī shèn shǐ ér jìng zhōng; lǜ yōng bì, zé sī xūxīn yǐ nà xià, jù chán xié, zé sī zhèng shēn yǐ chù è; ēn suǒ jiā, zé sī wú yīn xǐ yǐ miù shǎng; fá suǒ jí, zé sī wú yīn nù ér làn xíng. Zǒng cǐ shí sī, hóng cǐ jiǔ dé. Jiǎn néng ér rèn zhī, zé shàn ér cóng zhī, zé zhìzhě jìn qí móu, yóngzhě jié qí lì, rénzhě bō qí huì, xìnzhě xiào qí zhōng. Wén wǔ bìng yòng, chuí gǒng ér zhì. Hébì láo shén kǔ sī, dài bǎi sī zhī zhí yì zāi!

—《Wèi Zhènggōng Wénjí》

臣闻求木之长者，必固其根本；欲流之远者，必浚其泉源；思国之安者，必积其德义。源不深而望流之远，根不固而求木之长，德不厚而思国之安，臣虽下愚，知其不可，而况于明哲乎？人君当神器之重，居域中之大，不念居安思危，戒奢以俭，斯亦伐根以求木茂，塞源而欲流长也。

凡百元首，承天景命，善始者实繁，克终者盖寡。岂取之易，守之难乎？盖在殷忧，必竭诚以待下；既得志，则纵情以傲物。竭诚，则吴、越为一体；傲物，则骨肉为行路。虽董之以严刑，振之以威怒，终苟免而不怀仁，貌恭而不心服。怨不在大，可畏惟人，载舟覆舟，所宜深慎。

诚能见可欲，则思知足以自戒；将有作，则思知止以安人；念高危，则思谦冲而自牧；惧满溢，则思江海下百川；乐盘游，则思三驱以为度；忧懈怠，则思慎始而敬终；虑壅蔽，则思虚心以纳下；惧谗邪，则思正身以黜恶；恩所加，则思无因喜以谬赏；罚所及，则思无因怒而滥刑。总此十思，宏此九德。简能而任之，择善而从之，则智者尽其谋，勇者竭其力，仁者播其惠，信者效其忠。文武并用，垂拱而治。何必劳神苦思，代百司之职役哉！

——《魏郑公文集》

【注】

神器：帝位。Shénqì: dì wèi.

居域中之大：占据天地间的一大。《老子·上篇》：“道大，天大，地大，王亦大。域中有四大，而王居其一焉。”Jū yù zhōng zhī dà: zhànjù tiāndì jiān de yí dà.《Láozǐ · Shàngpiān》：“Dào dà, tiān dà, dì dà, wáng yì dà. Yù zhōng yǒu sì dà, ér wáng jū qí yī yān.”

域中：天地间。Yù zhōng: tiāndì jiān.

景：大。Jǐng: dà.

殷：深。Yīn: shēn.

董：督责，监督。Dǒng: dūzé, jiāndū.

作：兴作，建筑。指兴建宫室之类。Zuò: xīngzuò, jiànzhù. Zhǐ xīngjiàn gōngshì zhīlèi.

谦冲：谦虚。Qiānchōng: qiānxū.

自牧：自我修养。Zìmù: zìwǒ xiūyǎng.

盘游：打猎游乐。Pányóu: dǎliè yóulè.

三驱：一年打猎三次。Sānqū: yìnián dǎliè sān cì.《礼·王制》：“天子诸侯无事，则岁三田（猎）。”《Lǐ · Wángzhì》：“Tiānzǐ zhūhóu wú shì, zé suì sān tián (liè).”

九德：指忠、信、敬、刚、柔、和、固、贞、顺。Jiǔdé: zhǐ zhōng, xìn, jìng, gāng, róu, hé, gù, zhēn, shùn.

简：选拔。Jiǎn: xuǎnbá.

【译】

Wǒ tīngshuō, yào xiǎng shǐ shùmù shēngzhǎng màoshèng, bìxū wěngù tā de gēnbù, yīnwéi gēn shēn fāng néng yè mào; yào xiǎng shuǐliú chánchán, jīng jiǔ bù xī, bìxū shūtōng tā de yuántóu, yuányuǎn cáinéng liúcháng.Tóngyàng de dàoli,rúguǒ xiǎng shǐ guójiā āndìng, tǒngzhì wěngù, jiù bìxū jījù dàodé hé rényì, huǎnhé yǔ bǎixìng jiān de máodùn. Fǎnzhī, yuánliú bù shēn què yào tā liúcháng, gēn bù láogù què yào shù zhǎng de màoshèng, déyì bú hòu què xiǎng shǐ guójiā āndìng, wǒ suīrán wúzhī, zhī qí bù kě, gèng hékuàng xiàng nín zhèyàng de míngjūn ne! Zuòwéi tǒngzhì tiānxià de guójūn, rúguǒ bù jū ān sī wēi, jiè shē yí jiǎn, cóng chángyuǎn lìyì chūfā, nà jiù děngyú shì páo le shùgēn xīwàng shùmù màoshèng, dǔ le yuánquán háiyào liúshuǐ chàngtōng a!

Lìdài de dìwáng chéng tiān jǐng mìng zhìlǐ tiānxià, shànshǐzhě shí duō, ér shànzhōng zhě què shǎo. Nándào qǔ zhī róngyì ér shǒu zhī jiānnán ma? Yuánlái shì zài dǎ tiānxià de shíhou, dìwáng duìdài chénmín chéng xīn chéng yì, yídàn dé zhì,biàn zòngqíng àowù; rúguǒ bícǐ jiéchéng xiāngdài, suī yuǎn gé yìfāng xīn yě huì zài yìqǐ; rúguǒ yuǎnlí chénmín, jíshǐ shì gǔròu zhī qīn, yě xíng tóng mòlù. Rúguǒ zhǐshì yòng yánxíng jiāndū, yòng wēishì zhènyā bǎixìng, jiù huì shǐ bǎixìng wàibiǎo gōngshùn ér nèixīn bùfú. Shíjiān jiǔ le bìrán huì jīqǐ mínfèn. Yuàn búzài dàxiǎo, kěpà de shì rénmín de lìliang, yīnwéi chuán néng zǎi zhōu, yì néng fù zhōu. Yídìng yào shènzhòng a!

Yīncǐ kénqǐng guójūn jiēnà chénxià de jiànyì: yù qí suǒhào, lǐ yīng "sī zhīzú yǐ zì jiè", yào dǒng de zhīzú; yào xiūjiàn shénme, jiùyào kèzhì zìjǐ, yǐ āndìng bǎixìng shēnghuó wéi qiántí; xiǎng dào gāo chǔ bú shèng hán, jiùyào qiānxū bìng jiāqiáng zìjǐ de xiūyǎng; dānxīn jiāoào zìmǎn huì zhāo lái sǔnshī, jiù yīng yǒu jiānghǎi róngnà bǎichuān de dùliàng; xǐhuān yóulè, jiù yào yángé ànzhào guójūn yìnián dǎ sān cì de guīdìng; hàipà zìjǐ xièdài, jiù yīng shèn shǐ shèn zhōng; yōulǜ zìjǐ shòudào méngbì, jiù yào xūxīn nàjiàn; hàipà chányán hé xié'è, jiù yào zìshēn xíng de zhèng; yǒu suǒ shǎngcì, jiù búyào yīnwéi gèrén de xǐhào luàn jiā shǎngcì; shīxíng xíngfá, yě búyào yīnwéi zìjǐ yìshí de nùqì ér lànyòng. Zǒngzhī, rúguǒ guójūn nín néng fāyáng guāngdà shídiǎn chénshù de huà, xuǎnbá néngzhě rèn zhī, zé qí shànzhě cóng zhī, nà yídìng huì shǐ zhìzhě jìn qí móu, yǒngzhě jié qí lì, rénzhě bō qí huì, xìnzhě xiào qí zhōng; wén wǔ bìng yòng, zìrán kéyǐ dádào chuí gǒng ér zhì de qíngjǐng le. Nálǐ xūyào nín láoshén kǔsī, dàiguǎn bǎiguān de zhíshì ne?

我听说，要想使树木生长茂盛，必须稳固它的根部，因为根深方能叶茂；要想水流潺潺，经久不息，必须疏通它的源头，源远才能流长。同样的道理，如果想使国家安定，治理稳固，就必须积聚道德和仁义，缓和与百姓间的矛盾。反之，源流不深却要它流长，根不牢固却要树长得茂盛，德义不厚却想使国家安定，我虽然无知，知其不可，更何况像您这样的明君呢！作为统治天下的国君，如果不居安思危、戒奢以俭，从长远利益出发，那就等于是刨了树根希望树木茂盛，堵了源泉还要流水畅通啊！

历代的帝王承天景命治理天下，善始者实多，而善终者却少。难道取之容易而守之艰难吗？原来是在打天下的时候，帝王对待臣民诚心诚意，一旦得志，便纵情傲物；如果彼此竭诚相待，虽远隔一方心也会在一起；如果远离臣民，即使是骨肉之亲，也形同陌路。如果只是用严刑监督，用威势镇压百姓，就会使百姓外表恭顺而内心不服。时间久了必然会激起民愤。怨不在大小，可怕的是人民的力量，因为船能载舟，亦能覆舟。一定要慎重啊！

因此恳请国君接纳臣下的建议：遇其所好，理应"思知足以自戒"，要懂得知足；要修建什么，就要克制自己，以安定百姓生活为前提；想到高处不胜寒，就要谦虚并加强自己的修养；担心骄傲自满会招来损失，就应有江海容纳百川的度量；喜欢游乐，就要严格按照国君一年打三次的规定；害怕自己懈怠，就应慎始慎终；忧虑自己受到蒙蔽，就要虚心纳谏；害怕谗言和邪恶，就要自身行得正；有所赏赐，就不要因为个人的喜好乱加赏赐；施行刑罚，也不要因为自己一时的怒气而滥用。总之，如果国君您能发扬光大十点陈述的话，选拔能者任之，择其善者从之，那一定会使智者尽其谋，勇者竭其力，仁者播其惠，信者效其忠；文武并用，自然可以达到垂拱而治的情景了。哪里需要您劳神苦思，代管百官的职事呢？

【提示】

魏征（580—643)，唐初大臣，杰出的政治家，字玄成，馆陶（今河北省馆陶县）人，他在历史上以直言敢谏著称，前后陈谏二百余事，反复以隋亡为鉴戒提醒太宗，对太宗的行动及政策措施给以极有益的影响，为"贞观（guàn）之治"作出了贡献。死时，太宗大悲，亲自为他制碑文，并亲自手书。还曾慨叹说："人以铜为镜，可以正衣冠；以古为镜，可以见兴替；以人为镜，可以知得失。魏征殁，朕亡一镜矣！"魏征的言论多见于《贞观政要》。

《谏太宗十思疏》是魏征写于贞观十一年，劝谏唐太宗的上疏。全文围绕"思国之安者，必积其德义"的主旨，规劝唐太宗在政治上要慎始敬终，虚心纳下，赏罚公正；用人时要知人善任，简能择善；生活上要崇尚节俭，不轻用民力。这些主张虽以巩固李唐王朝为出发点，但客观上使人民得以休养生息，有利于初唐的强盛。本文以"思"为线索，将所要论述的问题连缀成文，文理清晰，结构缜密。并运用比喻、排比和对仗的修辞手法，说理透彻，音韵铿锵，气势充沛，是一篇很好的论说文。是一篇优秀的议论文。

Lòushì Míng
陋室铭

Táng · Liú Yǔxī

唐 · 刘禹锡

Shān búzài gāo, yǒu xiān zé míng; shuǐ búzài shēn, yǒu lóng zé líng. Sī shì lòu shì,wéi wǔ déxīn. Tái hén shàng jiē lǜ,cǎo sè rù lián qīng. Tánxiào yǒu hóngrú, wǎng lái wú báidīng. Kéyǐ tiáo sùqín, yuè jīnjīng. Wú sīzhú zhī luàn ěr, wú àndú zhī láo xíng. Nányáng Zhūgě Lú, Xīshǔ Zǐyún Tíng. Kóngzǐ yún: “Hé lòu zhī yǒu?”

山不在高，有仙则名；水不在深，有龙则灵。斯是陋室，惟吾德馨。苔痕上阶绿，草色入帘青。谈笑有鸿儒，往来无白丁。可以调素琴，阅金经。无丝竹之乱耳，无案牍之劳形。南阳诸葛庐，西蜀子云亭。孔子云：“何陋之有？”

【注】

斯：这。Sī:zhè. 陋室：陈设简单而狭小的房屋。Lòushì:chéngshè jiǎndān ér xiáxiǎo de fángjiān.

惟：只。Wéi:zhǐ. 德馨：品行高。Déxīn:pǐnxíng gāo.

鸿儒：指博学的人。Hóngrú:zhǐ bóxué de rén.

白丁：这里指不学习、没有知识的人。Báidīng:zhèli zhǐ bù xúexí, méiyǒu zhīshi de rén.

素琴：没有装饰的琴。Sùqín: méiyǒu zhuāngshì de qín.

金经：即《金刚经》。Jīnjīng:jí《Jīngāng Jīng》.

丝竹：弦乐、管乐。此处泛指乐器。Sīzhú:xuányuè,guǎnyuè. Cǐchù fànzhǐ yuèqì.

乱耳：使听力紊乱。Luàn ěr:shǐ tīnglì wěnluàn.

案牍：官府人员日常处理的文件。Àndú:guānfǔ rényuán rìcháng chúlǐ de wénjiàn.

【提示】

文章表现了作者不与世俗同流合污、洁身自好、不慕名利的生活态度。表达了作者高洁傲岸的节操，流露出作者安贫乐道的隐逸情趣。“铭”是古代刻在器物上用来警戒自己或者称述功德的文字。

Géyán
格言

Límíng jí qǐ, sásǎo tíng chú, yào nèiwài zhěngjié. Jì hūn biàn xī, guān suǒ ménhù, bì qīnzì jiándiǎn. Yì zhōu yí fàn, dāng sī lái zhī bú yì; bàn sī bàn lǚ, héng niàn wù lì wéi jiān, yí wèi yǔ ér chóumóu, wù lín kě ér juéjǐng. Zì fèng bìxū jiǎnyuē, yàn kè qiè wù liú lián ... Zǔzōng suī yuǎn, jìsì bù kě bú jiè, zǐsūn suī yú, jīng shū bù kě bù dú. Jū shēn wù qī zhìpǔ, jiào zǐ yàoyǒu yìfāng. Mò tān yìwài zhīcái, mò yǐn guòliàng zhī jiǔ. Yǔ jiān tiāo màoyì, wù zhàn piányi, jiàn qióngkǔ qīnlín, xū jiā wēn xù. Jiāmén héshùn, suī yōng sūn bú jì, yě yǒu yú huān; guó kè gōngshì zǎo wán, jí tuótuó wú yú, zì dé qí lè. Dúshū zhì zài shèngxián, fēi tú kē dì; wéi guān xīn cún jūn guó, qǐ jì shēn jiā.

黎明即起，洒扫庭除，要内外整洁。既昏便息，关锁门户，必亲自检点。一粥一饭，当思来之不易；半丝半缕，恒念物力维艰，宜未雨而绸缪，勿临渴而掘井。自奉必须俭约，宴客切勿流连。……祖宗虽远，祭祀不可不戒，子孙虽愚，经书不可不读。居身务期质朴，教子要有义方。莫贪意外之财，莫饮过量之酒。与肩挑贸易，毋占便宜，见穷苦亲邻，须加温恤。家门和顺，虽饔飧不继，也有余欢；国课公事早完，即橐橐无余，自得其乐。读书志在圣贤，非徒科第；为官心存君国，岂计身家。

【注】

饔：早饭。Yōng:zǎofàn.

飧：晚饭。Sūn:wǎnfàn.

国课：担任公职，公事。Guókè: dānrèn gōngzhí, gōngshì.

未雨绸缪：绸缪，绳索捆绑。原为下雨时用绳索捆绑门户。引申为事前要做好准备。Wèi yǔ chóumóu: chóumóu, shéngsuǒ kúnbǎng. Yuán wéi xiàyǔ shí yòng shéngsuǒ kúnbǎng ménhù. Yǐnshēn wéi shìqián yào zuòhǎo zhǔnbèi.

橐橐：原指口袋，引申为工薪（工资）。Tuótuó: yuánzhǐ kóudài, yǐnshēn wéi gōngxīn (gōngzī).

科第：应科第考取功名。Kēdì: yìng kēdì káoqǔ gōngmíng.

【提示】

朱熹（1130—1200），中国南宋思想家，字元晦，号晦庵，徽州婺源（今属江西）人，理学的集大成者，中国封建时代儒家的主要代表人物之一。主要哲学著作有《四书集注》《四书或问》《太极图说解》《通书解》《西铭解》《周易本义》《易学启蒙》等。此外有《朱子语类》，是他与弟子们的问答录。

《朱子家训》：又名《朱子治家格言》《朱柏庐治家格言》。一种说法认为此书为朱熹所著，一种说法认为此书为朱柏庐所著。《朱子家训》仅五百二十二字，精辟地阐明了修身治家之道，堪称家教名篇。自问世以来流传甚广，被历代士大夫尊为“治家之经”，清至民国年间一度成为童蒙必读课本之一。

朱柏庐（1617—1688），字致一，名用纯，明末清初江苏昆山人。

Jiāng Chéng Zǐ

江城子

Sòng · Sū Shì

宋 · 苏轼

Shínián shēng sǐ liǎng mángmáng, bù sī liàng, zì nán wàng, qiān lǐ gū fén wú chù huà qīliáng. Zòngshǐ xiāngféng yīng bù shí, chén mǎn miàn, bìn rú shuāng, yè lái yōu mèng hū huán xiāng. Xiǎo xuān chuāng, zhèng shū zhuāng, xiāng gù wú yán wéi yǒu lèi qiān háng. Liào dé niánnián duàn cháng chù, míng yuè yè, duǎn sōng gāng.

十年生死两茫茫，不思量，自难忘，千里孤坟无处话凄凉。纵使相逢应不识，尘满面，鬓如霜，夜来幽梦忽还乡。小轩窗，正梳妆，相顾无言惟有泪千行。料得年年断肠处，明月夜，短松冈。

【提示】

轩窗：意思为窗户。

这是一首悼亡词。作者写此词时正在密州（今山东诸城）任知州，他的妻子王弗在宋英宗治平二年（公元1065年）死于开封。作者结合自己十年来政治生涯中的不幸遭遇和无限感慨，形象地反映出对亡妻永难忘怀的真挚情感。

Shíhuī Yín

石灰吟

Míng · Yú Qiān

明 · 于谦

Qiān chuí wàn záo chū shēnshān, lièhuǒ fénshāo ruò děng xián.
Fén gǔ suì shēn dōu búpà, yào liú qīngbái zài rénjiān.

千锤万凿出深山，烈火焚烧若等闲。
粉骨碎身都不怕，要留清白在人间。

【提示】

于谦（1398—1457），字廷益，号节庵，浙江钱塘人，明朝名臣，著名军事家、政治家，性固刚直，官至宰相。有《于忠肃集》。

第二节 现代诗文阅读
Section II Reading Modern Poems, Stories and Essays

一 现代诗歌 Modern Poems

Zài Bié Kāngqiáo
再别康桥

Xú Zhìmó

徐志摩

Qīngqīng de wǒ zǒu le,
Zhèng rú wǒ qīngqīng de lái,
Wǒ qīngqīng de zhāoshǒu;
Zuò bié xītiān de yúncai.
Nà hépàn de jīnliǔ,
Shì xīyáng zhōng de xīnniáng;
Bōguāng li de yànyǐng,
Zài wǒ de xīntóu dàngyàng.

Ruǎnní shang de qīngxìng,
Yóuyóu de zài shuí dǐ zhāoyáo;
Zài Kānghé de róubō li,
Wǒ gānxīn zuò yì tiáo shuícǎo!

Nà yúyīn xià de yì tán,
Bú shì qīngquán, shì tiānshang hóng,
Róusuì zài fúzǎo jiān,
Chéndiàn zhe cǎihóng shì de mèng.

Xúnmèng? Chēng yì zhī cháng gāo,
Xiàng qīngcǎo gèng qīng chù mànsù,
Mǎnzài yì chuán xīng huī,
Zài xīng huī bānlán li fàng gē.

Dàn wǒ bù néng fàng gē,
Qiāoqiāo shì biélí de shēngxiāo;
Xiàchóng yě wèi wǒ chénmò,
Chénmò shì jīnwǎn de Kāngqiáo!

Qīngqīng de wǒ zǒu le,
Zhèng rú wǒ qīngqīng de lái;
Wǒ huī yi huī yīxiù,
Bú dài zǒu yí piàn yúncai.

Shíyī yuè liù rì, Zhōngguó Shànghǎi

轻轻的我走了，
正如我轻轻的来；
我轻轻的招手，
作别西天的云彩。

那河畔的金柳，
是夕阳中的新娘；
波光里的艳影，
在我的心头荡漾。

软泥上的青荇，
油油的在水底招摇；
在康河的柔波里，
我甘心做一条水草！

那榆荫下的一潭，
不是清泉，是天上虹
揉碎在浮藻间，
沉淀着彩虹似的梦。

寻梦？撑一支长篙，
向青草更青处漫溯，

满载一船星辉，
在星辉斑斓里放歌。

但我不能放歌，
悄悄是别离的笙箫；
夏虫也为我沉默，
沉默是今晚的康桥！

轻轻的我走了，
正如我轻轻的来；
我挥一挥衣袖，
不带走一片云彩。

十一月六日，中国上海

【提示】

箫：又名洞箫，吹奏乐器。这种单管竖吹的箫，早在汉代陶俑中已出现。其后在壁画、石刻中多有所见。

徐志摩（1897—1931），现代诗人、散文家，浙江海宁县硖石镇人，名章，字志摩，小字又申，曾经用过的笔名字有南湖、云中鹤。

《再别康桥》：此诗写于1928年11月6日，初载于1928年12月10日《新月》月刊第1卷第10号，署名徐志摩。

康桥：英国著名的剑桥大学所在地。1920年10月至1922年8月，诗人曾游学于此。

康桥时期是徐志摩一生的转折点。诗人在《猛虎集·序文》中曾经自陈道：在24岁以前，他对于诗的兴味远不如对于相对论或民约论的兴味。正是康河的水，开启了诗人的性灵，唤醒了久蛰在他心中的诗人的天命。因此，他后来曾满怀深情地说："我的眼是康桥教我睁的，我的求知欲是康桥给我拨动的，我的自我意识是康桥给我胚胎的。"

Yí Jù Huà

一句话

Wén Yīduō

闻一多

Yǒu yí jù huà shuō chūlai jiù shì huò,
Yǒu yí jù huà néng zháohuǒ,
Bié kàn wǔqiān nián méiyǒu shuōpò,
Nǐ cāide tòu huǒshān de chénmò?
Shuōbu dìng shì tūrán zháo le mó,
Tūrán qíngtiān li yí gè pīlì,
Bào yì shēng “Zánmen de Zhōngguó!”
Zhè jù huà jiào wǒ jīntiān zěnme shuō?
Nǐ bú xìn tiěshù kāihuā yé kě,
Nàme yǒu yí jù huà nǐ tīngzhe:
Děng huǒshān rěn bú zhù le jiānmò,
Yào fādǒu, shēn shétou, dùnjiǎo,
Tūrán qíngtiān li yí gè pīlì,
Bào yì shēng: “Zánmen de Zhōng guó!”

—《Sí Shuǐ》

有一句话说出来就是祸，
有一句话能着火。
别看五千年没有说破，
你猜得透火山的沉默？
说不定是突然着了魔，
突然晴天里一个霹雳，
爆一声 “咱们的中国！”
这句话叫我今天怎么说？
你不信铁树开花也可，
那么有一句话你听着：
等火山忍不住了缄默，
要发抖，伸舌头，顿脚，

突然晴天里一个霹雳，
爆一声 “咱们的中国！”

——《死水》

【提示】

《一句话》是篇散文诗，是现代新诗的突出代表，它寓情于理，集现实及情感于一体，从侧面展示了当时中国的国情和有志之士对国富民强的展望和期冀之情。

闻一多：本名家骅，字友三，亦字友山，后改名多，又改名一多。著名诗人、学者、爱国民主战士。出生于湖北省黄冈市浠水县。自幼爱好古典诗词和美术。早年加入文学社团“新月社”，并先后执教青岛大学、清华大学等。“皖南事变”后，积极投身于反对独裁、争取民主、反对内战的斗争中。1946 年，在昆明被国民党特务暗杀。

Wàng Dàlù Shī
望大陆诗

Yú Yòurèn
于佑任

Zàng wǒ yú gāoshān zhī shàng xī,
Wàng wǒ dàlù.
Dàlù bù kě jiàn xī,
Zhíyǒu tòngkū.
Zàng wǒ yú gāoshān zhī shàng xī,
Wàng wǒ gùxiāng,
Gùxiāng bù kě jiàn xī,
Yóngyuǎn bú wàng.
Tiān cāngcāng,
Yě mángmáng,
Shān zhī shàng,
Guó yǒu shāng.

葬我于高山之上兮，
望我大陆。
大陆不可见兮，
只有痛哭。
葬我于高山之上兮，
望我故乡。
故乡不可见兮，
永远不忘。
天苍苍，
野茫茫，
山之上，
国有殇。

【注】

国殇：祭奠为国捐躯的战士。古代称未成年而死或在外死去的人为“殇”。
Guóshāng:Jìdiàn wèi guó juānqū de zhànshì. Gǔdài chēng wèi chéngnián ér sǐ huò zàiwài sǐ qù de rén wéi “Shāng”.

【提示】

于右任（1878—1964），原名伯循，字右任，陕西三原县人，诗人，书法家，政治家。25岁时中举。1906年在日本得会孙中山，加入同盟会。1912年在南京临时政府任职。曾回三原任职，后长期担任国民政府监察院长。1949年去了台湾，1964年11月10日逝世于台北。

于右任是近代民主革命先驱，诗人，政论家，是沉雄博大的一代书法大师。当他滞留孤岛时，对大陆思念颇深。1962年1月24日，作了此诗，表达其思乡之情。

二 历史小故事 History Stories

Kǒng Róng Ràng Lí
孔融让梨

Kǒng Róng xiǎo shíhou cōngming hàoxué, cái sī mǐnjié, qiǎo yán miào dá, dàjiā dōu kuā tā shì qítóng. Sìsuì shí,tā yǐ néng bèisòng xǔduō shī fù, bìngqiě dǒng de lǐjié, fùmǔqīn fēicháng xǐ'ài tā. Yí rì, fùqīn mǎile yì xiē lí, tèdì jiǎnle yí gè zuìdà de lí gěi Kǒng Róng, Kǒng Róng yáoyáo tóu, què lìng jiǎnle yí gè zuìxiǎo de lí shuō: “Wǒ niánjì zuìxiǎo, yīnggāi chī xiǎo de lí, nǐ nà gè lí jiù gěi gēge ba.” Fùqīn tīng hòu shífēn jīngxǐ.

孔融小时候聪明好学，才思敏捷，巧言妙答，大家都夸他是奇童。四岁时，他已能背诵许多诗赋，并且懂得礼节，父母亲非常喜爱他。一日，父亲买了一些梨，特地拣了一个最大的梨给孔融，孔融摇摇头，却另拣了一个最小的梨说：“我年纪最小，应该吃小的梨，你那个梨就给哥哥吧。”父亲听后十分惊喜。

【提示】

赋：中国古典文学的一种重要文体，萌生于战国，兴盛于汉唐，衰于宋元明清，是介于诗、文之间的边缘文体。

孔融（153—208），东汉文学家，鲁国（今山东曲阜）人，字文举，孔子第二十世孙。

Cáo Chōng Chēng Xiàng
曹冲称象

Yǒu yí cì, Wú Sūn Quán sònggěi Cáo Cāo yì zhī yòu gāo yòu dà de dàxiàng. Dàxiàng yùn dào Xǔchāng nà tiān, Cáo Cāo dàilǐng wén wǔ bǎi guān hé xiǎo érzi Cáo Chōng, yì tóng qù kàn. Cáo Cāo duì dàjiā shuō: “Zhè zhī dàxiàng zhēn shì dà, kěshì dàodǐ yǒu duō zhòng ne? Nǐmen nǎ gè yǒu bànfǎ chēng tā yì chēng?” Yǒu rén shuō zào yì gǎn dǐngdà dǐngdà de chèng chēng. Yǒu rén shuō bǎ tā zǎi le, qiē chéng kuàir chēng. Dàchénmen wèicǐ xiǎng le xǔduō bànfǎ, gègè dōu xíng bùtōng. Zhèshí, Cáo Chōng duì Cáo Cāo shuō:

“Fùqīn, wǒ yǒu gè fǎr, kéyǐ chēng dàxiàng.” Cáo Chōng bǎ bànfǎ shuō le. Cáo Cāo yì tīng liánlián jiào hǎo, fēnfù zuǒyòu lìkè zhǔnbèi chēng xiàng. Zhòng dàchén gēnsuí Cáo Cāo láidào hébiān. Hé li tíngzhe yì zhī dà chuán, Cáo Chōng jiào rén bǎ xiàng qiān dào chuán shang, děng chuán shēn wěndìng le, zài chuánxián shang qí shuǐmiàn de dìfang, kèle yí dào héngxiàn zuòwéi jìhao. Zài jiào rén bǎ xiàng qiān dào àn shang, jiēzhe bǎ dàdà xiǎoxiǎo de shítou wǎng chuán shang zhuāng, chuánshēn jiù yìdiǎnr yìdiǎnr wǎng xià chén. Děng chuánshēn chén dào gāngcái kè de nà tiáo héngxiàn hé shuǐmiàn yíyàng qíle, Cáo Chōng jiù jiào rén tíngzhǐ zhuāng shítou. Dàchénmen kàndào zhèli bùyóude liánshēng chēngzàn: “Hǎo bànfǎ! Hǎo bànfǎ!” Xiànzài shuí dōu míngbai, zhǐyào bǎ chuán li de shítou dōu chēng yíxià, bǎ zhòngliàng jiā qǐlái, jiù zhīdào xiàng yǒu duō zhòng le.

有一次，吴孙权送给曹操一只又高又大的大象。大象运到许昌那天，曹操带领文武百官和小儿子曹冲，一同去看。曹操对大家说：“这只大象真是大，可是到底有多重呢？你们哪个有办法称它一称？”有人说造一杆顶大顶大的秤称。有人说把它宰了，切成块儿称。大臣们为此想了许多办法，个个都行不通。这时，曹冲对曹操说：“父亲，我有个法儿，可以称大象。”曹冲把办法说了。曹操一听连连叫好，吩咐左右立刻准备称象。众大臣跟随曹操来到河边。河里停着一只大船，曹冲叫人把象牵到船上，等船身稳定了，在船舷上齐水面的地方，刻了一道横线作为记号。再叫人把象牵到岸上，接着把大大小小的石头往船上装，船身就一点儿一点儿往下沉。等船身沉到刚才刻的那条横线和水面一样齐了，曹冲就叫人停止装石头。大臣们看到这里不由得连声称赞：“好办法！好办法！”现在谁都明白，只要把船里的石头都称一下，把重量加起来，就知道象有多重了。

【提示】

曹冲(196—208)，字仓舒，是曹操儿子之一，由环夫人所生。曹冲从小聪明仁爱，与众不同，深受曹操喜爱。曹操几次对群臣夸耀他，有让他继嗣的意思。不过曹冲还未成年就病逝，年仅13岁。

Huáng Xiāng Shān Zhěn Wēn Qīn
黄香扇枕温衾

Huáng Xiāng, Hàndài rén. Jiǔsuì shí mǔqīn sǐ le,āi tòng zhì qiè. Duì fùqīn hěn xiàoshùn, xiàtiān shǔ rè, gěi fùqīn shān liáng zhěnxí; dōngtiān hánlěng, yòng shēntǐ wēnnuǎn bèirù. Guānfǔ biǎoyáng tā shì “Xiàotóng”. Hòulái tā chéngwéi yí gè dàodé gāoshàng de yǒu xuéwèn de rén, guān zhì Shàngshū.

黄香，汉代人。九岁时母亲死了，哀痛至切。对父亲很孝顺，夏天暑热，给父亲扇凉枕席；冬天寒冷，用身体温暖被褥。官府表扬他是“孝童”。后来他成为一个道德高尚的有学问的人，官至尚书。

三 散文 Essays

Shuō Měi
说美
Qín Mù
秦牧

Rénmen cháng shuō: “Niǎo měi zài yǔmáo,rén měi zài línghún.” Línghún měi, jí dàodé pǐnzhì, jīngshén jìngjiè, sīxiǎng yìshí hé zhìqù qíngcāo zhī měi. “Rén bú shì yīnwéi měi cái kě'ài, érshì yīnwéi kě'ài cái měilì.” “Rén de měi bìng búzài wàimào, yīfu hé fàshì, ér zàiyú tā de běnshēn, zàiyú tā de xīn, yàoshi rén méiyǒu nèixīn de měi, wǒmen chángcháng huì yànwù tā de wàibiǎo.”

—《Yǒnggǎn de Zhuīqiú Zhēnzhèng de Měi》

人们常说：“鸟美在羽毛，人美在灵魂。”灵魂美，即道德品质、精神境界、思想意识和志趣情操之美。“人不是因为美才可爱，而是因为可爱才美丽。”“人的美并不在外貌、衣服和发式，而在于他的本身，在于他的心，要是人没有内心的美，我们常常会厌恶他的外表。”

——《勇敢地追求真正的美》

【提示】

秦牧（1919—1992），原名林阿书，又名林派光、林觉夫、林颀石，祖籍澄海东里樟林。我国著名文学大师，生于香港。1938年春到广州参加抗日救亡宣传活动，1941年在桂林的中山中学教书，并从事写作，开始涉足文坛。历任《中华论坛》《再生》《中国工人》诸杂志编辑。新中国成立后，历任广东省文教厅科长、中华书局广州编辑室主任、中国作家协会广州分会副主席、《羊城晚报》副总编辑，主编过《广东教育与文化》《中华通俗文库》《作品》等杂志。曾任广东省文联副主席、暨南大学中文系主任、全国文联委员、中国作家协会理事、广东省文联执行主席，并任《四海》杂志主编。曾率中国作家代表团访问美国，以作家身份访问过蒙古、古巴、新加坡和泰国。出版《秦牧全集》十卷，被喻为“一棵繁花树”。

Zhūzi
珠子
Bīng Xīn
冰心

Guòqù rénmen cháng bǎ xuéxí hé gōngzuò de tàidu bǐzuò sān zhǒng zhūzi: Yì zhǒng shì rúyìzhū, bù bō jiù dòng; yì zhǒng shì suànpán zhū, bōle cái dòng; yì zhǒng shì fódǐng zhū, bō yě bú dòng. Wǒmen... Xuéxí hé gōngzuò de tàidu, yídìng bú yào xiàng suànpán zhū, bō yíxià dòng yíxià, gèng bù néng xiàng fódǐng zhú, bō yě bú dòng, ér yào xiàng rúyì zhū nà yàng zhǔdòng .

—《Jiù Huà Chóng Tí》

过去人们常把学习和工作的态度比做三种珠子：一种是如意珠，不拨就动；一种是算盘珠，拨了才动；一种是佛顶珠，拨也不动。我们……学习和工作的态度一定不要像算盘珠，拨一下动一下，更不能像佛顶珠，拨也不动，而要像如意珠那样主动。

——《旧话重提》

【提示】

冰心 (1900—1999)，原名谢婉莹，现代著名女作家，儿童文学作家，福建长乐人，因一生刚好度过了一个世纪，所以被称为“世纪老人”，深受人民喜爱。

算盘：是中国人在长期使用算筹的基础上发明的。算盘呈长方形，四周是木框，里面固定着一根根小木棍，小木棍上穿着木珠，中间一根将算盘分成两部分，每根木棍的上半部有两个珠子，每个珠子当五；下半部有五个珠子，每个珠子代表一。

佛顶珠：这里比喻懒散呆滞、推拨不动的人。

如意珠：佛珠。梵语“真多摩尼”的意译。相传用佛舍利（佛骨）制成。

Tán Dúshū
谈读书
Péi Gēn
培根

Dú shǐ shǐ rén míngzhì, dú shī shǐ rén língxiù, shùxué shǐ rén zhōumì, kēxué shǐ rén shēnkè,lúnlǐ shǐ rén zhuāngzhòng, luóji xiūcí shǐrén shànbiàn, xiězuò zé shǐ rén jīngquè… Fán yǒu xīnxué, jiē chéng yì gé, rén zhī cáizhì ruò yǒu zhì'ài, wú bù kě dú shìdàng zhī shū, shǐ zhī chōngshí shùnchàng. Yì rú shēntǐ jíbìng, jiē kě jiè xiāngyí zhī yùndòng chú zhī. Gǔnqiú lì gāoshèn, shèjiàn lì xiōngfèi, mànbù lì chángwèi, qímǎ lì tóunǎo děng.

—《Tán Dúshū》

读史使人明智，读诗使人灵秀，数学使人周密，科学使人深刻，伦理使人庄重，逻辑修辞使人善辩，写作则使人精确……凡有新学，皆成一格，人之才智若有滞碍，无不可读适当之书，使之充实顺畅。一如身体疾病，皆可借相宜之运动除之。滚球利睾肾，射箭利胸肺，漫步利肠胃，骑马利头脑等。

——《谈读书》

【提示】

培根（1561—1626），英国哲学家、科学家。著有《学术的进步》《新工具》等。

四 童话故事 Tale Stories

Láng hé Xiǎoyáng
狼和小羊

Láng lái dào xiǎoxī biān, kànjiàn xiǎoyáng zhèngzài nàr hē shuǐ.

Láng fēicháng xiǎng chī xiǎoyáng, jiù gùyì zhǎochár shuō: “Nǐ bǎ wǒ hē de shuǐ nòng zāng le! Nǐ ān de shénme xīn?”

Xiǎoyáng chī le yì jīng, wēnhé de shuō: “Wǒ zěnme huì bǎ nín hē de shuǐ nòng zāng ne? Nín zhàn zài shàngyóu, shuǐ shì cóng nín nàr liú dào wǒ zhèr lái de, bú shì cóng wǒ zhèr liú dào nín nàr qù de.”

Láng qìchōngchōng de shuō: “Jiù suàn zhèyàng ba, nǐ zǒng shì gè huài jiāhuo! Wǒ tīngshuō, qùnián nǐ zài bèidì li shuō wǒ de huàihuà!”

Kělián de xiǎoyáng hǎndào: “Ā, qīn’ ài de láng xiānshēng, nà shì bú huì yǒu de shìr, qùnián wǒ hái méiyǒu shēng xiàlái na!”

Láng bù xiǎng zài zhēngbiàn le, zīzhe yá, bījìn xiǎoyáng, dàshēng rǎng dào: “ Nǐ zhè gè xiǎo huàidàn! Shuō wǒ huàihuà de bú shì nǐ jiùshì nǐ bàba, fǎnzhèng dōu yíyàng.” Shuōzhe jiù wǎng xiǎoyáng shēn shang pūqù.

狼来到小溪边，看见小羊正在那儿喝水。

狼非常想吃小羊。就故意找茬儿说：“你把我喝的水弄脏了！你安的什么心？”

小羊吃了一惊，温和地说：“我怎么会把您喝的水弄脏呢？您站在上游，水是从您那儿流到我这儿来的，不是从我这儿流到您那儿去的。”

狼气冲冲地说：“就算这样吧，你总是个坏家伙！我听说，去年你在背地里说我的坏话！”

可怜的小羊喊道：“啊，亲爱的狼先生，那是不会有的事儿，去年我还没有生下来哪！”

狼不想再争辩了，龇着牙，逼近小羊，大声嚷道：“你这个小坏蛋！说我坏话的不是你就是你爸爸，反正都一样。”说着就往小羊身上扑去。

Tùzi · Hóuzi · Mǎ · Huli
兔子 · 猴子 · 马 · 狐狸

Húli zài línzi li hài de línjūmen bù dé ānníng, dàn yě méi gè hǎo bànfǎ. Yì tiān hóuzi kànjiàn húli tōutōu mōmō de zǒu guòlai le, biàn tiàoxià shù shuō: “Húli dàgē, nǐ zhǎo shénme?” “Nǐ guǎn bu zháo! Shuōzhe húli yáozhe wěiba zǒu le. Hóuzi zhuī shàngqù yòu shuō: “ Húli dàgē bié zǒu, nǐ zhīdào shìjiè shang shénme dōngxi zuì hǎochī ma?” Húli yì tīngshuō hǎochī de dōngxi, biàn shùqǐle ěrduo shuō: “Nǐ shuō ne?” Hóuzi gǎnmáng shuō: “Zuì hǎochī de shì mǎ pìgu ròu! “ Shénme? Mǎ pìgu ròu!” Shuōwán jiù yáo le yáo tóu zǒu le. Hóuzi yòu zhuī shàngqù qiāoqiāo de shuō: “ Gāngcái wǒ kànjiàn mǎ zhèngzài shù xià shuì dà jiào ne, zhènghǎo, búguò nǐ chī de shíhou yào bǎ nǐ de wěiba hé mǎ wěiba shuān zài yìqǐ, cái néng chīshàng." Shuōzhe hóuzi tiàoshàng shù.Húli jiàn hóuzi zǒu le, kàn le kàn sìmiàn jiù qiāoqiāo de zǒudào shùxià, zhǐ tīngdào mǎ hū lūlu, hū lūlu de, biàn qīngqīng de bǎ zìjǐ de wěiba hé mǎ wěiba jǐnjǐn de shuān zài yìqǐ, ránhòu jiù duìzhǔn mǎ de pìgu hěnhěn de yǎole yì kǒu. Mǎ láolèile yì tiān zhèng shuì de xiāngtián, tūrán jué de pìgu téng de zuānxīn, bùguǎn sān qī èrshí yī tiàoqǐlái jiù pǎo, wěiba shuān de hěn jǐn, lā de húli zhí gǔn, téng de húli zhí hǎn: " Jiùmìng ā, jiùmìng…" Zhè shíhou dūn zài tǔpō shang de tùzi lè de hāhā dàxiào, bù xiǎoxīn bǎ shàng zuǐchún lièkāi le, hóuzi ne? Gāoxìng dé shóu wǔ zú dǎo, bù xiǎoxīn diàoxia shù lái bǎ pìgu dūn hóng le. Húli ne? Tā quánshēn de máo hēi yí kuài huī yí piàn de, jiù shì nà cì yǎo mǎ pìgu shí, ràng mǎ lāzhe móchūlái de. Mǎ ne? Tā zěnme yě bú yuàn wòzhe shuìjiào, pà húli zài lái yǎo pìgu. Nǐ bú xìn zǐxì kànkan, tùzi shì huōzi zuǐ, jiù nà cì xiào lièkāi de, dòngwùyuán de hóuzi pìgu shì hóngtōngtōng de, jiù shì nà cì shuāi de; húli pímáo zǒng bú shì yí sè de, jiù shì nà cì ràng mǎ lāzhe mó de; wǒmen kàndào de mǎ yìzhí shì zhànzhe shuìjiào de, jiù shì nà cì ràng húli yǎo pà le.

狐狸在林子里害得邻居们不得安宁，但也没个好办法。一天，猴子看见狐狸偷偷摸摸地走过来了，便跳下树说："狐狸大哥，你找什么？""你管不着！"说着狐狸摇着尾巴走了。猴子追上去又说："狐狸大哥，别走，你知道世界上什么东西最好吃吗？"狐狸一听说好吃的东西，便竖起了耳朵，说："你说呢？"猴子赶忙说："最好吃的是马屁股肉。""什么？马屁股肉！"说完就摇了摇头走了。猴子又追上去，悄悄地说"刚才我看见马正在树下睡大觉呢，正好，不过你吃的时候要把你的尾巴和马尾巴拴在一起，才能吃上。"

说着猴子跳上树。狐狸见猴子走了，看了看四面就悄悄地走到树下，只听到马呼噜噜，呼噜噜的，便轻轻地把自己的尾巴和马尾巴紧紧地拴在一起，然后就对准马的屁股狠狠地咬了一口。马劳累了一天正睡得香甜，突然觉得屁股疼得钻心，不管三七二十一跳起来就跑，尾巴拴得很紧，拉得狐狸直滚，疼得狐狸直喊："救命啊，救命……"这时候蹲在土坡上的兔子乐得哈哈大笑，不小心把上嘴唇裂开了，猴子呢？高兴得手舞足蹈，不小心掉下树来，把屁股蹾红了。狐狸呢？它全身的毛黑一块灰一片的，就是那次咬马屁股时，让马拉着磨出来的。

马呢？它怎么也不愿卧着睡觉，怕狐狸再来咬屁股。你不信仔细看看，兔子是豁子嘴，就那次笑裂开的；动物园的猴子屁股是红彤彤的，就是那次摔的；狐狸皮毛总不是一色的，就是那次让马拉着磨的；我们看到的马一直是站着睡觉的，就是那次让狐狸咬怕了。

【提示】

故事告诉我们：胜利了别骄傲，欢呼时要小心自己的嘴巴，高兴时别忘乎所以，睡觉时要提高警惕，防止坏人的偷袭！

Wūyā hé Húli

乌鸦和狐狸

Wūyā bù zhī shénme dìfang jiǎnlai le yí kuài nǎilào, tā qínzhe nǎilào dūn zài shùzhī shang, yí dòng bú dòng de chénsī mòxiǎngzhe, bù zhī rúhé xiǎngshòu zhè kuài měiwèi de dōngxi. Yí zhèn xiāngwèir zhāolái le yì zhī húli, tā qīngqīng de ràozhe shù zǒuzhe, shùqǐ ěrduo dīngzhe wūyā de zuǐ, xì shēng xì qì de shuō: “Yō! Qīn’ àide, nǐ! Nǐ zhǎngzhe yí gè zuì jiànquán de hóulóng, néng chàng chū shìjiè shang zuì měimiào de gēshēng, qīn’ àide, fàng kāi nǐ de hóulóng chàng ba! Ā, qīn’ àide, chàng ba! Rénmen dōu zài děngzhe nǐ ne, chàng ba!

Nàgè shǎ dōngxi tīngle húli de zànměi, biàn fàngkāi sǎngménr: “Ā! ā!... ” Nǎilào diào xiàqu le, húli yě méi yǐngr le.

乌鸦不知什么地方捡来了一块奶酪，它噙着奶酪蹲在树枝上，一动不动地沉思默想着，不知如何享受这块美味的东西。一阵香味儿招来了一只狐狸，它轻轻地绕着树走着，竖起耳朵盯着乌鸦的嘴，细声细气地说：“唷！亲爱的，你！你长着一个最健全的喉咙，能唱出世界上最美妙的歌声，亲爱的，放开你的喉咙唱吧！啊，亲爱的，唱吧！人们都在等着你呢，唱吧！”

那个傻东西听了狐狸的赞美，便放开嗓门儿，“啊！啊！……”奶酪掉下去了，狐狸也没影儿了。

五 笑话 Jokes

Guāng zhe Bǎngzi
光着膀子

Yì tiān, yì zhī máquè duì gēzi shuō: “Nǐ gǎn qù dǎ lǎoyīng ma?”

“Dāngrán gǎn le”, shuōwán gēzi jiù fēizǒu le, guòle yíhuìr, gēzi fēile huílai, shēnshang de yǔmáo yì gēn dōu méi le.

Máquè wèn: “Chūle shénme shì ?”

Gēzi shuō: “ Nà xiǎozi bù fúqi, wǒ guāng zhe bǎngzi zòule tā yí dùn.”

一天，一只麻雀对鸽子说：“你敢去打老鹰吗？”

“当然敢了”，说完鸽子就飞走了，过了一会儿，鸽子飞了回来，身上的羽毛一根都没了。

麻雀问：“出了什么事？”

鸽子说：“那小子不服气，我光着膀子揍了它一顿。”

Nǎ Yì Zhǒng Dòngwù
哪一种动物

Yī niánjí de lǎoshī jiāo xiǎo péngyou rènshi jiāqín dòngwù.

Lǎoshī shuō: “Yǒu yì zhǒng dòngwù liǎng zhī jiǎo, měitiān zǎoshang tàiyáng gōng gong chūlái shí, tā dōu huì jiào nǐ qǐchuáng, Érqiě jiào dào nǐ qǐchuáng wéizhǐ, shì nǎ yì zhǒng dòngwù?

Xiǎo péngyou shuō: “Māma!”

一年级的老师教小朋友认识家禽动物。

老师说：“有一种动物两只脚，每天早上太阳公公出来时，它都会叫你起床，而且叫到你起床为止，是哪一种动物？”

小朋友说：“妈妈！”

Tōu Píngguǒ
“偷”苹果

Nóngfū xúnshì guǒyuán, fāxiàn yí gè xiǎo nánhái pānshàngle píngguǒ shù.

“Xiǎo dǎodàn, nǐ děngzhe kàn, wǒ yào qù gàosu nǐ bàba!” Nánhái táitóu xiàng shàngmian hǎn dào: “Diē, shù dǐxià yǒu rén yào hé nǐ shuōhuà!”

“Ā! Shàngtou hái yǒu rén li?”

农夫巡视果园，发现一个小男孩攀上了苹果树。

“小捣蛋，你等着看，我要去告诉你爸爸！”男孩抬头向上面喊道：“爹，树底下有人要和你说话！”

“啊！上头还有人哩？”

六　人文常识 General Knowledge of Humanity

Zhōngguó Dìlǐ
中国地理

Zhōngguó wèiyú Yàzhōu dōngbù, Tàipíngyáng xī’àn, tā de bǎntú bèi xíngxiàng de bǐ zuò yì zhī tóu cháo dōng, wěi cháo xī de jīnjī. Qí lùdì miànjī yuē jiǔbǎi liùshí wàn píngfāng gōnglǐ, zài shìjiè gè guó zhōng, jǐn cì yú Éluósī, Jiānádà, jū dìsān wèi. Quánguó língtǔ dōng xī jùlí yuē wǔqiān èrbǎi gōnglǐ, héng kuà wǔ gè shíqū liùshí duō dù (jīngdù), nán běi jùlí yuē wǔqiān wúbǎi gōnglǐ, kuàyuè jìn wǔshí dù (wěidù), zuì běiduān zài Hēilóngjiāng Shěng Mò Hé yíběi de Hēilóngjiāng zhǔ hángdào zhōngxīnxiàn shang, zuì nánduān zhì Nánshā Qúndǎo de Zéngmǔ’ànshā (béiwěi sì dù fùjìn); zuìdōngduān zài Hēilóngjiāng Shěng Hēilóng Jiāng yǔ Wūsūlǐ Jiāng zhǔ hángdào zhōngxīnxiàn jiāohuìchù, zuì xīduān zài Xīnjiāng Pàmǐ’ěr Gāoyuán.

Zhōngguó dàlù hǎi’ànxiàn cháng yíwàn bāqiān duō gōnglǐ, yǒu dáoyǔ wǔqiān duō gè, zuìdà de dáoyǔ shì Táiwān Dǎo, dì’èr dà dǎo shì Hǎinán Dǎo, zuìdà de qúndǎo shì Zhōushān Qúndǎo, zuìdà de bàndǎo shì Liáodōng Bàndǎo, dì’èr dà bàndǎo shì Shāndōng Bàndǎo.

Zhōngguó suǒ bīnlín de hǎiyáng, cóng běi dào nán, yīcì wéi Bó Hǎi, Huáng Hǎi, Dōng Hǎi, Nán Hǎi, qízhōng Bó Hǎi shì Zhōngguó de nèihǎi.

Yǔ Zhōngguó lùdì xiānglín de guójiā yǒu shísì gè, fēnbié wéi Cháoxiǎn, Ménggǔ, Éluósī, Hāsàkèsītǎn, Jí'ěrjísīsītǎn, Tǎjíkèsītǎn , Ā fùhàn, Bājīsītǎn, Yìndù, Níbó'ěr, Bùdān, Miǎndiàn, Lǎowō, Yuènán; gé hǎi xiāngwàng de guójiā yǒu lìu gè, fēnbié wéi Hánguó, Rìběn, Fēilǜbīn, Mǎláixīyà, Wénlái , Yìndùníxīyà.

Zhōngguó de xíngzhèng qūyù jīběn fēn wéi shěng (Zìzhìqū, Zhíxiáshì, Tèbié xíngzhèng qū) , Xiàn (Zìzhìxiàn, Shì) , Xiāng (Zhèn) sān jí, gòng yǒu sānshísì gè shěng jí xíngzhèng dānwèi, èrshísān gè shěng, wǔ gè Zìzhìqū, sì gè Zhíxiáshì hé liǎng gè Tèbié Xíng zhèngqū.

中国位于亚洲东部、太平洋西岸，它的版图被形象地比做一只头朝东、尾朝西的金鸡。其陆地面积约九百六十万平方公里，在世界各国中，仅次于俄罗斯、加拿大，居第三位。全国领土东西距离约五千二百公里，横跨五个时区、六十多度（经度）；南北距离约五千五百公里，跨越近五十度（纬度），最北端在黑龙江省漠河以北的黑龙江主航道中心线上，最南端至南沙群岛的曾母暗沙（北纬四度附近）；最东端在黑龙江省黑龙江与乌苏里江主航道中心线交汇处，最西端在新疆帕米尔高原。

中国大陆海岸线长一万八千多公里，有岛屿五千多个，最大的岛屿是台湾岛，第二大岛是海南岛，最大的群岛是舟山群岛，最大的半岛是辽东半岛，第二大半岛是山东半岛。

中国所濒临的海洋，从北到南，依次为渤海、黄海、东海、南海，其中渤海是中国的内海。

与中国陆地相邻的国家有十四个，分别为朝鲜、蒙古、俄罗斯、哈萨克斯坦、吉尔吉斯斯坦、塔吉克斯坦、阿富汗、巴基斯坦、印度、尼泊尔、不丹、缅甸、老挝、越南；隔海相望的国家有六个，分别为韩国、日本、菲律宾、马来西亚、文莱、印度尼西亚。

中国的行政区域，基本分为省（自治区、直辖市、特别行政区）、县（自治县、市）、乡（镇）三级，共有三十四个省级行政单位，二十三个省，五个自治区，四个直辖市和两个特别行政区。

【提示】

自治区：自治区是一种行政区域划分名称。在我国成立初期，把民族自治地方统称为自治区；1954 年中华人民共和国宪法规定，分自治区、自治州和自治县（自治旗）三级。自治区的行政地位相当于省，为中国最高一级行政区——省级行政区。截至 2005 年底，中国共计有五个自治区。

直辖市：直辖市是直属中央政府管理的省级行政单位。中国有四个直辖市，分别是上海市、北京市、天津市和重庆市。

特别行政区：是指在中华人民共和国行政区域范围内设立的、享有特殊法律地位、实行资本主义制度和资本主义生活方式的地方行政区域。

Lóng de Chuánrén
龙的传人

Zhōnghuá mínzú wèihé bèi chēngwéi “lóng de chuánrén”, yǒu liáng zhǒng shuōfǎ: yì zhǒng rènwéi zhè yuán yú Fúxī hé Nǚwā de chuánshuō. Jù kǎozhèng Fúxī shēng yú jīn Gānsù Tiānshuǐ yídài, gù Tiānshuǐ sù yǒu “Xīhuáng Gùlǐ” zhī chēng. Tā wéi Zhōngguó shénhuà zhōng rén de shízǔ, jiāo rén jié wǎng, bǔ yú dǎliè, hái chuàngzào wénzì, huà bāguà, zuò jiǎlì, dìng sìjì, zào qínsè, xīng yīnyuè, fēng guānlì děng, wèi rénlèi de jìnbù zuòchūle hěndà de gòngxiàn. Chuánshuō, Fúxī hái chuàngzào hūnqǔ zhìdù, shǐ rénlèi déyǐ fányǎn. Gǔdài yí cì hóngshuǐ, tūnmò rénqún, Fúxī hé Nǚwā jiǎoxìng tuōxiǎn, yúshì jiéwéi fūqī, rénlèi cái miǎn yú mièjué. Hòulái, rénmen biàn chēng Fúxī hé Nǚwā wéi rénlèi de shízǔ. Chuánshuō Fúxī shì “lóngshēn rénshǒu”, Nǚwā shì “shéshēn rénmiàn”, yīncǐ, Zhōnghuá Mínzú bèi chēngwéi “Lóng de Chuánrén”.

Yě yǒu rén rènwéi shì yuán yú Xuānyuán Huángdì chéng lóng dào Huánglíng de chuánshuō.

Wúlùn zěnyàng, chuánshuō zhōng de Fúxī, Huángdì, dōu yǔ “Lóng” de shénhuà liánxì zài yìqǐ, yīncǐ wǒmen yán-huáng zǐsūn yě bèi chēngwéi “Lóng de Chuánrén”.

中华民族为何被称为“龙的传人”，有两种说法，一种认为这源于伏羲和女娲的传说。据考证伏羲生于今甘肃天水一带，故天水素有“羲皇故里”之称。他为中国神话中人的始祖，教人结网，捕鱼打猎，还创造文字，画八卦、作甲历、定四季、造琴瑟、兴音乐、封官吏等，为人类的进步作出了很大的贡献。传说，伏羲还创造婚娶制度，使人类得以繁衍。古代一次洪水，吞没人群，伏羲和女娲侥幸脱险，于是结为夫妻，人类才免于灭绝。后来，人们便称伏羲和女娲为人类的始祖。传说伏羲是“龙身人首”，女娲是“蛇身人面”，因此，中华民族被称为“龙的传人”。

也有人认为是源于轩辕黄帝乘龙到黄陵的传说。

无论怎样，传说中的伏羲、黄帝，都与“龙”的神话联系在一起，因此我们炎黄子孙也被称为“龙的传人”。

【提示】

龙：起源于新石器时代早期，距今天不少于八千年，是原始社会形成的一种图腾崇拜的标志。在早期，古人对大多数的自然现象无法作出合理的解释，于是便希望自己民族的图腾具备风、雨、雷、电的力量，群山的雄姿，能像鱼一样在水中游弋，像鸟一样在天空飞翔。因此许多动物的特点都集中在龙身上，龙渐渐形成骆头、蛇脖、鹿角、龟眼、鱼鳞、虎掌、鹰爪、牛耳的样子。这种复合结构，意味着龙是万兽之兽，万能之兽，万能之神。它又能兴云致雨，为众鳞虫之长，四灵之首，后成为皇权象征，历代帝王都自命为龙，使用器物也以龙为装饰。前人分龙为四种：有鳞者称蛟龙；有翼者称为应龙；有角者称虬龙；无角者称螭龙。

伏羲：又作宓羲、庖牺、包牺、伏戏，亦称牺皇、皇羲、太昊，史记中称伏牺。是中华民族人文始祖。所处时代约为旧石器时代中晚期，相传为中国医药鼻祖之一。

女娲：又称女阴、女娲娘娘，风姓，生于成纪，一说她的名字为风里希（或为凤里牺）。中国上古神话中的创世女神。传说她与伏羲是兄妹，与伏羲结婚而产生人类。

天水：市名，位于甘肃东南部，自古是丝绸之路必经之地。全市横跨长江、黄河两大流域。现辖武山、甘谷、秦安、清水、张家川回族自治县五县和秦州、麦积两区，总人口三百二十八万。境内四季分明，气候宜人，物产丰富，素有西北“小江南”之美称。

黄帝：古史传说中的人物，关于他的传说中最精彩的要数黄帝与炎帝、蚩尤的战争了。最终黄帝取得了胜利，被各部落拥戴为部落联盟领袖。在黄帝时期，养蚕、舟车、文字、音律、医学、算数都先行发明，并得到发展，他的功劳为后世所称赞。

甲历：用甲子记载岁时的日历。

第三节 汉字的书写
Section III The Writing of Chinese Characters

一 汉字的特点 Nature of Chinese Characters

汉字是记录汉语的符号。汉字和世界上其他的文字一样，有共同的特点，这是文字的共性。汉字也有自己的特点，这是它的个性。

Chinese characters are the written form of Chinese language. They have the common nature both Chinese characters and others, but Chinese characters have their own features. Following are the main features.

汉字具有哪些特点呢？

1. 汉字是代表音节的表意文字。

汉字同其他文字一样，它是由直接记事图画而来的文字，它是通过描绘实物的形体来显示字义的，是表意文字的初级阶段。如：

1. Chinese characters has an ideographic writing system.

As other characters, Chinese characters evolved directly from pictographic, which refer to their meanings, are shown by depicting the shapes of things. Pictographic are initial stage of the ideography of Chinese characters. For example:

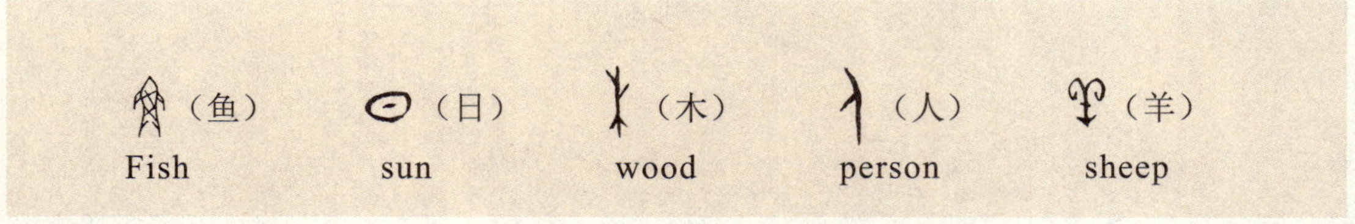

2. 汉字是方块形的形声文字。

汉字近五万个，占汉字总数90%左右的是形声字。这类形声字是由图画形的独体表意字构成的，合成形声字的部件有两个或两个以上的独体字，他们一个是表示意义的叫“意符”，一个是表示读音的叫“音符”（声符）。由于这类独体字在造字时是刻画在骨头等上面的，往往是长而细瘦的笔画。两个独体字合起来也就构成了一个“方块”形，经过长时期的演变，汉字也就成为方块字了。如：

2. Most Chinese characters are pictophonetic characters.

There are a total more than 50,000 Chinese characters, making up more than 90% of all Chinese characters. Phonograms are compound characters that contain both a form component that indicates the character’s meaning and a sound component that indicates its pronunciation. Because the independent characters were written on the bones, so their strokes are long and thin. A square character is usually made up of two independent characters. With evolution for a long history, Chinese characters became square characters. For example:

氵	（水） water	（江）jiāng river	
山	（山） hill	（峰）fēng mountain peak	
木	（木） wood	（枷）jiā cangue	
⺮	（竹） bamboo	（符）fú symbol	

这类形声字既能表意又能读音，解决了大部分汉字的读音问题，但还有不少的字要一个个口耳相传，代代相教，才能读出音来，就是我们常说的"会意"字。它也是由两个或两个以上的独体字结合而成的。两个独体字组合出了一个新的会意字。如：

Pictophonetic characters represent the characters meaning and pronunciation. It is often the case that we can guess the pronunciation of a pictophonetic characters by looking at one or both of these elements. But some characters are learned to read from generation to generation, which are associative characters. They are made up of two or more elements, to creat new characters new meanings by combining two or more than independent characters, and characters constructed in this way are known as associative characters. For example:

（目 eye）+ （人 person） = （见 see）

（手 hand）+ （木 wood） = （采 pick）

（日 sun）+ （一 one） = （旦 dawn morning）

（手 hand）+ （目 eye） = （看 look）

3. 汉字是形、音、义紧密结合的整体。

3. A Chinese character is the integration of its appearance, pronunciation and meaning.

汉字是方块字，一个方块字（形）就是一个音节，一个读音（音），表示一个意义（义），是形、音、义紧密结合的整体。这样近五万个汉字就有四万多个读音（同音字除外），近五万个形体，近五万个意义。再加上，它尽管是一个平面的方块形，但其笔画（线条）却是向四面八方发展的。也正由于如此，就给学习汉字上带来了“难认、难读、难写”的困难。

Chinese characters are known as “square character”, i.e. each character is endowed with a certain pronunciation and meaning. It is the integration of its appearance, pronunciation and meaning. As a result, about 50,000 Chinese characters are more than 40,000 kinds of pronunciation (besides homophone), 50,000 appearance and 50,000 meaning. Though they are square characters, their strokes have the different combination. As a result, there are difficulties in reading and writing for students to learn Chinese characters.

语言是人类最重要的交际工具，文字是人类最重要的辅助性交际工具。因此，学习语言还需要学习记录该种语言的文字。学习汉语也一样，必须学习记录汉语的书写符号系统——汉字。汉字是表意体系的文字，是用大量的表意符号来记录汉语的词和语素，从而间接代表了词和语素的声音。正是如此，就使汉字形成了一字、一形、一词、一个语素、一个意义、一个声音的特点。汉字有四五万个形体，在记录汉语的方式、方法上，不同于表音文字。一个汉字不管笔画有多少，都要写得清晰、准确、方方正正，书写时通常不连写。那么，这种特殊的书写形式又是如何形成的呢？

Language is the most important communicating tool between people, and characters are the most important supplementary communicating tools. Therefore, learning characters is necessary for learning a language. One who wants to learn Chinese should also learn the writing system — Chinese characters, as learning other languages. Chinese characters system, one type of ideograms, uses a large quantity of marks to record words and morphemes, and then indirectly stands for voices of words and morphemes. Therefore, it forms those characteristics, such as character, form, syllable, meaning and sound. There are about forty thousand to fifty thousand forms in Chinese, different from phonograms in the way of recording. No matter how many strokes a character has, it must be written clearly, correctly and smoothly. So, it’s stroke is not connected. However, how does the special writing form be developed?

二 汉字的形体 Shapes of Chinese Characters

（一）汉字形体的演变 I. The Shapes of Chinese Characters Originate from

汉字的形体从古至今，大致经过了三个阶段性的变化：图形化、线条化、笔画化。汉字的字体经历了甲骨文、金文、小篆、楷书、草书、行书阶段的发展。

Throughout history, the shapes of Chinese characters have greatly evolved from pictography, line presentation to strokes. Chinese character have gone through the stages of *Jiaguwen, Jinwen, XiaoZhuan, Lishu, Kaishu, Caoshu* and *Xingshu.*

七种汉字对照表

The Comparing Table of Seven Forms of Chinese Characters

印刷体	甲骨文	金文	小篆	隶书	楷书	草书	行书
虎				虎	虎		虎
象				象	象		象
鹿				鹿	鹿		鹿
鸟				鳥	鳥 乌		鸟
鼎				鼎	鼎		鼎
鬲				鬲	鬲		鬲
壶				壺	壺 壶		壶
尊				尊	尊		尊
受				受	受		受
兴				興	興 兴		兴

（二）汉字的形体分类　II. The Classification of Chinese Character's Shapes

1. 独体字

独体字是依据客观事物的具体形状描画而成的。如：

1. Single Characters

They are always created according to the concrete forms of things. For example:

 （人）	rén	 （口）	kǒu
 （目）	mù	（山）	shān
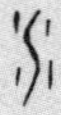 （水）	shuǐ	 （木）	mù
 （牛）	niú	 （羊）	yáng
（日）	rì	 （月）	yuè
 （虎）	hǔ	 （鸟）	niǎo
 （马）	mǎ	 （虫）	chóng
 （火）	hǔo	 （壶）	hú
 （鱼）	yú	 （竹）	zhú
 （刀）	dāo	 （井）	jǐng
 （车）	chē	 （舟）	zhōu
 （禾）	hé	 （瓜）	guā

具体事物可以象形，抽象概念无法描绘。为了避免多造新字，人们便在一些象形字上加一点或一画，表示所指事物和想象的意义。例如：

Concrete things could be hieroglyphic, but abstract ideas couldn't be described. In order to avoid too many new words, people add a point or a stroke on some hieroglyphic scripts to express a new meaning. For example:

“口”kǒu，在口中加一点是 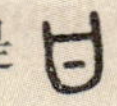 ，“甘”gān，表示甜美，今有“甘甜”。

“刀”dāo，在刀上加一点是  ，“刃”rèn，表示刀口锋利，今有“刀刃”“刀口”。

“木”mù，在木下加一画是  ，“本”běn，表示树根，今有“根本”“根据”。

“木”mù，在木上加一画是  ，“末”mò，表示树梢，今有“末梢”“末了”。

这类象形独体字在汉字的发展演变中，除了继续发挥它本身的形、音、义功能外，还成为造出更多的新合体汉字的基础字和重要的结构部件。

During the development of these hieroglyphic scripts, besides their original functions of form, sound and meaning.

2. 合体字

合体字是由两个或两个以上的象形独体字作为部件组合而成的。例如：

2.Compound Characters

A Compound Character is composed by two or more hieroglyphic single characters as its parts. For example:

“日”“月”组合为“明”míng，表示光明。

“人”“木”组合为“休”xiū，表示人依木休息。

“水”“目”组合为“泪”lèi，表示眼睛流泪。

三“日”组合为“晶”jīng，表示夜空众星闪亮。

“水”“步”组合为“涉”shè，表示两只脚从水中走过。

两“手”组合为“斗（鬥）”dòu，两人两手纠缠，表示搏斗。

“文”“止”“戈”组合为“斌”bīn，表示文质兼备。

三　现行汉字合体字的结构 The Structure of Compound Characters

构成合体字的方式有以下几种：

There are four ways to form a compound character with components:

左右结构

Left and Right Structure

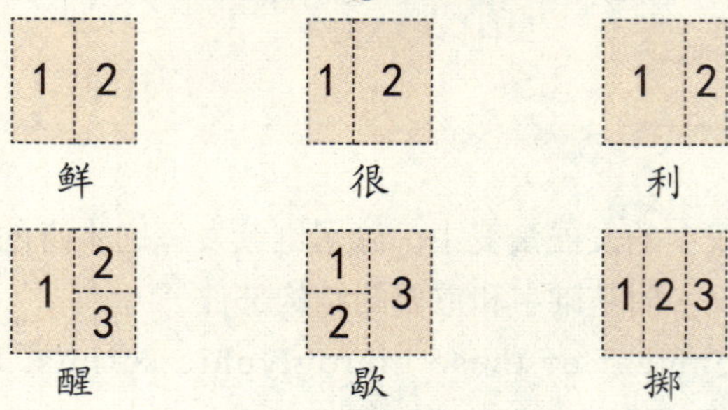

上下结构

Upper and Lower Structure

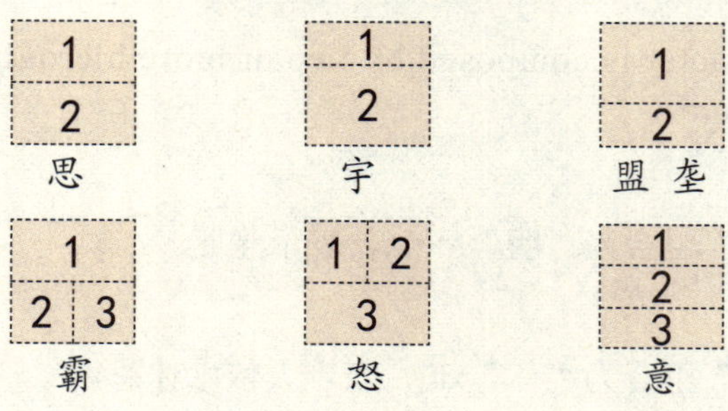

外半包围结构

Half-round Structure

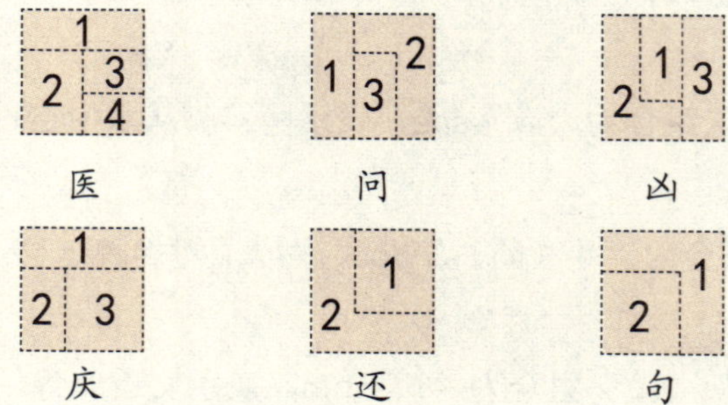

全包围及其他结构

Round Structure and Others

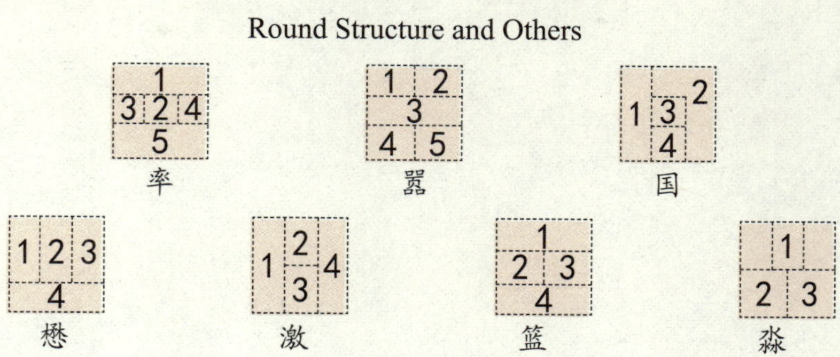

四　现行汉字的笔画　Rules of Strokes in Chinese Characters' Calligraphy

现行汉字的笔画有五种基本的类型，即“一”（横 héng）、“丨”（竖 shù）、“丿”（撇 piě）、“丶”（点 diǎn）、“乛”（折 zhé）。每种笔画都包含不同的变体，所以汉字的实际笔画在 30 种以上。

There are five basic types of Chinese characters, namely, “ 一 ”(horizontal stroke), “ 丨 ” (vertical stroke), “ 丿 ” (left-falling stroke), “ 丶 ” (dot stroke) and “ 乛 ” (turning stroke). In fact, there are more than 30 Chinese strokes because each basic stroke includes variants.

为了便于学习，传统的方法是把汉字的笔画分为八种。学习汉字，首先要掌握这八种基本笔画的写法。

For the convenience of study, Chinese characters are traditionally divided into eight categories. Grasping the eight basic strokes is a prerequisite for learning Chinese characters.

汉字中的“永”字包括了汉字的基本笔画，多写“永”字对写好汉字、理解意义有很大的帮助。下面对“永”字的笔画笔顺作一解析（1, 2, 3, 4, 5, 6, 7, 8 是下笔的先后顺序）。

The character “ 永 ” includes most of the basic strokes of Chinese characters. It is a great help for a better writing and understanding of Chinese character. Here are some analyses on the strokes of “ 永 ” (1, 2, 3, 4, 5, 6, 7, 8 is writing order).

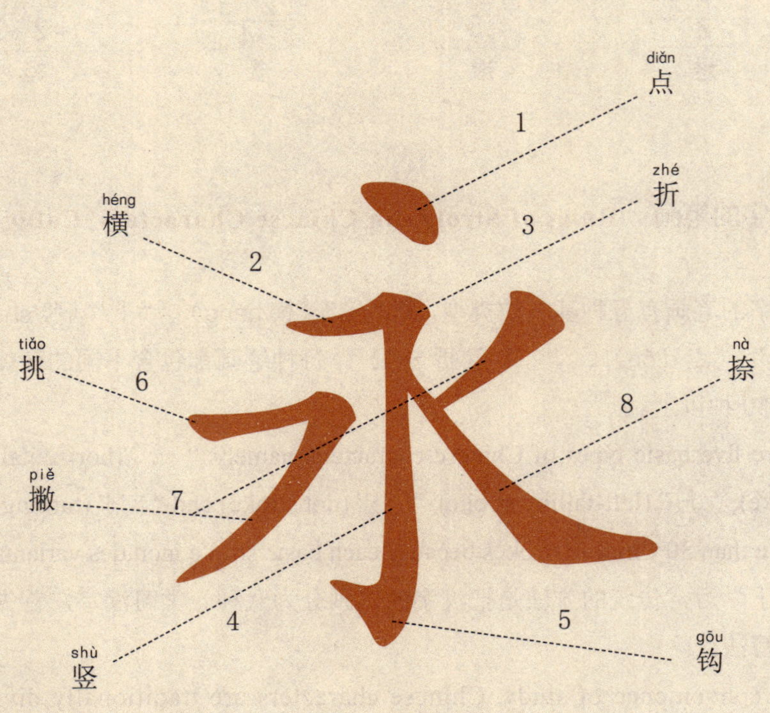
diǎn
点
1
héng
横
2
zhé
折
3
tiǎo
挑
6
nà
捺
8
piě
撇
7
shù
竖
4
5
gōu
钩

笔画表

TheTable of Strokes

名 称 Name		笔画 Stroke	例字 Example	名 称 Name		笔画 Stroke	例字 Example
点 Dot	斜点	、	主 内	捺 Right-falling stroke	平捺	㇏	之 这
	竖点	㇔	宝 心		斜捺	㇏	义 水
	长点	㇏	这 卜	钩 Hook Stroke	竖钩	亅	可 到
	撇行点	㇒	学 初		竖弯钩	㇟	儿 已
	挑行点	㇀	习 江		竖折折钩	㇉	马 弓
	撇点	㇛	女 巡		卧钩	㇃	心 必
横 Horizontal Stroke	长横	一	十 喜		横钩	㇖	买 饮
	短横	一	天 二		横折钩	㇆	向 报
横 Horizontal Stroke	长竖	丨	止 川		横折折钩	㇡	乃 杨
	短竖	丨	工 刊		横折右弯钩	㇈	九 瓦
竖 Vertical Stroke	竖挑	㇙	饮 以		横折左弯钩	㇌	陈 邓
	斜挑	㇀	地 打		斜钩	㇂	戈 民
	横折挑	㇊	说 辩		横折斜钩	⺄	风 飞
撇 Left-falling	平撇	㇒	千 后	折 Turning Stroke	竖折	㇗	匡 母
	斜撇	丿	人 方		撇折	㇜	公 红
	直撇	丿	月 师		横折	㇕	日 片
	横折撇	㇇	又 水		横折折	㇅	凹
	横折折撇	㇋	及 廷		横折折折	㇎	凸

五　现行汉字的笔顺　The Order of Chinese Characters' Calligraphy

笔顺是汉字书写时笔画的先后顺序。了解汉字书写的笔顺，可以让我们知道怎么写汉字，怎样写得更快、更好。了解汉字的笔顺，还可以帮助我们查字典。当不知道一个汉字的发音时，如果知道这个字的笔顺，就可以确定起笔、末笔，通过笔画查字典、部首查字典，就能在词典上找到所要查的汉字。

Stroke orders refers to the orders of writing stokes of Chinese characters. Understanding rules of stroke orders allows us to know how to write Chinese characters and write them fast and better. And what's more, it helps us look up a dictionary. If we don't know the pronunciation of a Chinese character but know its stoke order, we can make sure of the starting and ending strokes and find the location of the character through the stroke indexing method or radical indexing method.

笔顺规则
Common Rules of the Strokes in Chinese Characters' Calligraphy

1. 先横后竖

From Horizontal Character Stroke to Straight down Character Stroke For example: 一、十、丁、干。

2. 先撇后捺

From the Falling Left Stroke to the Falling Right Stroke For example: 人、入、八。

3. 从上到下

From the Upper Part to the Lower Stroke For example: 三、工、王、文。

4. 从左到右

From Left to Right For example: 九、月、阝、州。

5. 由外到内

From Outside to Inside For example: 园、日、田、回、耳、门、冈、风、凡。

6. 由中间到两边

From the Middle to the Left and Right For example: 小、水、办、忄。

7. 先两点后中下

From the Two Dots to the Middle and Lower For example: 火、尘、父、半。

8. 由左边角到中间

From the Left Corner to the Middle For example: 巨、区、匹、医、臣。

9. 由右边角到中间

From the Right Corner to the Middle For example: 刁、习、句、勾。

10. 由内到外

From Inside to Outside For example: 还、这、廷、延。

11. 其他

Others For example: 厂、历、厉、厄、厕。

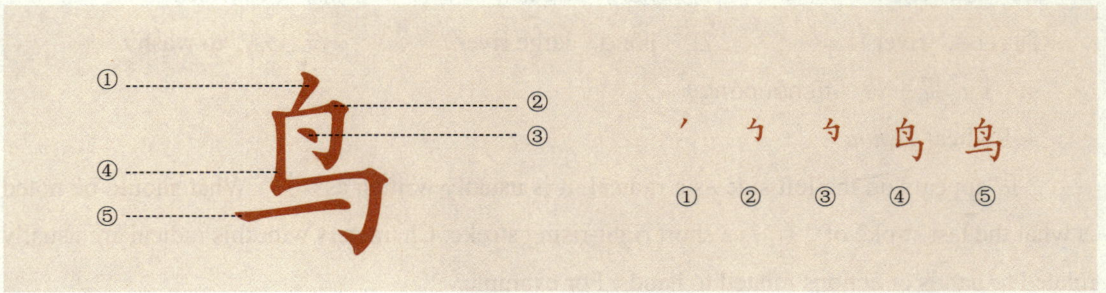

六 现行汉字常用偏旁（部首） Common Radicals of Chinese Characters

组成合体字的结构单位，叫做偏旁（部首）。了解汉字的偏旁（部首）是学会查汉语字典的关键。

The components, which compose a character, are called the Sides. Some of the Sides are used as radicals in Chinese dictionaries, So it is of key importance to know the Sides or Radicals before you learn know to consult a Chinese dictionary.

下面介绍一些常用的偏旁（部首）：

The following are some frequently used the sides (radicals)

1. 讠（言）言字旁（yán zì páng）

1. Radical *Yan*

"言"在左边做偏旁的时候简化为"讠"。这个偏旁的字大多和说话有关系。如：

When "言" appears on the left as a radical, it is simplified as "讠". Characters with this radical are usually related to "speaking". For examples:

说（shuō, to speak） 读（dú, to read） 语（yǔ, language） 谢（xiè, to thank）

2. 亻（人）单人旁（dān rén páng）

2. Radical *Ren*

"人"字在左边的时候一般写成"亻"。有"亻"旁的字大多跟人或者人的活动有关。如：

When"人"appears on the left as a radical, it is simplified as "亻". The character with this radical are usually related to "people"or "people's activities". For example:

你（nǐ，you） 他（tā，he） 住（zhù，to live）
信（xìn，to believe） 休（xiū，to rest） 位（wèi，a measure word）

3. 氵 三点水旁（sāndiǎnshuǐpáng）

3. Radical *Sandianshui*

“氵”象征流水，通常在一个字的左边。如：

This side symbolizes flowing water. It is usually on the left of a character. For example:

泪（lèi，tear） 汗（hàn，sweat） 海（hǎi，sea）
河（hé，river） 江（jiāng，large river） 洗（xǐ，to wash）

4. 扌 提手旁（tíshǒupáng）

4. Radical *Tishou*

“手”appears on the left side as a radical, it is usually written as “扌”. What should be noted is what the last stroke of “扌” is a short right-rising stroke. Characters with this radical are usually related to hands or actions related to hands. For example.

打（dǎ，to hit） 抢（qiǎng，to rob） 扫（sǎo，to sweep）
扔（rēng，to throne） 抓（zhuā，to grab） 拍（pāi，to pat）

5. 日 日字旁（rì zì páng）

5. Radical *Ri*

This side symbolizes the sun and characters with “日” are related to season, etc. Examples:

昨（zuó，yesterday） 明（míng，tomorrow） 春（chūn，spring）
早（zǎo，morning） 晚（wǎn，night） 时（shí，time）

6. 口 口字旁（kǒuzìpáng）

6. Radical *kou*

用口做旁的字常常和嘴有关系，如：

Characters with this radical “口”are usually related to “mouth”. For example:

吃（chī，to eat） 喝（hē，to drink） 唱（chàng，to sing）
问（wèn，to ask） 吹（chuī，to blow） 吻（wěn，to kiss）

7. 辶 走之旁（zǒuzhīpáng）

7. Radical *Zouzhi*

用“辶”做偏旁的字常跟行走有关系。例如：

Characters with this radical “辶”are often related to “walking”. For examples:

进（jìn，to enter） 送（sòng，to send） 道（dào，road）
远（yuǎn，far） 近（jìn，near） 逃（táo，run away）

8. 冫 两点水（liǎngdiǎnshuǐ）

8. Radical *Liangdianshui*

“冫”古代表示冰凝结的形状，带“冫”旁的字大多表示和冰或者和寒冷有关。如：

“冫” denotes the shape of clotted water. Characters with this radical are usually related to “ice”or “coldness”. For example:

冰（bīng，ice）　冷（lěng，cold）　凉（liáng，cool）
凝（níng，coagulate）　冻（dòng，freeze）　凌（líng，ice）

9. 心　心字底（xīnzìdǐ）

9. Radical *Xinzidi*

“心”看起来像心脏的形状，古人认为心脏是思想和感情的器官。带心字底的字与思想、感情有关。如：

This side loves like the shape of a heart. The ancients, people took the heart for the organ of thinking emotions. Characters with the “ear bottom” are usually related to thinking and emotions in meaning. For examples:

忘（wàng，to forget）　想（xiǎng，to think）　思念（sīniàn，to miss）
愁（chóu，to worry about）　恋（liàn，to love）　悲（bēi，sad）

10. 忄　竖心旁（shùxīnpáng）

10. Radical *Shuxin*

“心”作为一个部首字，出现在一个字的下部多写为“心”，出现在左边时多写“忄”。竖心旁的字大多和心理活动有关系。例如：

As a radical characters, “心”is mostly written as it’s original form when appearing in the lower part of a word, while “忄” is written when appearing on the left side. Characters with “忄”are also usually related ones psychological activities. For example:

忙（máng，busy）　恨（hèn，to hate）　怕（pà，to fear）
快（kuài，fast）　慢（màn，slow）　情（qíng，feeling）

11. 钅　金字旁（jīnzìpáng）

11. Radical *Jinzi*

“金”表示金属，在左边做偏旁时简化为“钅”。有这个偏旁的字大多和金属有关。例如：

“金”indicates “metal”. When it appears on the left side as a radical, it is usually written as “钅”. Characters with this radical are usually related to “metal”. For example:

银（yín，silver）　铁（tiě，iron）　钱（qián，money）
钢（gāng，steel）　针（zhēn，needle）　锁（suǒ，lock）

12. 月　肉字旁（ròuzìpáng）

12. Radical *Rouzi*

“肉”的本义是指禽兽的肉。肉字旁的字大多与人或动物的身体或肉食有关。后来，“肉”的字形发生了改变，变得和“月亮”的“月”同形，但肉的本意没变，这是要注意区别的。例如：

“肉”means the flesh of animals, characters with this radical are also usually related to the bodies of people or animals. Later, the shape of“肉”evolves into“月”, but with different meaning for that in“月亮”. For example:

脸（liǎn，face）　脑（nǎo，brain）　肥（féi，fat）

胖（pàng，fat）　脖（bó，neck）　肚（dù，belly）

13. 月　月字旁（yuèzìpáng）

13. Radical *Yuezi*

月字旁的字大多与月亮和时间（古代人用日、月、星的变化来估计时间）有关。例如：

Characters with this radical“月”are usually related to“the moon”or“time”(the ancients estimated time by the change of the sun, the moon and stars). For example:

明（míng，bright）　望（wàng，to look over）　星期（xīngqī，week）

朔（shuò，new moon）　朗（lǎng，bright）

14. 目　目字旁（mùzìpáng）

14. Radical *Muzi*

“目”的本义是人的眼睛，所以目字旁的字大多和眼睛或和眼睛的动作有关系。例如：

“目”means peoples's eyes, so characters with this radical are usually related to eyes or actions of the eyes. For examples:

眼睛（yǎnjing，eyes）　看（kàn，to look）　眉（méi，eyebrow）

瞎（xiā，blind）　睡（shuì，to sleep）　盼（pàn，to look forward to）

15. 纟　绞丝旁（jiǎosīpáng）

15. Radical *Jiaosi*

有“纟”旁的字大多和线绳或者丝织有关。例如：

Characters with“纟”are usually related to“thread”“rope”or“silk”. For example:

线（xiàn，thread）　绳（shéng，rope）　绸（chóu，silk）

编织（biānzhī，to weave）　纸（zhǐ，paper）　红（hóng，red）

16. 衤　衣字旁（yīzìpáng）

16.Radical *Yizi*

“衣”是个部首字，在左边做偏旁时写做“衤”，“衤”是“衣”的变形，所以也叫衣字旁。有这个偏旁的字大多和衣服或是做衣服的布制品有关。例如：

“衣”is a radical world. When it appears on the left side as a radical, it is usually writlen as “衣”, “衤”is the variant of “衣”, so it is also called Yizipang. Characters with this radical are usually related to “clothes” or “cloth”. For example:

裤（kù, trousers） 裙（qún, skirt） 袜（wà, stockings）
袖（xiù, sleeves） 被（bèi, quilt） 补（bǔ, to patch）

17. 礻 示字旁（shìzipáng）

17. Radical *Shizi*

“示”本义与“祭祀”有关，“示”是个部首字，在字的下面时一般写做“示”。

“示”means “worship”, it is a radical word. When it appears at the bottom as a radical, it is usually writhen as it’s orginal form. For example,

祝福（zhùfú, to wish） 祥（xiáng, lucky） 祸（huò, disaster）
祈祷（qídǎo, to pray） 宗（zōng, ancestor） 崇（chóng, to worship）

18. 火 火字旁（huǒzipáng）

18. Radical *Huozi*

火字旁的字大多与火或者燃烧有关。例如：

Characters with “火” are usually related to “fire” or “burning”. For example:

灯（dēng, lamp） 烟（yān, smoke） 烧（shāo, to burn）
炸（zhá, to fry） 烫（tàng, very hot） 燥（zào, dry）

19. 灬 四点底（sìdiǎndǐ）

19. Radical *Sidiandi*

“火”在字的下边时多写成“灬”。有这个偏旁的字也大多和火有关。例如：

When “火” appears at the bottom of a character, it is written as “灬”. Characters with this radical are usually related to “fire”. For example:

照（zhào, to light） 热（rè, hot） 煮（zhǔ, to boil）
熟（shú, cooked） 焦（jiāo, burnt） 燃（rán, burning）

练习一 汉字书写
Exercise I Writing of Chinese Characters

人

家

燕

祖国

纱窗

巧克力

沉鱼落雁

言简意赅

天才来自勤奋！

业精于勤，荒于嬉。

但愿人长久，千里共婵娟。

同一个世界，同一个梦想。

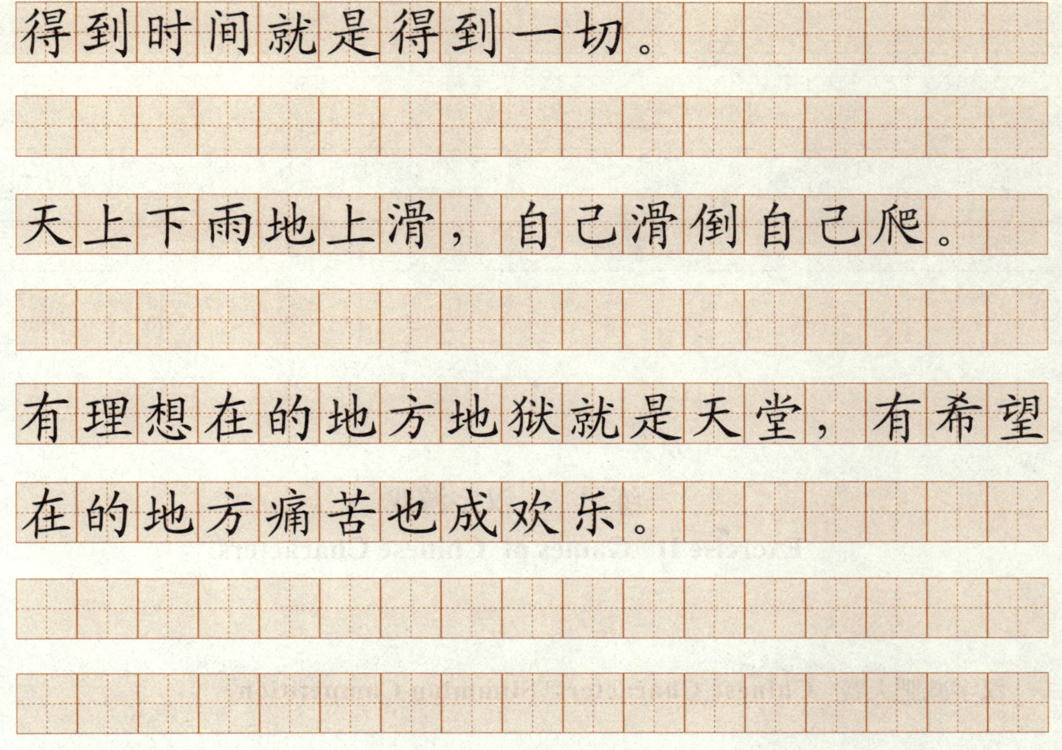

杀鸡取蛋

很久以前，有一个农夫，生活很苦，靠养鸡为生。有一天，他发现自己养的母鸡有一只每天能下一个金蛋。他非常高兴，只要母鸡下了金蛋就拿到集市上去卖。很快他就有了钱，生活过得很好。

过了一段时间，他想：要是我把母鸡杀了，把它肚子里的金蛋都卖了，我就马上能变得更有钱。于是，他把这只母鸡杀了，但是没有看到一个金蛋。从此他的生活又变得很艰苦。

练习二 汉字游戏
Exercise II Games of Chinese Characters

一 汉字减肥大赛 Chinese Characters' Slimming Competition

许多汉字在多次去掉部分笔画后，每次又成为另外一个字，很像美女们减肥。现在汉字减肥大赛正式开始，看谁减得最巧妙，看谁减得次数最多，先定几条规则：1. 不要用生僻字；2. 最后的那个字笔画不少于两笔；3. 笔画只能减少不能移动。如：

谜—迷—米—木—十

语—吾—五—工—二

嘴—觜—角—用—甲—田—王—土—十

箱—相—目—日—口

懈—解—角—用—田—王—土—二

潼—童—里—早—旦—日—口

你不妨自己找一些汉字按照上面的方法试一试。

二 成语不离“舌” Idioms about “Tongue”

形容惊诧无言。（张口结舌） 形容说话轻薄。（闲嘴淡舌）

形容不善辞令。（笨嘴拙舌） 形容随声附和。（鹦鹉学舌）

三 数字俗语 Proverbs about Numbers

表示实实在在，不可更改时用。（一是一，二是二）
表示做事考虑不周到，干了再说时用。（一不做，二不休）
表示一样东西两人平分时用。（二一添作五）
表示某人干事麻利时用。（三下五除二）
表示差不多时用。（八九不离十）
表示某人爱打小算盘时用。（小九九）
表示归根到底时用。（九九归一）
表示把握大时用。（十有八九）
表示很不容易时用。（九牛二虎之力）
表示信心十足时用。（十拿九稳）
表示距离远时用。（十万八千里）

四 下面人名各取自什么成语? Which Proverb Does Each of the Following Names Come from?

王鹏程（鹏程万里）
苟任重（任重道远）
李慧中（秀外慧中）
刘若愚（大智若愚）
时残云（风卷残云）
康海粟（沧海一粟）
甘如饴（甘之如饴）

五 成语填空 Complete Proverbs by Filling the Suitable Chinese Characters

（ ）服（ ）服　（ ）德（ ）德　（ ）讹（ ）讹
（ ）牙（ ）牙　（ ）老（ ）老　（ ）计（ ）计
神（ ）（ ）神　精（ ）（ ）精　痛（ ）（ ）痛
（ ）欺欺（ ）　将（ ）（ ）将　日（ ）（ ）日
微（ ）（ ）微　神（ ）（ ）神　年（ ）（ ）年

答案：（心）服（口）服，（以）德（报）德，（以）讹（传）讹，（以）牙（还）牙，（倚）老（卖）老，（将）计（就）计，神（乎）（其）神，精（益）（求）精，痛（定）（思）痛，（自）欺欺（人），将（门）（有）将，日（复）（一）日，微（乎）（其）微，神（乎）（其）神，年（复）（一）年

六　宝塔诗如何读？　How to Read the "Pagoda Poem"

开
山满
桃山杏
山好景山
来山客看山
里山僧山客山
山中山路转山崖

山中山路转山崖，山客山僧山里来，山客看山山景好，山杏山桃满山开。

七　数字猜成语　Guess the Proverbs from the Numbers

12345609　（七零八落）　　1256789（丢三落四）
1+2+3　（接二连三）　　333 555（三五成群）
3.5　（不三不四）　　1510　（一五一十）
9 寸 +1 寸 =1 尺　（得寸进尺）

八　猜谜语　Riddles

十五天　（打一字）
吃尽苦头有出头。　（打一字）
闪电之后，彩虹之前。　（打一电影名）
当你没有钥匙的时候，你怎么办？　（打一地名）
一堆草。　（打一花）
一口咬掉牛尾巴。　（打一字）

答案：胖 胡 《雷雨》 厦门 梅花 告

后 记

我在兰州大学文学院（原中文系）讲授本科生课程“现代汉语”、研究生课程“汉语方言调查与研究”及留学生课程“汉语”时，深感汉语语音存在着老师不好教、学生不爱学的问题，这主要是由于语音一发即逝，把握不住。再者，也由于当时语言课内容较单一，知识点琐碎，不易掌握，致使大部分学生觉得枯燥无味。尽管在当时也有简单的静态语音示意图，有点示意的直观性，但对语音是如何形成的仍然是“纸上谈兵”。在此期间，我一直在思考、探讨如何才能使静止的示意图动起来，并看到口腔中的活动。

从 1984 年起，我边教课边了解动画片的制作过程，发现动画片仍然是用手工画图后拍摄而成的。我就自己学着画，然后请别人试拍。起初将元音和辅音的每个音各画了 13 张，便有了一些动态的雏形，但为了使图像的动态性更直观，后来每个音的图片增至 23 张。终于在 1986 年元月在给示意图配音后完成了《现代汉语语音》动画录像教学片。经过数次播放后，觉得此片通过电视荧屏可以看出语音是由人体发音器官的开合、起落活动而产生的。如果学习者依照录像教学片学习发音，对汉语语音的认识便会一目了然，讲授者也省去了不少讲解之烦。

同年 3 月份，我携带此片去北京国家语委请求审定，欣逢语委语文影像出版社接纳，并向国家教委普通话推广处推荐，双方商定由出版社邀请国家语委有关领导和专家审定。当时参加者有北京师范大学语言学教授、国家教委普通话推广处副处长徐世荣，中国社科院语言文字应用研究所研究员、国家语委语文影像出版社副社长、副总编李行健，国家语委汉语拼音处副研究员李乐毅，国家教委孙修章等多人。审定会后参加者对该片给予肯定和很高的评价，认为这是语言教学的重要改革和创新，也提了很好的意见，建议修改后及早出版，但后因各种原因未得付梓。

时光荏苒，从 1986 年迄今二十多个春秋里，如何让发音动画出现在语言教学课堂的想法一直萦绕于心。特别是近年来，随着国际上学习汉语的热潮继续升温，孔子学院遍布全球，成百上千的各国留学生也进入我国各地高校学习汉语，但学习汉语首先就要学习汉语语音。如此，就更激发了我编撰摄制一部语音动画教学片的决心。尽管当时我早已退休，也步入耄耋之年，但自认为精力尚可，于是说干就干，在几位研究生的协助下，确定目标，制订计划，编写提纲，安排任务，查阅资料，并了解先进的多媒体数字制作技术，等等。自2007年迄今的四五年中，案头的修订稿不断增高，动画的制作者在酷暑之下挥汗如雨，而我来来回回奔波于家和制作中心，比上班还要“敬业”。总之，反反复复做了许多艰苦而细致的工作，虽说是对原动画片的修订，但又可以说是改弦易辙、重新编撰。现在，此教材将在兰州大学出版社发行，就我个人而言，虽然掉了几斤肉，却了了心愿！

本教材在编撰过程中，主要参考了黄伯荣、廖序东两位先生的《现代汉语》（笔者也参与编写）中“语音”和“文字”的部分内容，还借鉴了徐世荣教授编著的《普通话语音知识》中的部分语音图片。特此说明，并对三位先生表示诚挚的感谢和敬意！

此教材的出版，首先感谢兰州大学社科处、教务处及兰州大学文学院在科研经费方面的大力支持和帮助；感谢兰州大学新闻传播学院影视动画研发中心的技术支持；感谢陕西师范大学党委书记甘晖同志对此书的写作给予的鼓励和支持，书成之时并欣然赐序，不胜感激；在本书的出版过程中，感谢兰州大学出版社各位领导和编辑对本书的认真审阅和修改；此外，还要感谢兰州大学文学院硕士生吕文瑞、李彩霞和硕士生张竞婷及华侨大学文学院的侯然等，她们在文稿的电脑录入和编排以及提供材料上花费了大量时间。在此，深致谢意。

最后，衷心感谢家人的支持，感谢所有支持我的亲友。

限于作者水平，本教程出版后肯定还有不足之处，欢迎读者多多批评、指教。

主编　刘伶
2011年7月底

《秋思》

《无题》

《从军行》

《人儿人儿今何在》

《赠从弟》

《行宫》

《赤壁》

《天净沙·秋思》

《题西林壁》

《江雪》

《乌衣巷》

《一剪梅》

《饮酒》

《回乡偶书》

《声声慢》

《子夜歌》

《清明》

《春夜喜雨》

《踏莎行》

《蜀相》